AIR TRAFFIC CONTROL
HANDBOOK

Other books by this author include:

Action Stations 3.
Military Airfields of Wales and the North-West
PSL 1981 and 1990

Action Stations 7.
Military Airfields of Scotland, the North-East
and Northern Ireland
PSL 1983, 1989 and 1993

Britain's Military Airfields 1939-45
PSL 1989

**Britain's Aviation Memorials and
Mementoes**
PSL 1992

International Air Band Radio Handbook
PSL 1995

AIR TRAFFIC CONTROL
HANDBOOK

THE COMPLETE GUIDE FOR ALL AVIATION AND AIR BAND ENTHUSIASTS

NINTH EDITION

Previously titled
Air Band Radio Handbook

David J. Smith

Haynes Publishing

First published as *Air Band Radio Handbook* in 1986 by Patrick Stephens Limited
Second edition 1987
Reprinted (with revisions) 1988
Third edition 1990
Reprinted (with revisions) 1990
Reprinted 1991
Fourth edition 1992
Reprinted (with revisions) 1993
Fifth edition 1994
Sixth edition 1997
Seventh edition 2002
Eighth edition, published by Sutton Publishing Limited, 2005
This ninth edition, retitled *Air Traffic Control Handbook*, was published by Haynes Publishing, in January 2010

A catalogue record for this book is available from the British Library

ISBN 978 1 84425 832 1

Library of Congress catalog card no 2009936759

Unless otherwise credited, the photographs are by the author.

Published by Haynes Publishing, Sparkford, Yeovil, Somerset BA22 7JJ, UK
Tel: 01963 442030 Fax: 01963 440001
Int. tel: +44 1963 442030 Int. fax: +44 1963 440001
E-mail: sales@haynes.co.uk
Website: www.haynes.co.uk

Haynes North America Inc., 861 Lawrence Drive, Newbury Park, California 91320, USA

Designed and typeset by James Robertson
Printed and bound in the UK

Contents

Introduction

IT IS NOW well over 20 years since the first edition of *Air Band Radio Handbook* was published. I have always aimed the content at several distinct groups of readers, primarily the air band listener to whom it is an aircraft spotting tool, but also the aviation enthusiast who is fascinated by air traffic control and wants to know how it all works. Then there is both the student and qualified private pilot who, I hope, will learn a lot from this book and, finally, the person who is considering a career in ATC but has only a rudimentary knowledge of its workings. In fact a colleague assures me that it was reading my book that inspired him to choose ATC as a career! And, he claims, its contents helped him to pass the NATS tests and interviews.

A great many enthusiasts have bought air band radios and found that the jargon they hear is almost incomprehensible. It is easy to pick out call-signs but most VHF listeners I have talked to would like to build up a better picture of what is going on and to unravel the 'mysteries' of air traffic control. This book aims to do just that. People embarking upon a course of flying lessons for a Private Pilot's Licence will find it very useful to acquire an air band radio and listen to how the professionals do their R/T. My experience shows that, for the majority of trainee pilots, learning how to use the radio is almost as big a hurdle as mastering their aircraft. The terse messages, so confusing at first hearing, follow a definite pattern known as 'standard phraseology'. This verbal shorthand is designed to impart the maximum amount of unambiguous information in the shortest possible time. Since English is the international language of Air Traffic Control it must be understood easily by those with a different native tongue.

With careful listening, and the aid of the examples in this book, the R/T exchanges on the air band will soon become both logical and familiar. A magazine reviewer of the previous edition of this book observed that the key to understanding the basics of air band transmissions lay in a careful reading of Chapter 2.

What of the future of air band listening? Back in 1999, mandatory carriage of 8.33kHz channel spaced radios was introduced in Europe. It was seen originally as an interim stop, providing a means of alleviating frequency congestion prior to the introduction of new digital systems. In practice, the arrival of a new generation communication system is taking rather longer than expected and 8.33 may still be around for many years to come! It is now firmly entrenched in UK upper airspace and it may be necessary to introduce it at lower levels in the future.

The spread of datalink has reduced some listening opportunities, mainly so-called 'housekeeping' tasks to reduce controller workload. Some of these services are already operational in the UK; Oceanic Route Clearance Authorisation service (ORCA), Datalink

LEFT: Remote transmitter site at Kelsall, Cheshire, for area control frequencies.

Volmet (D-Volmet) and Datalink Automatic Terminal Information Service (D-ATIS). D-ATIS is currently restricted to a few airports, including Heathrow and Gatwick. Pre-Departure Clearance System is planned for both airports and a trial is currently running at Gatwick. As for the use of datalink in more dynamic situations such as area control, controllers remain sceptical about several factors, not least being pilot response times to instructions. Datalink does not keep talking in a pilot's ear, nor does it have the ability to express urgency as effectively as a controller's voice!

It must be emphasised that, in the extremely complex world of Air Traffic Control, procedures are changing all the time; new air lanes may be brought into use, others replaced or re-routed. Similarly, new beacons and reporting points are always being introduced. The fact that radio navigation charts are updated every month or so shows just how frequently changes are liable to occur. Frequencies tend to stay the same for many years but the ever-evolving complexity of controlled airspace has resulted in many new allocations, some of them 8.33kHz spaced. The military UHF band has been entirely overhauled since the last edition of this book.

I hope that I have distilled a readable narrative from the mass of official data listed in Chapter 19 as primary sources. Most of this is available for download or reading online if you really want to immerse yourself in the subject. I have attempted to de-mystify a very complex subject which is growing ever more specialised. Four more chapters have been added, covering careers in ATC, virtual radar systems, UFOs and ATC, and Hijackings. Virtual radar is an enormous leap in technology, enabling the enthusiast to see a picture of traffic over a wide area much the same as the real controller is seeing on his or her display.

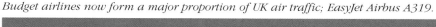

Budget airlines now form a major proportion of UK air traffic; EasyJet Airbus A319.

Acknowledgements

THANKS GO TO Ken Cothliff of Air Supply in Leeds for his help with updating the scanner chapter, Roger Hall, Editor of *RadioUser* magazine, who kindly supplied a selection of scanner photographs, John Locker (satcom.website.orange.co.uk) who provided a lot of information on virtual radar systems, and Steven Hill at CAA for granting permission to use certain charts from the Aeronautical Information Publication.

Beluga lift-off from Liverpool.

Abbreviations and Q-Codes

*Abbreviations marked with an asterisk are normally spoken on R/T as a complete word or without use of phonetics.

AAC	Air Arrivals Control	CAA	Civil Aviation Authority
ACARS*	Aircraft Communications Addressing and Reporting System	CAVOK*	Ceiling and Visibility OK
		CDA	Continuous Descent Approach
		CFMU	Central Flow Management Unit
ACC	Area Control Centre		
ACMI*	Air Combat Manoeuvring Instrumentation	CHAPI*	Compact Helicopter Approach Path Indicator
ADD	Allowable Deferred Defect	CPDLC	Controller–Pilot Data Link Communications
ADF*	Automatic Direction Finder		
ADR*	Advisory Route	CVR	Cockpit Voice Recorder
ADS-B*	Automatic Dependence Surveillance-Broadcast	D&D	Distress and Diversion
ADT	Approved Departure Time	D/F*	Direction Finding
AEF	Air Experience Flight	DFR	Departure Flow Regulation
AEW	Airborne Early Warning	DGPS	Differential Global Positioning System
AFIS*	Aerodrome Flight Information Service		
AGL*	Above Ground Level	DME	Distance Measuring Equipment
AIAA	Area of Intense Aerial Activity	DVP	Digital Voice Protection
AIS	Aeronautical Information Service	EAT	Expected Approach Time
AMSL	Above Mean Sea Level	ETA	Estimated Time of Arrival
APU	Auxiliary Power Unit	ETD	Estimated Time of Departure
ARINC*	Aeronautical Radio Inc		
ASU	Air Support Unit	FDPS	Flight Data Processing System
ATA	Aerial Tactics Area	FDR	Flight Deck Recorder
ATD	Actual Time of Departure	FIR	Flight Information Region
ATIS*	Automatic Terminal Information Service	FISO	Flight Information Service Officer
ATM	Air Traffic Monitor	FL	Flight Level
ATU	Aerial Tuning Unit	FM	Frequency Modulation
ATZ	Aerodrome Traffic Zone	FMS	Flight Management System
		FMU	Flow Management Unit
BAA	British Airports Authority	FTR	Fighter
BFO	Beat Frequency Oscillator	FTU	Flying Training Unit

GAT	General Air Traffic	MHz	Megahertz
GHFS	Global High Frequency System	MLS*	Microwave Landing System
GLONASS*	Global Orbiting Navigation Satellite System	MNPS	Minimum Navigation Performance Specification
GMC	Ground Movement Control	MOR*	Mandatory Occurrence Report
GMP	Ground Movement Planning	MRA	Military Reserved Airspace
GPS	Global Positioning System	MRSA	Mandatory Radar Service Area
GPU	Ground Power Unit	MTA*	Military Training Area
GPWS	Ground Proximity Warning System		
		NATS	Now company title but stood for National Air Traffic Services
HF	High Frequency		
HMR	Helicopter Main Route	NDB*	Non-Directional Beacon
HPZ	Helicopter Protected Zone	NFM	Narrow (band) Frequency Modulation
IAS	Indicated Air Speed	NM	Nautical Miles
IATA	International Air Transport Association	NOTAM*	Notice to Airmen
		NPR	Noise-Preferential Route
ICAO	International Civil Aviation Organisation	OACC	Oceanic Area Control Centre
ICF	Initial Contact Frequency	OAT	Operational Air Traffic or Outside Air Temperature
IFR*	Instrument Flight Rules		
ILS*	Instrument Landing System	OCA	Oceanic Control Area
IMC*	Instrument Meteorological Conditions	OCH	Obstacle Clearance Height
		ORCAM*	Originating Region Code Assignment Method
INS	Inertial Navigation System		
IRVR*	Instrumented Runway Visual Range	OTS	Organised Track System
		PAPI*	Precision Approach Path Indicator
kHz	Kilohertz		
		PAR	Precision Approach Radar
LARS*	Lower Airspace Radar Service	PIREP*	Pilot Report of weather conditions encountered en route
LATCC*	London Area and Terminal Control Centre		
		PPR	Prior Permission Required
LDOCF	Long Distance Operational Control Facilities	QAR	Quick Access Recorder
		QDM	Magnetic track to the airfield with no allowance for wind
LITAS*	Low Intensity Two-colour Approach Slope Indicator		
LJAO	London Joint Area Organisation	QFE	Barometric pressure at aerodrome level
LSB	Lower Side Band		
LVPs*	Low Visibility Procedures	QGH	Controlled descent through cloud
MACS	Military Aeronautical Communication System	QNH	Barometric pressure at sea level
		QRA	Quick Reaction Alert
MATO	Military Air Traffic Operations	QSY	Change frequency to ...
MATZ*	Military Aerodrome Traffic Zone	QTE	True bearing from the aerodrome
MDH	Minimum Descent Height		
MDI	Minimum Departure Interval		
MEDA	Military Emergency Diversion Aerodrome	RA	Resolution Advisory
		RCC	Rescue Co-ordination Centre
METRO*	US Military Met Office	RP	Reporting Point

R/T*	Radio Telephony	TMA	Terminal Manouevring Area
RTOW*	Regulated Take-Off Weight	TOS	Traffic Orientation Scheme
RTTY*	(pronounced 'Ritty') Radio Teletype	TRACON*	Terminal Radar Control (USA)
RVR*	Runway Visual Range		
RVSM*	Reduced Vertical Separation Minima	UAC	Upper Area (Control) Centre
		UAR	Upper Air Route
		UAS	University Air Squadron
SAR	Search and Rescue	UAV	Uninhabited Aerial Vehicle
SID*	Standard Instrument Departure	UHF*	Ultra High Frequency
SLP	Speed Limit Point	UIR	Upper (Flight) Information Region
SMR	Surface Movement Radar		
SOTA*	Shannon Oceanic Transition Area	USAF	United States Air Force
		USB	Upper Side Band
SPECI*	Special Met Observation	UTC	Universal Time Constant (or Co-ordinated)
SRA	Surveillance Radar Approach		
SSB	Single Side Band		
SSR*	Secondary Surveillance Radar	VASI*	Visual Approach Slope Indicator
STAR*	Standard Terminal Arrival Route		
STOL*	Short Take-off and Landing	VCR	Visual Control Room
		VDF*	VHF Direction Finder
TA	Traffic Advisory	VFR*	Visual Flight Rules
TACAN*	Tactical Air Navigation	VHF*	Very High Frequency
TAD*	Tactical Air Designator	VMC*	Visual Meteorological Conditions
TAF*	Terminal Aerodrome Forecast		
TAS	True Air Speed	VOR*	VHF Omni-directional Range
TC	Terminal Control	VRP*	Visual Reference Point
TCA	Terminal Control Area		
TCAS*	Traffic Alert and Collision Avoidance System	WFM	Wide (band) Frequency Modulation

Chapter 1

Listening

WHAT YOU CAN hear, and in turn relate to aircraft you see flying overhead, obviously depends on your location relative to airports and air lanes. Since VHF radio waves follow approximate lines of sight, the higher the aircraft, the further away you can hear messages from it. Transmitter power is also a factor but, generally speaking, high-flying aircraft can be received up to 200 miles away. Certain atmospheric conditions can produce freak ranges far in excess of normal but this is a fairly rare occurrence. As a rule of thumb, frequencies below 123MHz are allocated to Tower and Approach units at airports and those above 123MHz to Area Control Centres (ACCs), although there are many exceptions to this.

Ground stations may be screened by hills, buildings and other obstructions, so you may not be able to pick up the replies from the tower or approach if you live more than ten miles away from the airport. The coverage for the ACCs at London and Prestwick is very much better, however, there being few places in the flatter parts of the British Isles out of range of

The most common cockpit noise the air band listener hears when a pilot transmits a message to ATC is the buzzer which sounds when an aircraft, such as this Titan Airways Boeing 757, is climbing or descending towards a cleared level.

one or more of the powerful transmitters. This is because they are sited at some distance from their associated ground stations, usually on high ground. There may, however, be some 'blind spots' in reception for no apparent reason.

The first thing to do after acquiring a new scanner is to establish which ground stations are within range and which can help you to identify aircraft flying in your local area. You can set up the appropriate frequencies on the scanner and monitor them when required. With experience you will soon know which station an aircraft is likely to be 'working', its height being a good clue as to whether the pilot is talking to the local airfield, ACC, radar unit etc.

Unfortunately, in parts of Britain there are so many ATC units capable of providing a radar service that it may be difficult to discover to which a transit aircraft is talking. A flight below airways in the north Midlands, for example, might be in contact with Birmingham, East Midlands or Shawbury Radar, or simply the London Flight Information Region frequency. Of course, the pilot may not be talking to anyone, nor does he need to if he remains clear of aerodrome traffic zones and other restricted airspace.

If you live beneath an air route, the relevant airways control frequency can be selected and you can relax and wait for something interesting to appear. Unfortunately, it is not just a simple case of running outside at the right moment (if it isn't cloudy) and rapidly filling up one's notebooks. Aircraft do not always use their registrations or military serial numbers as call-signs, and most commercial flights use a call-sign totally unrelated to what is painted on the aircraft.

The answers to many of the questions that arise from air band monitoring can be found in the network of enthusiasts' magazines, which keep most airfields under surveillance and publish detailed lists of visitors, usually tabulated by call-sign as well as registration letters. The information is often acquired by courtesy of the airport management or ATC, the ranks of which are riddled with enthusiast 'moles'. Since most transatlantic flights from NW Europe have to cross Britain at some point, even those anonymous airliners on contrails can be identified. There are several publications available that match the call-sign and registration of most of them. Identifying military aircraft can be very difficult as few, apart from some USAF transports, use the actual serial number. Military airfields generally use UHF frequencies to communicate with their own aircraft. Unfortunately, the call-signs of first-line combat aircraft are changed frequently for security reasons.

Background noise

Air band listeners can often hear all kinds of background cockpit noises when a pilot transmits a message to ATC. The most common one is the buzzer which sounds when an aircraft is climbing or descending towards a cleared level. The level is pre-set on the Flight Management Computer (FMC) and the warning sounds a thousand feet below when climbing, and a thousand feet above when descending. It alerts the pilots so that they can request a higher or lower level and, if so cleared, avoid having to level off. Automatic radio altimeter callouts are a customer option on the Boeing 737 series and other types, using a synthetic voice. Cockpit aural warnings include fire bell, take-off configuration, cabin altitude, and landing gear configuration. Take off configuration warnings are a frequent cause of aborted take-offs. Maybe the flap setting is not quite right for the conditions or it can just be a spurious warning. Only certain warnings can be silenced while the condition exists.

There are a number of sites on the web that incorporate sound files of cockpit warnings. You can listen to such sharp annunciations as 'Terrain, Terrain'; 'Glideslope, Glideslope'; 'Wind Shear, Wind Shear'; 'Sink Rate, Sink Rate', all accompanied by a 'whoop, whoop' sound and guaranteed to grab the pilots' attention! TCAS (Traffic Collision Avoidance System – see page 42) has its own menu of warnings designed to resolve conflictions. TCAS generates a Traffic Advisory (TA) when another aircraft becomes a potential threat and is approximately 40 seconds from the closest point of approach. No manoeuvres are required for a TA. If the intruder continues to close and becomes an imminent threat, a Resolution Advisory (RA) is generated when the other aircraft is approximately 25 seconds from the closest point of approach. The RA provides a vertical restriction or manoeuvre to maintain or increase separation from the traffic.

A TA is indicated by the aural annunciation 'Traffic, Traffic' which sounds once, and is then reset until the next TA occurs. If the other aircraft's transponder is operating in Mode C or S, altitude information and vertical motion, if applicable, are also displayed. RAs are indicated by one or more aural phrases, ranging from 'Monitor Vertical Speed', meaning avoid deviations from the current vertical speed, to the self-evident 'Climb, Climb, Climb', 'Descend, Descend, Descend', 'Reduce Climb, Reduce Climb', and 'Reduce Descent, Reduce Descent'. 'Clear of Conflict' is announced once the RA encounter is resolved. TCAS alerts are inhibited by Ground Proximity Warning System, and Windshear warnings, and at low altitudes where the Traffic Avoidance Manoeuvre would be inappropriate.

ATC transmissions are often accompanied by background noise as well. Visitors unused to control rooms always behave as though they are in church, but the working environment is not always quiet. The controller's assistant calls out bits of information about last-minute parking stand changes and the like, ground vehicles blare on UHF loudspeakers, telephones ring and so on. I once flew into Liverpool in the jump seat of a Viscount and it sounded like a party going on in the background, much to the pilots' amusement!

Legalities

A reminder about the law relating to air band listening; it is illegal for the unlicensed! Strangely enough, owning a scanner or any radio that can receive air band transmissions is not against the law. It is a myth that listening is permitted if one does not impart the information to anyone else. Judging by the number of radios blasting out across public viewing areas at airports, it would appear that officialdom turns a blind eye to what is essentially a harmless activity.

The Civil Aviation Authority is currently very concerned by what it calls Malicious Interference to VHF Communications Services. For some time, certain irresponsible, if not criminal, persons have been deliberately impersonating air traffic controllers and the types of messages they broadcast. CAA says that problems caused by these incidents have so far been minimised owing to the experience of pilots and controllers receiving the transmissions. All such incidents are investigated and evidence is gathered for prosecution, especially messages taped by the ground station. The local Radio Investigation Office, part of the Radiocommunications Agency, will then investigate.

I am sure that readers would not dream of sending spurious messages, whether they be on air traffic or any other radio channels. Air band listening, while technically illegal, harms no one so let's keep it that way! If you hear what you believe to be fake messages, take notes on content, times and any background noises. Better still, try to record them as evidence for an investigation as they may not be picked up by ATC receivers and thus not recorded in the normal way. I am sure that a blind eye would be turned to the fact that you were listening in the first place!

Listening to police messages is most definitely illegal, and there have been a number of cases involving heavy fines and confiscation of scanners. Merely having these frequencies in the receiver's memory is considered proof of guilt. You have been warned!

Chapter 2

ATC terminology

THE MAJORITY OF air band listeners use their radios as a means of logging aircraft registrations but there are others for whom this is of no more than academic interest. Their listening pleasure is derived from learning how aircraft are controlled and the way the ATC system operates. Those in the second category will soon begin to grasp the principles, and will want to find out more, whilst those in the first will recognise that a basic knowledge will assist in tracking the aircraft in which they are interested.

Before I embark upon a more detailed description of ATC I should like first to cast some light on the jargon words which always puzzle the new air band listener. The most obvious are the terms QNH, QFE and Flight Level. The first two are codes rather than abbreviations and refer to the current atmospheric pressure at sea level and aerodrome level respectively. When the value in millibars is set on the aircraft's altimeter the instrument will indicate the distance above the appropriate datum. The term QFE Threshold refers, by the way, to the barometric pressure converted to that at the end of the runway.

Above a point known as the transition altitude, normally between 3,000ft and 6,000ft in the United Kingdom, a standard setting of 1013.2 millibars is used, producing what is termed a Flight Level (abbreviated to FL). This ensures that all aircraft, particularly within controlled airspace, are flying on the same altimeter setting and can thus easily be separated vertically by the required amount. This removes the necessity of continually adjusting the altimeter to allow for local pressure variations over the route, any error being common to all aircraft in the system. FL70 is roughly equivalent to 7,000ft, FL230 to 23,000ft and so on.

Times are given in the form of two figures; for example 14, pronounced one four, indicates 14 minutes past the hour, four two 42 minutes past the hour and so on. The standard ATC time in the United Kingdom, and indeed in the entire aviation world, is Universal Time Constant (or Co-ordinated) known as UTC. In the winter it is the same as local or Alpha time in the United Kingdom but British Summer Time is one hour ahead of it. This use of UTC ensures that there is no confusion with Flight Plans on aircraft flying through time zones.

The word squawk is often heard, particularly in route clearances, along with a four-figure code. This is set on the aircraft's transponder, a device which responds to automatic interrogations from a ground station by sending a return signal in coded form. The information appears on the radar screen as a label giving call-sign, height and destination, adjacent to the appropriate aircraft position symbol. The word blip is obsolete, the image on the display (screen is obsolete too!) on modern radars being produced electronically via a computer. The centre sweep familiar in films is long gone, as even relatively old radar equipment can be processed to produce an excellent picture.

The term clearance or cleared is a legal one meaning that the aircraft may proceed under certain explicit conditions and that it will not be impeded by other traffic. It has, in the past, been rather over-used by controllers in circumstances where its use was unnecessary, so the authorities have narrowed it down considerably. It is now confined mainly to route clearances

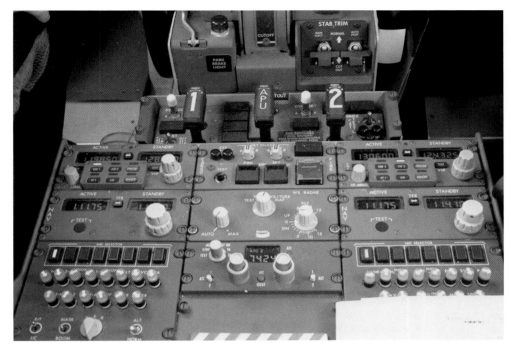

Boeing 737-800 radio control panel. Frequencies selected or on standby are Liverpool Approach, Manchester Control, Servisair and Liverpool ATIS. The Nav panel has Wallasey VOR and Liverpool 27 ILS dialled up. SSR code in centre foreground.

and runway occupancy for take-off and landing, thus avoiding any possible confusion with the meaning.

Directions are given in degrees magnetic so that if an aircraft is heading 360° it is flying due north, 090° due east and so on. Note the difference between heading and actual path over the ground (track). If there is a strong cross-wind an aircraft may be pointing (heading) in a particular direction but travelling over the ground in a considerably different direction. There is an analogy here with rowing a small boat across a fast-flowing river; although you may be aiming for a point on the opposite bank, the current will also be deflecting you sideways. Simple right and left are used for direction changes, as in the instruction 'Turn right heading 340 degrees', port and starboard being long outmoded in aviation.

Speed is expressed in knots, one knot being equal to one nautical mile per hour. The exception to this is on transatlantic and similar long-haul flights where a Mach Number is employed, speed being expressed as a ratio of the speed of sound. Jet transports cruise at around Mach 0.8 and Concorde, when it was operational, at Mach 2, twice the speed of sound.

Distances are measured in nautical miles (approx 2,025yd). References to DME, as in 'Report 8 DME Wallasey', relate to the Distance Measuring Equipment carried aboard aircraft. This receives radio transmissions from ground beacons and enables the distance to or from the particular position to be presented automatically to the pilot as a continuous read-out in miles and tenths. The 'time to go' to the beacon can also be displayed to the pilot.

Runways are designated by two numbers derived from the heading in degrees magnetic. The runways at Manchester, for example, are 05/23 Left and Right. This is rounded down from the actual direction of 051/231° Magnetic and the end zero omitted. Similarly a heading of

064/244° would be presented as 06/24. Other familiar examples are 09 Right/27 Left and 09 Left/27 Right at Heathrow and 08 Right/26 Left at Gatwick. Note that small annual changes in the bearing of the Magnetic Pole can affect the designation of runways. For example, Heathrow's directions were 10/28 until 1987 when the exact alignment became nearer to 090/270° than 100/280° Magnetic.

Somewhat confusing to the layman are the terms VFR, IFR, VMC and IMC, so I shall explain them at some length because they are of paramount importance in ATC. Flight conditions are divided thus:

(a) Visual Flight Rules (VFR) which apply under Visual Meteorological Conditions (VMC);
(b) Instrument Flight Rules (IFR) which apply under Instrument Meteorological Conditions (IMC).

The minima for VFR flight are quite complicated but can be summarised as follows. At or below 3,000ft AMSL at an indicated air speed (IAS) of 140 knots or less, an aircraft must remain in sight of ground or water and clear of cloud in a flight visibility of at least 1,500 metres. If the IAS is more than 140kt up to a limit of 250kt, the flight visibility must be at least 6km. Above 3,000ft up to FL 100 the minima are 5km visibility and at least 1,500 metres horizontally, or 1,000ft vertically clear of cloud. At FL 100 and above, the speed limit no longer applies and the visibility minimum is increased to 8km.

Since it is his or her responsibility to keep clear of other traffic, the pilot must maintain a good look-out. Furthermore, under certain conditions, climbs or descents maintaining VMC may be authorised for aircraft flying under IFR so as to expedite traffic; it is then the pilot's responsibility to avoid other traffic. In R/T transmissions the terms VFR or Victor Fox are used freely by pilots. In the same way, VMC may be referred to as Victor Mike. The phrase 'VMC on top' means that the aircraft is flying in VMC conditions above a cloud layer.

IFR comes into force when the visibility requirements described above cannot be met, and at all times during the hours of darkness. It is then mandatory for an aircraft to be flown on instruments by a suitably qualified pilot. It must also carry a minimum scale of navigational and other equipment. Within controlled airspace, responsibility for separation from other aircraft is in the hands of the ground controllers.

Outside controlled airspace, pilots flying above the transition altitude of 3,000ft must reset their altimeters to the standard setting of 1013 millibars and fly in accordance with what is known as the quadrantal rule. This is intended to ensure that aircraft on converging headings at levels below 24,500ft remain clear of each other by at least 500ft, as the following table explains:

Magnetic track	Cruising level
Less than 90°	Odd thousands of feet
90° but less than 180°	Odd thousands of feet plus 500ft
180° but less than 270°	Even thousands of feet
270° but less than 360°	Even thousands of feet plus 500ft

Above 24,500ft the semi-circular rule applies:

Magnetic track	Cruising level
Less than 180°	25,000ft
	27,000ft
	29,000ft or higher levels at intervals of 4,000ft
180° but less than 360°	26,000ft
	28,000ft
	31,000ft or higher levels at intervals of 4,000ft

See note on RVSM, page 50

A final variation on the IFR/VFR theme is Special VFR, an authorisation by ATC for a pilot to fly within a control zone, even though he is unable to comply with IFR, and in certain airspace where provision is made for such flights. Depending on the visibility, amount of cloud and its height and the limitations of the pilot's licence, a Special VFR clearance may be requested and issued.

Standard separation is provided between all Special VFR flights, and between such flights and other aircraft operating IFR. In practice much use is made of geographical features to keep Special VFR traffic apart, routeing along opposite banks of an estuary for instance. When flying on this type of clearance a pilot must comply with ATC instructions and remain at all times in flight conditions which enable him to determine his flight path and to keep clear of obstructions. It is implicit in all Special VFR clearances that the aircraft stays clear of cloud and in sight of the surface. ATC almost always imposes a height limitation which will require the pilot to fly either at or below a specific level. A typical clearance at Liverpool, for example, is 'GYE is cleared to the zone boundary via Chester, Special VFR not above altitude 1,500ft Liverpool QNH 1002'.

The phonetic alphabet

The use of phonetics on radio to overcome the problems of confusing similar sounding letters like 'B' and 'P' or 'M' and 'N' dates back to the First World War when it was essential that such information as map references were passed accurately by aircraft spotting for the artillery. The phonetic alphabet of the time began A – Ack, B – Beer and has left us with such familiar phrases as 'Ack-Ack' for anti-aircraft fire. By the time of the Second World War it had been replaced by an alphabet beginning A – Able, B – Baker and C – Charlie. In the 1950s, by international agreement, the British wartime code was superseded by a new alphabet designed to be more easily pronounced by aircrew whose native language was other than English. Some of the original phonetics were retained but a number of words known throughout the world were now employed. The resulting alphabet was almost identical to that in use today, the exceptions being M – Metro, N – Nectar and X – Extra. The new offering sparked off some ribald comment that its originators seemed to have spent a lot of time hanging around in bars and dance halls, such was the emphasis on these admirable pursuits! The alphabet was overhauled once more in 1956 and remains in use to this day.

Certain universally accepted codes and abbreviations, such as QNH, QFE, ILS, SRA, QDM are not put into phonetics but said as written. There is also a standard way of pronouncing numbers and the word decimal, as used in radio frequencies, is supposed to be said as 'dayseemal' although this rarely happens in practice.

Current phonetic alphabet

A – Alpha	H – Hotel	O – Oscar	V – Victor
B – Bravo	I – India	P – Papa	W – Whiskey
C – Charlie	J – Juliet	Q – Quebec	X – X-Ray
D – Delta	K – Kilo	R – Romeo	Y – Yankee
E – Echo	L – Lima	S – Sierra	Z – Zulu
F – Foxtrot	M – Mike	T – Tango	
G – Golf	N – November	U – Uniform	

Transmission of numbers

0 – Zero	3 – Tree	6 – Six	9 – Niner
1 – Wun	4 – Fower	7 – Seven	Thousand – Tousand
2 – Too	5 – Fife	8 – Ait	

Examples of number transmissions are: 10 – Wun Zero; 583 – Fife Ait Tree; 2,500 – Too Tousand Fife Hundred; 3,000 – Tree Tousand. Exceptions are Flight Level Wun Hundred, Too Hundred and Tree Hundred, said in this way to avoid the confusion that has sometimes occurred in the past with FL100/110 and FL200/210. All six figures are spoken when identifying radio frequencies, irrespective of whether they are 25kHz or 8.33kHz spaced. Exceptionally, when the two final digits of the frequency are both zero, only the first four digits need be given. 119.000 – Wun Wun Niner dayseemal Zero; 122.500 - Wun Too Too dayseemal Fife. Since the last edition of this book, the use of the R/T prefix 'Channel' for 8.33kHz frequencies has been discontinued.

The Q-Code
A further note concerns the Q-Code, long obsolete in aviation, apart from certain enduring terms like QGH, QNH and QFE. It was an expansion of the Q-Code already in use by the merchant marine and it became possible to exchange information on practically all subjects that might be needed in aviation communications. These three letter groups could be sent by Wireless Telegraphy (W/T) in Morse with great speed and overcame any inherent language difficulties. For example, an operator would send the code 'QDM' to a ground station, which meant 'What is my magnetic course to steer with zero wind to reach you?'. The ground operator would transmit 'QDM' and the appropriate figure.

Standard words and phrases used in R/T communications

Word/Phrase	Meaning
Acknowledge	Let me know that you have received and understood this message
Affirm	Yes
Approved	Permission for proposed action granted
Break	Indicates the separation between messages
Break break	As above but in a busy environment
Cancel	Annul the previously transmitted clearance
Check	Examine a system or procedure (no answer is normally expected)
Cleared	Authorised to proceed under the conditions specified
Climb	Climb and maintain
Confirm	I request verification of clearance, instruction, action or information
Contact	Establish radio communications with ...(The obsolete code 'QSY', which meant the same thing is often still used by pilots)
Correct	True or accurate
Correction	An error has been made in this transmission (or message indicated). The correct version is ...
Descend	Descend and maintain
Disregard	Ignore
Fanstop	I am initiating a practice engine failure after take-off. (Used only by pilots of single engine aircraft.) The response should be 'Report climbing away'
Freecall	Call (unit) your details have not been passed. Mainly used by military ATC
Hold short	Stop before reaching the specified location
How do you read	What is the readability of my transmission?
I say again	I repeat for clarity or emphasis
Maintain	Continue in accordance with the conditions specified in or in its literal sense eg 'Maintain VFR'
Monitor	Listen out on (frequency)
Negative	No or permission not granted or that is not correct
Over	My transmission is ended and I expect a response from you. (Not normally used in VHF communications
Out	My transmission is ended and no response is expected
Pass your message	Proceed with your message

Read back	Repeat all, or the specified part, of this message back to me exactly as received
Report	Pass required information
Request	I should like to know, or I wish to obtain
Roger	I have received all your last transmission. (Note: under no circumstances to be used as an affirmative or negative)
Say again	Repeat all, or the following part of your last transmission
Standby	Wait and I will call you. (Note: No onward clearance should be assumed)
Unable	I cannot comply with your request
Wilco	I understand your message and will comply with it

Also note that controllers who are recently ex-military sometimes use standard RAF phrases such as 'Wait' (for 'Stand by') and 'Wrong' (for 'Correction').

If a pilot wants a check on the quality of his radio transmissions he will say: 'Tower, GCD radio check'. The tower may reply: 'GCD, readability 5.' The clarity of radio transmissions is expressed by the following scale:

Readability 1 – Unreadable
Readability 2 – Readable now and then
Readability 3 – Readable but with difficulty
Readability 4 – Readable
Readability 5 – Perfectly readable

Note that controllers in exasperation sometimes use non-standard phrases like 'Strength a half' for really awful radios! Another phrase in common usage is 'Carrier wave only', indicating that an unmodulated transmission is being received by the ground station, ie it is just noise without the accompanying speech.

Communications
Aeronautical ground stations are identified by the name of the location, followed by a suffix which indicates the type of service being given.

Suffix	Service
Control	Area Control Service
Radar	Radar (in general)
Director	Approach Radar Controller dealing only with arriving traffic
Arrivals	As Director
Approach	Approach Control
Tower	Aerodrome Control
Ground	Ground Movement Control
Delivery	Ground Movement Planning (Clearance Delivery)
Talkdown	Precision Approach Radar (Military)
Information	Flight Information Service
Radio	Aerodrome Air/Ground Communications Service

When satisfactory two-way communication has been established, and provided that it will not be confusing, the name of the location or the call-sign suffix may be omitted. The basic rule is that the full call-signs of both stations must be used on the first transmission. For example:

Aircraft: 'Southend Tower GABCD.'
ATC: 'GABCD Southend Tower pass your message.'

Aircraft call-signs may take various forms but they must remain the same throughout the flight. However, if aircraft on the same frequency have similar call-signs ATC may instruct them to alter the format temporarily to avoid confusion. Aircraft in the heavy wake turbulence category must include the word 'Heavy' immediately after the call-sign in the initial call. For the Airbus A380 'Super' is used as a suffix. In both cases, this is to remind the controller that increased separation may be necessary for following aircraft. To alert controllers to the fact that a student pilot is flying solo, the call-sign prefix 'Student' is used in the initial call and then usually dropped until contact is made with another ATC unit. The controller can then make due allowance for the limited experience of student pilots and keep instructions as simple and straightforward as possible. 'Helicopter' is another possible call-sign prefix.

When receiving a radar service, certain ex-military aircraft types have been granted an exemption from the Air Navigation Order requirement to fly at an indicated airspeed less than 250kt below Flight Level 100. In order to alert the controller to this higher speed profile, pilots of exempted aircraft will, on initial contact, prefix the aircraft call-sign with 'Fastjet' or 'Fastprop' depending on the type of propulsion. Use of the prefix is confined to initial contact with ATC agencies for periods of flight during which speeds in excess of 250kt are intended.

Aircraft are identified by one of the following types of call-sign:

(a) The registration of the aircraft, eg GBFRM, N753DA
(b) The registration of the aircraft preceded by the approved telephony designator of the operating company, eg Speedbird GBGDC
(c) The flight identification or trip number, eg Speedbird 501.

Once satisfactory two-way communication with an aircraft has been established, controllers are permitted to abbreviate the call-sign but only to the extent shown in the table below.

Full call-sign	Abbreviation
GBFRM	GRM
Speedbird GBGDC	Speedbird DC
N31029	N029
Cherokee GBGTR	Cherokee TR
Speedbird 501	No abbreviation

In practice other variations are to be heard, some pilots using their company three-letter designator and flight number rather than the normal company name and flight number, eg SKS232 or Sky Service 232. Either is correct and it is quite common for controllers, faced with an unfamiliar company designator on a flight progress strip, or simply forgetting what it stands for, to revert to the three-letter prefix.

The aim is to prevent incidents and potential accidents caused by call-sign ambiguities but they still occur in sufficient numbers to cause concern. Regular bulletins of Mandatory Occurrence Reports (MORs) are circulated amongst pilots and controllers and they often contain reports of aircraft with similar call-signs taking instructions meant for each other by mistake.

Private aircraft normally use the aircraft registration letters or numbers as a call-sign, as do some taxi and executive aircraft and sometimes airliners on training or empty positioning flights. Otherwise, commercial operators use their company designator and flight number as in (c) above. Intensive use of flight numbers often leads to call-sign confusion when two aircraft with the same flight number are on frequency together, for example Air France 532 and Air Malta 532. The problem is under constant scrutiny and a possible solution is the use of alpha-numerics. Further confusion has been caused by call-signs resembling flight levels or headings, so operators have agreed, as far as possible, not to allocate flight numbers which end in zero or five. In practice, this means figures below 500.

Glossary of aviation terms heard on radio

See also Abbreviations and lists on pages 20, 21 and 50

Abeam	Passing a specified point at 90 degrees to the left or right
Abort	Abandon take-off or return prematurely
Active	The runway-in-use
Actual	The current weather conditions
Airprox	Official term for a near-miss
Alternate	Alternate airfield if unable to land at destination
Approach plate	Another term for approach chart
Approach sequence	Position in traffic on to final approach
Approved Departure Time	See page 104
Autorotation	Helicopter practice forced-landing
ATIS (Ay-Tiss)	Automatic Terminal Information Service
Avgas	Aviation gasoline
Backtrack	Taxi back along the runway
Bandboxed	Two or more frequencies monitored by one controller during quiet periods
Base check	Periodic training flight to check the competency of commercial flight crew
Base turn	Turn on to final from an instrument approach when it is not a reciprocal of the outbound track
The Bell	Colloquial term for the Belfast VOR
Blind transmission	A transmission from one station to another when two-way communication cannot be established but where it is believed that the called station is able to receive the transmission
The Boundary	Boundary between Flight Information Regions or alternatively the edge of a Control Zone
Box	Radio, Box One being the main set and Box Two the standby
Breakthrough	Transmissions on one frequency breaking through on to another
Build-ups	Cumulo-nimbus clouds
CAVOK	See page 92
CB	Also referred to as Charlie Bravo. Cumulo-nimbus clouds
Centrefix Approach	Self-positioning to final approach using the aircraft Flight Management System
Charlie	That is correct (common HF usage)
Chopping to approach	Military term for changing frequency
Clearance limit	A specified point to which an ATC clearance remains effective
Closing heading	Heading to intercept the ILS
Coasting in/out	Crossing the coast inbound/outbound
The company	As in 'Follow the company', ie an aircraft belonging to the same operator as the subject
Conflict Alert	See pages 42 and 43
Conflicting traffic	Other aircraft in the vicinity which may prove a hazard
The Cross	Colloquial term for Dean Cross VOR
Crosswind component	Strength of wind from the side on final approach
CTOT	See-Tot, Calculated Take-Off Time (Slot)
The Data	Temperature, QNH, runway-in-use, etc

Detail	Intentions during a particular training flight
Direct	Flying from one beacon or geographical point straight to another
Discrete	Separate frequency usually devoted to one aircraft for PAR talk-down, etc
Div Arrival	Arrival message sent to destination and other agencies when an aircraft diverts en route
Dogleg	Flying a zig-zag to lose height, etc
Drift	The effect of wind on an aircraft (see page 17)
En route	As in 'Report going en route', ie changing to another frequency
Established	Aligned or 'locked on' with the ILS
Expected Approach Time	See page 54
Fanstop	Practice engine failure
Flag	Warning flag on cockpit instrument that ILS or other ground-based aid has failed or is not being received correctly
Fod	Jargon word for airfield debris, derived from the abbreviation of 'foreign object damage' but now deemed to be 'foreign object debris'
Four Dee etc	4 miles DME
Free call	A call to a ground station without prior co-ordination by landline between this and the previous ATC unit with which the aircraft was in contact
Glidepath	The final descent path to the runway on an ILS approach
Go around	Overshoot runway and rejoin circuit or carry out missed approach procedure
Going en route	Changing to another frequency
Good rate	Unofficial abbreviation for a good rate of climb or descent
The GOW	Colloquial term for Glasgow VOR
GPU	Ground Power Unit
Guard frequency	International Distress Frequency which is monitored continuously by aircraft flying long-distance routes
Guesstimate	Just what it implies!
Heading	Direction in which the aircraft is pointing. (See also Track)
Heavy	See page 101
Intentions	Course of action after a missed approach etc
IR Test	Instrument Rating Test
Jet A-1	Turbine fuel
Land after	See page 61
Localiser	See page 38
LVPs	Low Visibility Procedures (spoken as written)
Mach	Speed expressed as a ratio of the speed of sound (Mach 1)
MOR	Mandatory Occurrence Report
Navex	Navigational Exercise
No ATC speed	Unofficial abbreviation for 'no ATC speed restriction'
Nosig	No significant change in weather
Notam	Notice to Airmen
Off blocks	The time the aircraft commenced taxying or pushback
On task	Aircraft reporting on scene or job
Orbit	Circle, usually over a specified point
The Park	Colloquial term for Brookmans Park VOR
Pattern	American equivalent of circuit
Pax	Passengers
The Pole	Colloquial term for Pole Hill VOR
Popup traffic	Traffic which suddenly appears on radar perhaps because it has just climbed into coverage

Powerback	Reversing off an apron stand under an aircraft's own power
PPR	Prior permission by telephone required for landing
Practice asymmetric	Engine failure simulation on multi-engined aircraft
Procedure turn	Similar to base turn except that the aircraft retraces its steps on an exact reciprocal of the outbound leg
Pushback	Reversing out of an apron stand with the aid of a special tractor
QAR	Quick Access Recorder
Radar heading	Heading imposed by a radar controller
Radar overhead	Radar blind spot above aerial
Radar vectoring	Specified headings given by radar (see page 54)
Radial	Magnetic bearing line from or to a VOR
Ready message	Sent to CFMU in the hope of an earlier CTOT (slot)
Ready in sequence	Ready for departure on reaching head of queue at holding point
Recovery	Military jargon for land back at base
Release(d)	Control of a particular aircraft handed over from area controller to approach, or authorisation from area for an aircraft to take-off
Regional	The QNH for a defined area
Rejected take-off	Abandoned take-off procedure which is sometimes practised during pilot check-outs
Resume own navigation	Revert to self-navigation after a period of radar vectoring
RVR	Runway Visual Range (see page 93)
Sector	Each leg of a series of (usually) scheduled flights. Also sub-divisions of an area control service
Securité	Prefix to RAF flight safety message
Selcal	Selective Calling (see page 81)
SID	Standard Instrument Departure
SIGMET	Significant met conditions (see page 93)
Slot time	See pages 65 and 104
SNOCLO	Airfield closed during snow-clearing operations
SNOWTAM	See page 94
Special flight	A police, photographic survey or other flight for which special permission has been granted by the CAA
Speed Limit Point	Position before which an inbound aircraft entering a TMA must have slowed to the speed limit (normally 250kt). For departing traffic speed restriction is lifted here
Squawk	SSR code (see pages 16 and 199)
Stand	Numbered parking position on apron
Standard Missed	Procedure to be followed if an aircraft is unable to land from an instrument approach
Stepdown Fix	A defined point on the final approach track indicating that a critical obstacle has been safely overflown and descent to the next specified level may be commenced
Stepped on	Someone else transmitted over you
Stratus	Low-lying cloud layer
Stud	Military pre-set frequency
TAD	Tactical Air Directive (frequency)
TAF	Terminal Aerodrome Forecast
Teardrop	A 180 degree turn to land back on the runway from which one has just departed. Often used by circuit training aircraft when runway-in-use is changed
Tech stop	En route diversion for technical reasons such as refuelling

Tempo	Forecast temporary weather change
Three greens	Indication of wheels down and locked
Toppo chart	Topographical chart
Track	The path of an aircraft over the ground
Traffic	Other aircraft known to be in the vicinity
U/s	Unserviceable
Volmet	See page 95
Wake turbulence	See page 101
Waypoint	A pre-selected geographical position used with a Flight Management System
Wind shear	See page 94

There are certain other basic R/T rules with which pilots must comply. Aircraft flying in controlled airspace must obtain permission from the controlling authority before they can change frequency to another station. They should not, for example, call the tower until approach instructs them to do so. Pilots sometimes take instructions intended for other aircraft, particularly if the call-signs are similar. Controllers need to be constantly vigilant to the possibility of such errors.

When a ground station wishes to broadcast information to all aircraft likely to receive it, the message is prefixed by the call-sign 'All stations'. No reply is expected to such general calls unless individual aircraft are subsequently called upon to acknowledge receipt. Direct communications between pilots and controllers can be adversely affected by simultaneous transmissions which, effectively, block all or part of intended messages. The controller is usually alerted to the fact that he has transmitted over another aircraft by a distinctive change in the sidetone in his headset. The word 'blocked' may be used when the controller hears simultaneous transmissions, also by a pilot hearing simultaneous transmissions and wanting to alert aircraft and ATC alike.

Another important point is that an ATC route clearance is not an instruction to take off or enter an active runway. The words take-off are used only when an aircraft is cleared for take-off; at all other times the word 'departure' is used. The disaster at Tenerife in 1977 was caused mainly by a flight crew interpreting a route clearance as also implying a take-off clearance. They must have known better but there were pressing distractions and so the fatal error was made.

There is also a stringent requirement to read back certain information because of the possible seriousness of a misunderstanding in the transmission and receipt of these messages. If the controller does not receive a read-back, the pilot will be asked to give one. Similarly, the pilot is expected to request that instructions be repeated or clarified if they are not fully understood. The following ATC instructions must be read back in full by the pilot: level, heading and speed instructions, airways or route clearances, runway-in-use, clearance to enter, land on, take off on, backtrack, hold short of, or cross an active runway, Secondary Surveillance Radar operating instructions, altimeter settings, VDF information, frequency changes and type of radar service.

For example:

ATC: 'GBFVM cleared to cross Lima 975 at Malud Flight Level 180.'
Aircraft: 'Cleared to cross Lima 975 Malud Flight Level 180, GVM.'

ATC: 'GTE contact East Midlands Approach 134.175.'
Aircraft: 'East Midlands 134.175 GTE.'

Levels may be reported as altitude, height or Flight Level, according to the phase of flight and the altimeter setting, but a standard form of reporting is adhered to. An aircraft climbs, descends, maintains, passes, leaves or reaches a level.

For example:

'Shamrock 920 climb FL 190.'
'Midland 581 maintain altitude 3,500ft.'
'Speedbird 58 report passing FL160.'
'Ryanair 842 report reaching FL190.'

Aircraft: 'Midland 581 request descent.'
ATC;   'Midland 581 descend FL60.'
Aircraft: 'Midland 581 leaving FL140 for FL60.'

Sometimes a changing traffic situation may necessitate an intermediate halt to a descent or climb. 'Shamrock 920 stop descent FL150.' Or perhaps for traffic reasons, a higher than normal rate of climb or descent may be requested to avoid eroding separation. 'Speedbird 58 climb to FL 190, expedite passing FL150.'

Clearances to climb and descend must include the expression 'Flight Level', 'Altitude' or 'Height'. The word 'to' after the verb must be used when clearing an aircraft to an altitude or height. It must not be used when a Flight Level is involved.

Separations
The rules for separation of IFR traffic, particularly when radar is not available, are quite complicated and probably of little interest to the layman. Suffice it to say that the basic radar separations are five miles laterally (but three and up to ten in certain cases) and/or 1,000ft vertically up to FL290. Above this level, 2,000ft vertical separation is applied unless aircraft have been approved for RVSM (Reduced Vertical Separation Minima) operations. RVSM is mandatory over the UK and much of Europe so aircraft unable to comply with the conditions have to remain below FL290. Above FL410, 2,000ft is the required vertical separation.

For aircraft departing from an airport the minimum separation is one minute, provided the aircraft fly on tracks diverging by 45 degrees or more immediately after take-off. Where aircraft are going the same way, and provided the first has filed a true air speed (TAS) 40kt or faster than the second, the separation is two minutes. With a TAS of 20kt or more faster than the second aircraft it becomes five minutes and in all other cases it is ten minutes. Radar will reduce some of these times and they are also affected by the demands of wake turbulence separation and local procedures.

Conditional clearances
These comprise the call-sign of the aircraft being given the clearance, identification of the subject of the condition, eg aircraft, reporting point, level, etc and the clearance. Examples are:

'Speedbird 123, after passing Burnham, fly heading 305.'
'Lufthansa 456, below FL150, speed 220 knots.'
'Scandinavian 721, after the landing 757, line up Runway 22 via Alpha One.'

In the last example, the Scandinavian may respond: 'Behind the landing 757, line up behind.' This is the ICAO phraseology used in mainland Europe

Categories of priority
Requests for clearances are normally dealt with in the order in which they are received and issued according to the traffic situation. However, certain aircraft are given priority over others in the following descending order:

Liverpool Tower Controller's position.

Category A	Aircraft in emergency and ambulance/medical aircraft when the safety of life is involved. Aircraft that have declared a 'Police Emergency'
Category B	Search and Rescue and post-accident flight checks of navigation aids
Category C	Royal Flights
Category D	Certain flights carrying Heads of Government or very senior government officials
Category E	Flight check aircraft engaged in, or in transit to, time- or weather-critical calibration flights
Normal	Those that have filed a flight plan in the normal way and are conforming with normal route procedures. Initial instrument flight tests conducted by CAA (callsign 'Exam')
Category Z	Non-standard and other flights, particularly training

Non-deviating Status: aircraft, both civil and military, that have been allocated this status have an operational requirement to maintain a specific track and level(s) or a particular route and level(s). It is imperative that an NDS aircraft is not moved from its pre-planned flight path unless absolutely necessary because this could render it operationally ineffective.

Chapter 3

Types of airspace

Flight Information Regions (FIRs)

THE UNITED KINGDOM is divided into two FIRs, the London and the Scottish, the boundary between them being the 55 N line of latitude. Above 24,500ft these areas are known as Upper Flight Information Regions, abbreviated to UIR. The London FIR comes under the London Area Air Traffic Control Centre at Swanwick in Hampshire and the Scottish FIR under Scottish Area Control Centre at Atlantic House near Prestwick. Southern Ireland comes under the jurisdiction of the ACCs at Shannon and Dublin, the stretches of the Atlantic to north and south being controlled by Reykjavik and Shanwick Oceanic Controls, respectively.

The UK follows the ICAO system, which aims to classify airspace internationally so that it is perfectly clear to users from anywhere in the world which flight rules apply and what air traffic services they can expect within a particular airspace. The seven different categories of airspace are represented by the letters A to G, although Class C has yet to be adopted in the UK.

Class A

This consists mainly of airways which are normally ten miles wide (five miles each side of centreline) and generally have a base between 3,000ft and FL55. With some exceptions they extend vertically to FL245, the base of upper airspace in Britain. Aircraft flying in them are required to operate under IFR and are separated positively by ATC, using radar or procedural methods. 'Westbound' flights, which could in practice also be on north–west or south–west headings, fly at even numbered flight levels and 'eastbound' flights at odd numbers. Some airways are activated for peak periods only, usually weekends and national holidays.

Other Class A airspace includes the London Control Zone and Control Area, the Worthing, Daventry and Cotswold Control Areas, and the Shannon Oceanic Control Area.

A, B, G, and R signify regional air routes, prefixed by U when in the upper airspace (ie above FL245). Regional area navigation routes are designated UH (Link Route to Polar Tracks), UL (Link Route to oceanic airspace), UN and UP, while UT is a non-regional area nav route. Suffixes N, S, E and W indicate compass points, eg R1N and R1S are parallel one-way routes. Advisory Routes (Class F airspace) are suffixed D.

Class B

No UK airspace is currently designated as Class B.

Class C

This comprises the London and Scottish FIR above FL195, including all Control Areas and Airways, plus the London and Scottish UIR between FL245 and FL660 which includes the Hebrides Upper Control Area (UTA).

Class D
In general, these are Control Zones and Control Areas around airports.

Class E
Parts of Scottish TMA airspace below 6,000ft (above 6,000ft is Class D), Belfast TCA and Prestwick TCA.

Class F
This is reserved for Advisory Routes, normally referred to as ADRs, which have been established where public transport aircraft use certain routes but not in sufficient quantity to justify the full protection of an airway. To distinguish them from airways, the suffix 'Delta', eg Whiskey Two Delta, is used. Most of the ADRs are to be found in Scotland and Northern England. In contrast to airways, the quadrantal rule is applied for level allocation (see page 18).

Class G
All UK airspace, including that above FL660, not included in Classes A to F. This is unregulated airspace in the open FIR within which pilots are allowed to fly as they wish without hindrance or radio calls. In instrument conditions pilots are expected to conform to a simple procedure called the quadrantal rule which regulates altitude according to the aircraft's heading.

Classification of airspace
The classification of the airspace within a Flight Information Region determines the flight rules which apply and the minimum services which are to be provided. These are summarised below:

Class	Flight Rules	Aircraft Requirements	Minimum Services by ATC Unit
A	IFR only	ATC clearance before entry Comply with ATC instructions	Separate all aircraft from each other
B	IFR and VFR	ATC clearance before entry Comply with ATC instructions	Separate all aircraft from each other
C	IFR and VFR	ATC clearance before entry Comply with ATC instructions	(a) separate IFR flights from other IFR and VFR flights (b) separate VFR from IFR flights (c) pass traffic information to VFR flights on other VFR flights and give traffic avoidance advice if requested
D	IFR and VFR	ATC clearance before entry Comply with ATC instructions	(a) separate IFR flights from other IFR flights (b) pass traffic information to IFR flights on VFR flights and give traffic avoidance advice if requested
E	IFR and VFR	IFR flights to obtain ATC clearance before entry and comply with ATC instructions	(a) separate IFR flights from other IFR flights (b) pass traffic information, as far as practicable, to IFR flights on VFR flights
		VFR flights do not require clearance	(c) VFR flights in contact are to be given traffic information as far as practicable
F	IFR and VFR	Participating IFR flights are expected to comply with ATC instructions	Separate participating IFR flights from each other
G	IFR and VFR	None	None

Special zones and areas

Aerodrome Traffic Zones
The dimensions of ATZs relate to the midpoint of the longest runway and its length. For example, if the longest runway is greater than 1,850 metres, the boundary of the ATZ will be a circle of radius 2nm from the midpoint of that runway. Aerodromes with shorter runways have smaller ATZs but the vertical limit remains 2,000ft above aerodrome level. Both within or outside controlled airspace pilots must either avoid the ATZ or obtain permission to fly through it.

Military Aerodrome Traffic Zones
The purpose of a MATZ is to provide a volume of airspace within which increased protection may be given to aircraft in the critical stages of circuit, approach and climb-out. It normally comprises the airspace within five nautical miles of the airfield from the surface up to 3,000ft. In addition a 'stub' out to five miles protects the final approach path of the most used runway. Although it is not mandatory for civil pilots to request permission to penetrate a MATZ, it is obviously highly desirable for them to do so.

Helicopter Main Routes and Protected Zones
The concentration of offshore oil and gas installations in the North Sea and increasingly the Irish Sea, with their busy helicopter support operations, has resulted in the introduction of protected airspace. Helicopter Main Routes (HMRs) and Overland Corridors have been established when helicopters operate on a regular basis from and to the mainland or between platforms. A Helicopter Protected Zone (HPZ) is sometimes established around two or more installations and a Helicopter Flight Information Service may also be provided. Apart from the East Shetland Basin, in which procedural separation is provided, the airspace is uncontrolled but its dimensions are published and military and civil pilots must obtain clearance to penetrate an HPZ and keep a good look-out when in proximity to an HMR.

Military Training Areas and Temporary Reserved Airspace
MTAs are defined areas of upper airspace, within which intense military flying takes place during weekdays and occasionally, with prior notification, at weekends. Certain airways, including UN864 and UL18 are affected when MTAs are active. The two areas are the Valley MTA over North Wales and the East Anglian MTA.

Aerial Tactics Areas and Air-to-Air Refuelling Areas
ATAs are used for air-to-air combat training over the North Sea. Lakenheath ATA is situated off Cromer and The Wash ATA is off the Humber Estuary. Within The Wash ATA is NSAR, the North Sea ACMI Range, otherwise known as Playground, the ACMI element standing for Air Combat Manoeuvring Instrumentation. Fixed sensor towers monitor activity and send information by data-link to the mainland for subsequent analysis and debrief of aircrew.

There are 14 Refuelling Areas, mostly over the North Sea, with others over the West Country and the Scottish Highlands. Tankers orbit in the ARA to allow the receiving aircraft to home on to them. When 'on boom', the operation begins along a specific track within the ARA.

E-3 AWACS Orbit Areas
There are 11 of these around the UK, mainly off the coast , where an E-3 Sentry can hold in order to direct battle exercises.

Danger Areas
The most common Danger Areas are weapons ranges, but the term also embraces parachuting and other activities potentially hazardous to aircraft. Radar crossing services are available for

Lower Airspace Routes, South sheet (used with the permission of and copyright of UK CAA).

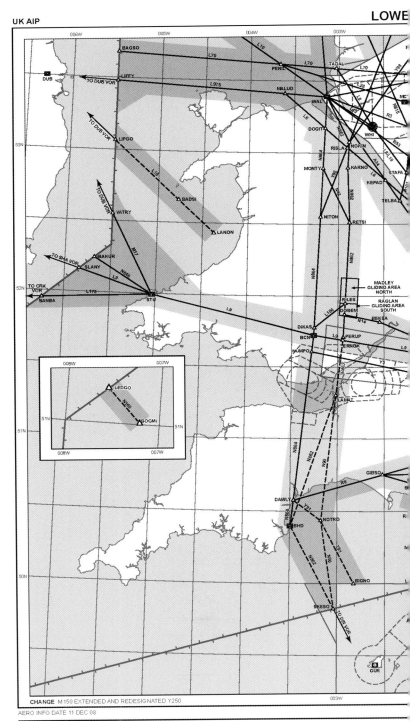

ROUTES (South Sheet)

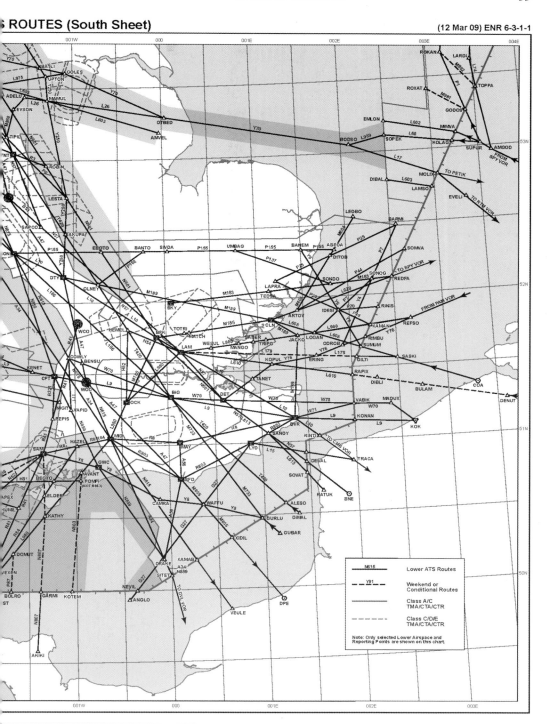

ALTIMETER SETTING REGIONS

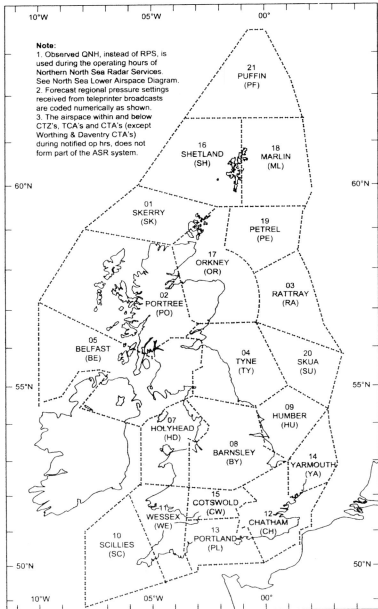

Note:
1. Observed QNH, instead of RPS, is used during the operating hours of Northern North Sea Radar Services. See North Sea Lower Airspace Diagram.
2. Forecast regional pressure settings received from teleprinter broadcasts are coded numerically as shown.
3. The airspace within and below CTZ's, TCA's and CTA's (except Worthing & Daventry CTA's) during notified op hrs, does not form part of the ASR system.

21 PUFFIN (PF)
16 SHETLAND (SH)
18 MARLIN (ML)
01 SKERRY (SK)
19 PETREL (PE)
17 ORKNEY (OR)
02 PORTREE (PO)
03 RATTRAY (RA)
05 BELFAST (BE)
04 TYNE (TY)
20 SKUA (SU)
09 HUMBER (HU)
07 HOLYHEAD (HD)
08 BARNSLEY (BY)
14 YARMOUTH (YA)
15 COTSWOLD (CW)
11 WESSEX (WE)
12 CHATHAM (CH)
13 PORTLAND (PL)
10 SCILLIES (SC)

United Kingdom Altimeter Setting Regions.

some of them, depending on activity status. In the initial stages of a disaster or emergency incident, a Temporary Danger Area is always introduced to prevent flight by aircraft not engaged in the associated support or rescue action.

Prohibited and Restricted Areas

Most Prohibited Areas are centred on nuclear power stations, over-flight being prohibited below 2,000ft above ground level within a radius of two miles. Restricted Areas include certain prison sites.

Low Flying

The UK Military Low Flying System (UKLFS) extends across the whole of the UK and surrounding overseas areas, from the surface to 2,000ft. This permits a wide distribution of activity, which contributes to flight safety and reduces the environmental impact of low flying. Military pilots are directed to avoid major conurbations, built-up areas, controlled airspace, aerodrome traffic zones and other sensitive locations. Inevitably, the protection given to these areas creates unavoidable concentrations of military low flying activity where corridors are formed between them. Where necessary, military pilots follow unidirectional flows below 2,000ft to reduce the risk of confliction.

For administrative purposes, the UKLFS is divided geographically into low flying areas (LFA). Certain LFAs are nominated Dedicated User Areas (DUA), are allocated for special use (such as concentrated helicopter training) and are managed under local arrangements. Civil pilots should be aware that what is known as Unusual Air Activity and night exercises are frequently conducted in DUAs. These exercises can include aircraft operating without, or with restricted, navigation lights. In the north of Scotland, the Highlands Restricted Area (HRA) is used for special training, often in Instrument Met Conditions (IMC). To ensure safety, entry by civil and non-participating military aircraft is normally prohibited during published operating hours.

Military fixed wing aircraft (except light aircraft) are considered to be low flying when at less than 2,000ft Minimum Separation Distance (MSD), which is the authorised minimum separation, in all directions, between an aircraft and the ground, water or any obstacle. The lowest height at which military aircraft normally fly is 250ft MSD. However, in three specially designated areas, known as Tactical Training Areas (TTAs), located in mid-Wales, the Borders of Scotland and the north of Scotland, a small number of flights may be authorised to fly down to 100ft MSD. Military light propeller aircraft and helicopters are considered to be low flying when operating below 500ft. In practice, most military low flying takes place between 250 and 600ft MSD, decreasing in intensity up to 1,000ft MSD and reducing further in the 1,000–2,000ft height band. Occasionally, however, military aircraft perform high-energy manoeuvres between 250ft and 2,000ft, during which rapid changes in height, speed and direction will occur.

UAVs (Unmanned (or Uninhabited) Aerial Vehicles)

Eurocontrol has published Air Traffic Management (ATM) specifications that set out how military UAVs should fly in European airspace. Eurocontrol says that currently, when UAVs operate outside specifically designated areas, they are subject to numerous restrictions to ensure the safety of other airspace users. These restrictions are preventing the full use of UAVs' operational capabilities. Since 2003, when a pan-European high-level military conference asked Eurocontrol to develop an ATM framework that would allow UAVs to operate in all classes of airspace and across national borders, the issue has become more urgent with the increased use and capability of more advanced UAVs.

Before military UAVs are allowed to fly routinely outside segregated airspace, additional technology such as sense-and-avoid needs to be developed. It will also be necessary to do additional work in a range of other fields, including airworthiness, security and operator training. Once these issues have been addressed, the specifications will ensure that ATM procedures for UAVs mirror those applicable to manned aircraft, and the provision of air traffic services to UAVs will be transparent to controllers. Safety of all users of airspace is paramount and the new specifications ensure that UAV operations will be carried out with the same level of safety as for manned aircraft.

Chapter 4

Navigational aids and ATC-related equipment

RADIO NAVIGATIONAL AIDS or 'navaids' assist a pilot in threading his way through the airways, letting down at destination and then, if an Instrument Landing System is installed, following its beam down to the runway. The main types of navaid in the United Kingdom are described briefly below.

Non-Directional Beacon (NDB)
The most common, and one of the simplest of aids is the Non-Directional Beacon. It is used to mark airways when its useful range may be up to 100 miles and as an approach and landing aid, sometimes referred to as a Locator Beacon, when its range will be about 15 miles. It consists merely of a radio transmitter in the medium frequency band that sends out a continuous steady note in all directions. A call-sign of three letters in morse code (two for airport locator beacons) is superimposed at regular intervals as a check that the desired beacon has been selected. The Automatic Direction Finder (ADF), or radio compass, fitted in an aircraft will, when tuned to the appropriate frequency, indicate the relative position of the transmission source by means of a needle on a dial. The great disadvantage of the NDB is that it is very prone to interference. For example a thunderstorm cell in the area will often cause the cockpit needle to point to it in preference to the beacon, not a happy state of affairs!

VHF Omni-directional Range (VOR) and Doppler VOR (DVOR)
VORs broadcast their signals in all directions but the signals vary around the compass in such a way that each direction has its own signal which cannot be confused with that of any other direction. If an aircraft receiver can pick up and decode the signal from a VOR, it can tell the bearing (or radial as it is termed) from the station. Doppler VOR is a recent development that improves the accuracy of the signal and reduces errors caused by obstructions and high ground.

Strong rumours suggest that a number of UK VOR beacons are going to be withdrawn from service in the not-too-distant future, one of them being Dean Cross to the west of Carlisle. The Newcastle VOR has already gone. This is part of a European plan for future navigation, based on the ability of area navigation systems to work out the most accurate track-keeping by means of multiple DMEs. It is expected that by 2010 around 60% of existing VORs will be taken out of service, leaving the rest as back-up for aircraft RNAV system failures.

RIGHT: ILS/DME chart for Runway 27L at London/Heathrow (used with the permission of and copyright of UK CAA).

INSTRUMENT APPROACH CHART - ICAO

LONDON/HEATHROW
ILS/DME I-LL
RWY 27L
(ACFT CAT A,B,C,D)

APP 119.725, 120.400, 127.525, 134.975	HEATHROW APPROACH	AD ELEVATION	83
TWR 118.500, 118.700, 124.475	HEATHROW TOWER	THR ELEVATION	77
RAD 125.625, 127.525	HEATHROW RADAR	OBSTACLE ELEVATION	
ATIS 128.075, 113.750, 115.100	HEATHROW INFORMATION	1087 AMSL (1010) (ABOVE THR)	

MSA 25NM ARP

OBSTACLE ELEVATION 1087 AMSL (1010) (ABOVE THR)

BEARINGS ARE MAGNETIC

TRANSITION ALTITUDE **6000**

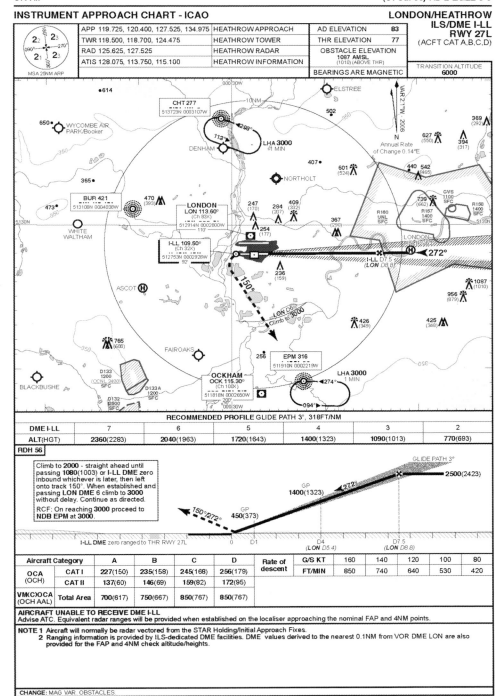

RECOMMENDED PROFILE GLIDE PATH 3°, 318FT/NM

DME I-LL	7	6	5	4	3	2
ALT(HGT)	2360(2283)	2040(1963)	1720(1643)	1400(1323)	1090(1013)	770(693)

RDH 56

Climb to **2000** - straight ahead until passing **1080**(1003) or I-LL DME zero inbound whichever is later, then left onto track 150°. When established and passing LON DME 6 climb to **3000** without delay. Continue as directed.
RCF: On reaching **3000** proceed to **NDB EPM** at **3000**.

I-LL DME zero ranged to THR RWY 27L

Aircraft Category	A	B	C	D	Rate of descent	G/S KT	160	140	120	100	80
OCA (OCH)	CAT I	227(150)	235(158)	245(168)	256(179)		FT/MIN	850	740	640	530	420
	CAT II	137(60)	146(69)	159(82)	172(95)							
VM(C)OCA (OCH AAL)	Total Area	700(617)	750(667)	850(767)	850(767)							

AIRCRAFT UNABLE TO RECEIVE DME I-LL
Advise ATC. Equivalent radar ranges will be provided when established on the localiser approaching the nominal FAP and 4NM points.

NOTE 1 Aircraft will normally be radar vectored from the STAR Holding/Initial Approach Fixes.
  2 Ranging information is provided by ILS-dedicated DME facilities. DME values derived to the nearest 0.1NM from VOR DME LON are also provided for the FAP and 4NM check altitude/heights.

CHANGE: MAG VAR. OBSTACLES.

AERO INFO DATE 19 MAY 08

Distance Measuring Equipment

While VOR gives accurate, specific directional information, it cannot make explicit distance measurements. The pilot, however, may find his distance from the station by taking an intersection of radials from two VORs, or by doing a timed radial manoeuvre with a single VOR. A simpler answer is to use DME which is associated closely with VOR, the combination providing an accurate position fix. A special transmitter in the aircraft sends out pulses in all directions and these are received at the DME station on the ground. As each pulse is received an answering pulse is transmitted automatically and this is picked up in the aircraft. It is in fact the reverse of secondary radar (see below).

As the speed of radio waves is constant at 186,000 miles per second, a computer in the aircraft, which measures the time interval between the transmission of the pulse and the receipt of the response, can convert this time interval into a distance and display it to the pilot in nautical miles. The presentation is either by means of a mechanical meter or more often nowadays by a computer display. In both cases the distance is in miles and tenths.

It should be noted, incidentally, that the height of the aircraft affects the distance measurement; when directly above the station at 36,000ft the instrument will show the aircraft as still being six miles from it. This is because the DME measures slant range rather than ground distance, but it is of little importance except when very close to the station.

DMEs are normally co-located with VORs and the frequencies of the two installations are 'paired'. For example, the VOR frequency of 112.7MHz is always matched by a DME on Channel 74, a VOR on 114.9 by a DME on Channel 96 and so on. This means that aircraft equipment can be arranged so that the selection of a particular VOR frequency means that the related DME channel is selected at the same time.

Instrument Landing System (ILS)

ILS is a pilot-interpreted aid which gives a continuous indication of whether the aircraft is left or right of the final approach track and also its position in relation to an ideal glide path to the runway. The latter is a standard 3 degrees, giving an approximate rate of descent of 300ft per minute. Certain airfields may have greater angles owing to high ground on the approach or other local considerations. London City with its steep 5.5° approach to reduce noise footprint is one example.

This information is augmented by marker beacons on the ground showing range; the outer marker at about four miles from touchdown and a middle marker at around 3,500ft. As the aircraft passes over them they give an audible signal. The outer marker transmits low-toned dashes and the middle marker alternates dots and dashes on a medium tone. These markers cannot only be heard, they also light up lamps on the instrument panel. The outer marker illuminates a blue lamp and the middle an amber, each flashing in time with the codes. These signals are transmitted on a standard 75MHz. Few civil airports have these markers nowadays because increased use of airport-sited DME has rendered them redundant. The pilot now has a continuous read-out of his range from touchdown.

A transmitter with a large aerial system known as the Localiser is sited at the far end of the runway, transmitting its signals on either side of the centreline of the runway and approach. These signals, called blue on the right of the approach path and yellow on the left, overlap in a beam about 5 degrees wide exactly along the approach centreline. A second unit, the glide path transmitter, is sited at the nearer end and slightly to one side of the runway. ILS Localiser/ DME systems dispense with the glide path beam but the DME ranges enable the pilot to monitor his rate of descent.

Initial approach on to the ILS is normally achieved by Approach Radar, the aim being to place the aircraft on a closing heading of about 30 degrees to the final approach at a range of between seven and nine miles. The aircraft should be at an appropriate altitude so that the glide path can be intercepted from below rather than attempting to 'chase' it from above. The final turn-on can be done by radar direction, but these days it is usually done automatically by coupling the ILS with the FMS or autopilot. Where no radar is available a procedural ILS is flown, similar to an NDB approach with the exception that the procedure turn will intercept the ILS and enable the pilot to establish himself on it.

ILSs are divided into three categories as follows:

Category 1: Operation down to 60m decision height with Runway Visual Range in excess of 800m.

Category 2: Operation down to 60m decision height with RVR in excess of 400m.

Category 3: Operation with no height limitation to and along the surface of the runway with external visual reference during the final phase of landing with RVR of 200m.

Subdivisions are Category 3b with RVR of 45m and a planned Category 3c with RVR of zero. They both require guidance along the runway and the latter also to the parking bay. Special ground lighting is required for Category 2 and 3 ILSs, together with safeguarded areas around the sensitive aerial systems to avoid fluctuations caused by vehicles or taxying aircraft. Localiser/DME ILSs are non-precision and therefore uncategorised.

Microwave Landing System (MLS)

The MLS is so-called because it works in the much higher frequency microwave band. This creates a number of advantages, not the least of which is a high accuracy which means Category 3 for all installations. In addition, non-standard offset or curved approaches can be made to avoid obstacles or noise-sensitive areas and the glide path is adaptable to high-angle

Compton DVOR site.

approaches by STOL aircraft or helicopters. The CAA has been evaluating MLS equipment at Heathrow to gain the technical and operational experience necessary for the approval of future installations in the UK. BA Airbus crews operated the ongoing trials.

ICAO planned that MLS would replace ILS by 1998 but the decision has been deferred because of pending developments in satellite navigation. The datalink from the test MLS at Heathrow is being used to uplink Differential Global Positioning System (DGPS) corrections to a specially-equipped British Airways aircraft in order to demonstrate the feasibility of this concept. This integration of MLS and DGPS would enable precision approaches to be made and provide a cost saving of around 50% on each MLS installation because of the elimination of certain functions such as Precision DME and departure guidance. Both of these can be provided by DGPS. At the time of writing, MLS has just become operational on all four of Heathrow's runway directions.

Doppler

The Doppler navigation system is self-contained and produces the desired information on position through a measurement of aircraft velocity by means of Doppler radar, and measurement of direction by means of a sensor such as a gyro or magnetic compass. The two sets of information are then processed in a computer.

Inertial Navigation System (INS)

INS operates independently of ground stations, being based on a computer aboard the aircraft which derives its input from gyroscopic accelerometers. A pre-determined journey can be programmed in, the output of which will direct the autopilot or FMS to fly the required tracks. This enables aircraft to fly direct routeings without reference to radio beacons if first requested from, and approved by, ATC.

LORAN-C

A ground-based long-range radio navigation system which is interpreted by a cockpit computer. Its use is declining in favour of satellite navigation but it is being retained for the time being as a back-up.

Satellite Navigation (GLONASS and GPS)

Currently there are two systems: GLONASS, the GLobal Orbiting NAvigation Satellite System developed by the former USSR; and the American GPS, Global Positioning System. A joint system combining the GLONASS and GPS satellites is planned so that worldwide coverage will be increased significantly and a greater measure of redundancy introduced to guard against satellite failure. Two other Satnav systems are under development, Galileo in Europe and Compass in China. Global positioning is the most accurate form of navigation technology under development and it will play a major role in increasing airspace capacity as well as improving safety. Currently under evaluation is the concept of Differential GPS, whereby the integrity of the satellite-derived position information is constantly verified and corrected if necessary by a ground station using Mode S datalink to the aircraft. When perfected the system could enable precision approaches to be made in association with ILS or MLS. GPS operates in the band 1559–1610MHz.

Europe's Galileo will be interoperable with the US GPS, improving the accuracy and reliability of navigation and timing signals received across the planet. The final constellation of 30 satellites will more than double the number providing the American GPS. More importantly, it will eliminate reliance on GPS, which is in the hands of the US military and could be withdrawn or at least rendered less accurate at times of international crisis. The idea of the Europeans developing their own network had irked the US Department of Defense, which controls GPS, because of the potential for Galileo's signals to interfere with those intended for use by the military. The Pentagon was concerned that frequency clashes could have prevented American commanders from degrading navigation data in the theatre of war to all but their own forces, as is possible at present.

However, Washington and Brussels have now signed an agreement to adopt compatible operating standards. These technical parameters will allow either side to jam effectively the other's signal in a small area, such as a battlefield, without shutting down the whole system. More importantly, from the civilian perspective, the agreement allows the systems to be meshed seamlessly, greatly benefiting manufacturers, service providers and consumers. Better accuracy, especially in built-up areas where the current GPS signal can be patchy, should lead to an even bigger demand for positioning systems. Remember that aviation is just one of many users of satellite navigation.

GPS does have some limitations, namely its weak signal strength which is easily jammed. Apart from the effects of deliberate disruption, natural phenomena such as solar flares can affect the system too. Nevertheless, CAA has an on-going project to make GNSS (Global Navigation Satellite System) non-precision approaches available to UK GA pilots. The first one approved is at Shoreham Airport.

Precision Area Navigation (P-RNAV)

With the anticipated growth in air traffic, it is envisaged that P-RNAV will be employed to a greater extent for the design of terminal procedures, including Standard Instrument Departures (SIDs), Standard Terminal Arrival Routes (STARs) and Transitions to final approach. It is proposed that the changes to be made in parts of the London TMA and its associated airports in the near future will include procedures based on P-RNAV. After this date conventional procedures, supplemented where necessary by the use of radar vectors, will continue to be provided for a limited period for those aircraft not authorised to fly P-RNAV procedures. The aim is to make much greater use of the already existent potential of RNAV.

One of the major benefits is environmental, because conventional departure and arrival procedure design requires aircraft to overfly ground-based navigational aids. If it is possible to remove this restriction safely, it will enable aircraft to be more easily routed round noise sensitive or built-up areas. The accuracy and functionality afforded by modern RNAV systems means that aircraft can fly noise-preferential routes with a greater degree of accuracy than was previously possible. Continuous Descent Approaches can also be designed into the procedure, meaning reduced noise, fuel burn and therefore carbon emissions. An ability to separate arrival and departure routes strategically will reduce controller workload. The initial changes are likely to involve P-RNAV SIDs and STARs and RNAV holds at Stansted and Luton. At London City Airport it is proposed to introduce two P-RNAV SIDs for northerly departures, plus a single RNAV hold for arrivals from the north and east. Additionally, a number of new SIDs will be introduced at Heathrow. Currently, P-RNAV procedures are not envisaged in the Manchester and Scottish TMAs until 2011.

Automatic Dependent Surveillance-Broadcast (ADS-B)

For an aircraft to be capable of employing ADS-B, it must have a transponder which broadcasts not just Mode C but ADS-B information. Essentially, a GPS receiver (or the output from the aircraft's primary GPS) is piped into the transponder, along with other information from flight instruments. Then, once per second, the transponder transmits a code which contains the aircraft ID, its altitude, and its position as derived from GPS, along with information such as its rate of climb or descent and whether it is presently turning and in what direction. This transmission is intended to be received by two different types of receiver. First, it is intended to be received by other aircraft within approximately 200 miles. Those aircraft, if they are also equipped for ADS-B, will have a special computerised display in their cockpits which is able to show the position of every ADS-B transponder-equipped aircraft and its relative position and heading from the display aircraft. ADS-B updates once per second, and its transmissions are also meant to be received by ground stations, being nearly ten times more accurate than radar.

To illustrate this, whether primary or secondary, the controller's radar picture updates only as fast as the radar antenna can spin round, which can mean anything up to 12 seconds per sweep. During that time a jet can travel a mile or more, and usually the radar location information isn't very precise either, which means that, in congested airspace, a substantial margin of error must be maintained. This in turn means fewer aircraft can move through a given amount of airspace, leading to delays. Recognising this, the US Federal Aviation Agency (FAA) intends to move to an ADS-B-based system that will lay the groundwork for the Next Generation Air Transportation System, or NextGen. Eurocontrol is working towards similar goals and this may well be the future of ATC worldwide. Controllers will have a much more accurate idea where all the aircraft are, which could potentially allow them to move traffic through bottlenecks more quickly.

Transponder
The transponder is not a navigational aid in the true sense, but its use certainly improves the service which ATC is able to give. A small airborne transmitter waits until a radar pulse strikes its antenna and then instantly broadcasts, at a different frequency, a radar reply of its own – a strong synthetic echo. Since ordinary 'skin return' (the reflection of the ground radar pulse from the aircraft structure) is sometimes quite weak, especially at great distances or with small aircraft, the transponder helps the radar operator to track targets that might return an echo too weak to display. Interference from weather and other causes is virtually eliminated.

The transponder is simple in concept but in practice is a complex, sophisticated device. It is triggered into either of two modes of reply by the nature of the ground radar pulse. Without delving too deeply into the technicalities, Mode A is employed for identification and Mode C for altitude information. Mode B is in military use only and Mode S (S standing for Select) is a datalink for the exchange of operational information. At the UK Control Centres, radar replies are channelled into a computer which decodes the pulses, converts them into a letter and number display, and places a label alongside the appropriate target on the radar display. The information includes the call-sign and altitude of the aircraft.

Secondary Surveillance Radar (SSR) has many advantages. One of the most important is that aircraft identification is easy to achieve and eliminates the necessity of requesting a turn of at least 30 degrees from the original heading to confirm which blip is which on the display. R/T loading is reduced considerably because altitude information is presented continuously to the controller and the pilot no longer needs to make constant checks.

When Traffic Alert and Collision Avoidance System (TCAS) is fitted to aircraft, the equipment reacts to the transponders of other aircraft in the vicinity to determine whether or not there is the potential for a collision. TCAS is mandatory within UK airspace for all jet and turbo-prop aircraft with a maximum take-off weight of 5,000kg or more, or passenger capacity of more than 30, and there are frequent references to it on R/T.

Warnings are given in two steps: typically 40 seconds before the assumed collision, a Traffic Advisory (TA) warning indicates where the pilot must look for the traffic; then between 20 and 30 seconds before the assumed collision a Resolution Advisory (RA) gives the pilot advice to climb, descend or remain level. The two warnings, TA followed by RA, can only be received if the conflicting aircraft is transponding on Mode C or Mode S. Where both aircraft in an encounter are fitted with TCAS Mode S, the transponders will communicate with each other to agree which aircraft is to pass below, and which above, the other. Mode S is a datalink system which has a number of potential applications in ATC, one being the eventual replacement of many routine radio messages, such as route clearances and weather information. Warnings appear on the flight deck display indicating the relative positions of the conflicting aircraft in plan view and elevation, together with an aural warning spoken by a synthetic voice.

Ground Proximity Warning System (GPWS)

GPWS is not a navigational aid but it provides an audible warning to the pilot if an aircraft experiences any of the following conditions:

(a) Excessive sink rate
(b) Excessive terrain closure rate
(c) Altitude loss after take-off or overshoot
(d) Proximity to terrain when not in the landing configuration
(e) Deviation below the glide slope

In the first four conditions, the warning consists of an audible tone and a spoken warning over a cockpit loudspeaker, 'Whoop, whoop. Pull up'. For the last condition the warning 'Glide slope, glide slope' is used. The warning is repeated as long as the conditions exist.

Aircraft flight manuals instruct pilots to climb immediately to a level where the warning is no longer being received. If a pilot gets a 'pull up' warning, his recovery action is to establish the power setting and attitude which will produce the maximum climb gradient consistent with the aircraft configuration. If a 'glide slope' warning is received, recovery action is to apply power to regain the ILS glide slope.

Unfortunately, the GPWS is an extremely sensitive piece of equipment and spurious warnings can be caused by several factors. One of these is a sudden variation in terrain, even though it is well below the aircraft. GPWS incidents can occasionally be heard being discussed on air band frequencies. Enhanced GPWS (EGPWS) has made the system even more effective by issuing earlier warnings and reducing the number of failure alerts.

Short Term Conflict Alert

Again not a navaid as such, STCA (Short Term Conflict Alert, known colloquially as 'Stacker'), uses sophisticated software to examine radar track data in order to look for possible conflicts between pairs of aircraft. In London Terminal Control, for example, aircraft tracks are projected ahead and a low severity alert generated when the aircraft are predicted to come close vertically and laterally in the same time interval. The target labels on the controller's radar display change from green to white to indicate that a conflict is predicted and a white pairing line joins them. As the conflict situation becomes imminent, the labels change to red to indicate that the situation has deteriorated.

Flight Checks

Some of the navaids, particularly ILS, require regular flight checks to ensure that their performance remains consistent. These checks, normally flown by a Beech Super King Air of Cobham Flight Inspection, are not as intensive as those made when the equipment was first installed at a specific location but they are still quite time-consuming. As a more immediate safeguard, most navaids are self-checking and will shut down automatically if they are not operating within the correct parameters.

Tools of ATC

Flight Plans

Flight Plans are the standard method of providing ATC units with details of intended flights. They are mandatory for most IFR flights, any flight across international borders and flights into designated areas such as Air Defence Identification Zones (ADIZ) or anywhere the authorities deem to be difficult for search and rescue operations. For VFR flights in relatively populated countries such as the UK, Flight Plans are not required but pilots are encouraged to file them, particularly if they are flying over water or mountainous areas. A Plan must be filed at least 30 minutes before departure but sophisticated ATC systems such as the United Kingdom's may require considerably more than this if the flight is to operate within a complex route network. Scheduled flights to a regular timetable are covered by the so-called Repetitive Flight Plan, better known as a 'stored plan'. This refers to the fact that when a computer is being used to support the air traffic services, the information can be placed in what is termed the 'bulk store' and the computer programmed to produce the relevant data at a predetermined time. Where there is no ATC unit at destination, Flight Plans have to be 'closed' by the pilot as soon as practicable after landing to avoid unnecessary SAR operations.

Typical Flight Plan

Transmitted in abbreviated form on the AFTN, the flight plan message reads: FPL RYR953 IN B738/M SDHIR/C EGGP0700 NO436F370 UB3 HON UA1 VEULE UL612 PAS UA41 GRO UA26 CMP DCT LIRA0223 LIRN EET/LFFF0031 LSAS0116 LFFF0117 LIMM0124 LIRR0151 REG/EIDAZ. Decoded, this means Ryanair Boeing 737-800, wake turbulence category Medium, call-sign RYR953, IFR flight Liverpool to Rome Ciampino, standard navigation equipment, ETD 0700, true air speed 436kts at FL 370, routeing via Honiley VOR, VEULE on the French coast near Dieppe, Passeiry VOR near Geneva, Pisa VOR, Grosseto VOR, Ciampino NDB, estimated elapsed time to Rome 2 hours 23 mins, alternate airfield Naples. The estimated elapsed times to each FIR boundary en route are also included, as well as the aircraft registration EI-DAZ. The supplementary information (fuel endurance, total number on board, survival equipment, etc) is not sent but held on file at the departure airport.

Flight Progress Strips (FPS)

Amidst all the high-tech hardware of modern ATC, the humble paper flight progress strip, which is slotted into a plastic holder, still has an important part to play. It carries all the basic details of each aircraft's flight plan; its call-sign, type, required flight level, true air speed, route and destination, along with spaces in which the controller can annotate and update the information. They are still handwritten at many locations but machine-printed in busier ATC environments. The controller will annotate and update them with such information as take-off or landing times, route clearances (ticked when passed and acknowledged correctly), slot times, pressure settings and current ATIS code. Different colour pens may be used where several controllers write on

Typical outbound Flight Progress Strip: an easyJet Airbus A319 G-EZIO Liverpool to Krakow, ETD 0715 Flight Level 390 437 knots cruise, 0204 hours en route, DESIG 1V SID. Annotated with parking Stand 56, CTOT 0715, passed ATIS Alpha with QNH 1014, SID and squawk ticked as passed and acknowledged by crew, Runway 09, predicted airborne time of 13 passed to area control, actual airborne time 0711. The ticked 'R' confirms that a release for departure has been received from Liverpool Radar. Aircraft transferred to area control on 128.05MHz at 0712.

Boeing 737 Flight Director over the Baltic.

the same strip, ie Delivery, GMC and Tower. The trend is towards electronic presentation of FPSs alongside the radar display or as a 'window' in the display itself.

Electronic Flight Progress Strips

Heathrow, Gatwick and Stansted are now using the world's most advanced tower-airport flight data system. Developed by Nav Canada, it creates 'paperless' towers by eliminating the need for paper flight strips and is known as the Electronic Flight Progress System (EFPS). It allows tower controllers to manage electronic flight data online, using touch-sensitive display screens. This significantly reduces the need for voice communications among controllers and replaces the traditional method described above. It increases efficiencies by ensuring an instantaneous sharing of relevant flight information between workstations within the tower, and between the tower and terminal control. EFPS is fully interfaced with the Integrated Initial Flight Plan System (IFPS) and other flow management systems located at the Central Flow Management Unit (CFMU) in Brussels. It also interfaces with the BAA's Stand (or gate) Management System, NATS's National Airspace System (NAS) and it also performs datalink Departure Clearance (DCL) with aircraft flight decks.

Radar Data Processing (RDP)

On advanced radar systems automatic radar data processing removes unwanted signals such as ground and weather echoes and limits the information on the radar display to aircraft responses. This computer technology is used to decode the combined radar information from several antenna to produce the best possible picture. It also enables the transponder information to be displayed as a label alongside the radar position symbol, a computer-generated 'blip'. RDP can be correlated with Flight Data Processing to display call-sign, actual flight level and destination. The aircraft's ground speed and other information can also be displayed as required. All modern radar displays use colour to identify different types of airspace, land and water areas, active and pending traffic, as well as a variety of other operational features specified by the customer.

Chapter 5

Area or Airways Control

SINCE MESSAGES BETWEEN the Area Control Centres (ACCs) and aircraft on the UK airways system are those which are most easily monitored from all parts of the country, this seems a logical point at which to begin. There are two Centres, London and Scottish. The dividing line between London and Scottish is just north of Birmingham. It should be noted that the Manchester Area Control Centre, which used to cover NW England and the Irish Sea, closed in January 2010 and its functions are now performed by the Scottish ACC.

Transmitter/receiver stations are sited at various strategic positions around Britain and linked to the ACCs by land line. The aim is to achieve a balanced coverage over the whole area with no 'dead' spots. Similarly, the radar stations are 'remoted' on high ground, where possible, to improve range. London ATCC (LATCC) is served by radar heads at Heathrow, Ash near Canterbury, Ventnor on the Isle of Wight, Clee Hill in Shropshire, Burrington, Devon and St Annes near Blackpool. Additional service is provided on a Eurocontrol agency basis from Mount Gabriel in Eire, a station which extends SSR cover out to 15 degrees west in the south-west approaches.

More information on SSR will be found in a separate section of this book but, briefly, the main function of primary radar is to provide aircraft position. Secondary Radar, or SSR, depends for its operation on a transponder carried in the aircraft which, on receipt of pulses from a ground interrogator, will transmit coded reply pulses back to the ground. When these are decoded by the display equipment, they give the altitude or Flight Level of the aircraft together with a four-figure identifying number known as a squawk. The primary and secondary information received by the radar stations is processed in a common 'plot extractor', converting the base radar data into digital form and automatically sending the information to the ACCs over land lines.

At the ACC, display processing equipment employing modern computer technology is used to decode the combined radar information from several antennae and displays either a manually selected radar station or a composite area mosaic picture. The SSR squawk is paired with the aircraft call-sign in the computer and this call-sign label is displayed on the screen instead of the code. This enables the controller to match the radar picture with the strips on his flight progress board.

When the mosaic picture is selected at LATCC, the computer divides the London FIR into 16-mile squares, each of which has radar cover from a 'preferred' radar and a 'supplementary' radar. This avoids the blind spots possible if only one radar were in operation. Should the preferred radar fail, the supplementary will take over automatically, information from a third radar head being upgraded in turn to supplement it.

All incoming primary and secondary digital data is continuously recorded and the tapes are kept for 30 days before being erased and reused. The same applies to all ATC radio messages, whether they be Area, Tower or Approach. The purpose of these recordings is to help an investigating authority to build up a picture of the events surrounding an accident or incident.

London Area Control Centre and London Military Transmitter Sites.

To facilitate traffic handling, airspace under area control is broken up into sectors, each with its own radio frequencies, a primary and several 'as directed' channels to enable the sector to be split during busy periods. Aircraft are passed from one sector to the next with co-ordination between the controllers concerned. See 'Standing agreements' at the end of this chapter. From mid-evening, as traffic decreases, sectors are 'closed down', the frequencies being 'band-boxed', to use the jargon. Hence nothing may be heard on what is in daytime a busy airways frequency. By the early hours the whole FIR may be controlled by only two frequencies. When the morning shift comes on duty the sectors are activated again to meet the renewed traffic flow.

Before computers came on the scene in British ATC in the 1970s, flight progress strips at the ACCs were hand-written in vast quantities. Today the system is automated, apart from a shut-off period for computer maintenance in the small hours of the morning, and it would be advantageous to describe briefly what happens when a particular flight leaves, for example, Leeds for Heathrow.

If the flight is a scheduled one, it will be on a 'stored plan' in the LATCC computer's bulk store file, if not it will be input on a teleprinter at Scottish ACC. At the appropriate time as programmed into the computer, usually about 40 minutes before Estimated Time of Departure (ETD), warning strips will be printed by flight strip printers at Scottish and at any location at LATCC where advance information of the flight is required.

When Scottish receives an estimated time of departure from Leeds, based on the aircraft starting up, via a direct telephone link, an activation message will be input to the computer.

This will generate an update message for the sectors at the Scottish Centre and those sectors at London which have warning strips. Additionally 'live strips' will be printed at any sector or location concerned with the flight that did not have a warning strip. In all cases the computer will have calculated and printed times for en route reporting points based upon the airborne time input at Manchester. The forecast winds at various levels will have been programmed in and thus automatically taken into account.

The flight of an aircraft from Heathrow to Manchester serves as a good example of how traffic is fed through the airways system. When the departing aircraft comes on to the LATCC Departure Radar Controller's frequency and has complied with the minimum noise routeing element of its Standard Instrument Departure, it is started on its climb to cruising level, using radar separation where necessary between it and other arriving, departing or transiting traffic. To ease the task of the Departure Controller in regard to co-ordination with other sectors concerned with the airspace, there is an internal procedure which permits him to climb the aircraft to an arbitrary level without reference to other sectors. This is known as a Standing Agreement and is further described below.

However, before it reaches this Flight Level or, alternatively, when the aircraft is approaching the airspace for which the next Sector Controller is responsible, prior co-ordination is carried out. When this has been done, the aircraft is instructed to contact the next Sector (still with the same London Control call-sign).

Clearance is given for the aircraft's climb to its cruising level, once again using radar to resolve any conflict with other traffic. By this time it is also possible to check the computer on the elapsed time between reporting points and, if these deviate by three minutes or more, the estimates for the rest of the flight are revised and a new ETA is passed to Scottish.

As the flight nears the Manchester TMA boundary, co-ordination takes place between Daventry Sector and the TMA Controller. Descent instructions dependent upon the Manchester traffic situation are then issued and the aircraft transferred to the Scottish Control frequency. The TMA Controller has a radar display similar to that used by the Daventry Sector and, as the aircraft enters his airspace, its call-sign and level will be visible on his display. He will also have displayed in front of him the flight progress strips generated by the computer which have been updated by any revised estimates. The descent will be continued until the aircraft comes under the jurisdiction of the Manchester Approach Controller (call-sign Manchester Director) and is positioned on the ILS as described in the next chapter.

Ideally, traffic is given an uninterrupted climb to cruising level and, from a convenient point, a continuous descent to final approach. In practice, however, the presence of other traffic rarely makes this possible. Traffic climbing to, say, FL180 may be given an initial limit of FL120 against conflicting traffic at FL130. By the time it is approaching FL120, the other aircraft may be well out of the way and the controller will be able to instruct the pilot to continue his climb to the required level. Before the days of SSR height read-outs, the Area Controller in this example would ask the pilot to report passing FL110 and then would assess the situation with regard to further climb.

The phraseology used in Area Control is mainly self-evident and some, concerning level changes, has already been covered in an earlier chapter. Common phrases to be heard are as follows:

Aircraft: 'Speedbird 345 request descent.'
ATC: 'Speedbird 345 maintain FL110 expect descent after Lichfield.'
ATC: 'Air France 045 descend to cross Honiley FL170 or above. After Honiley descend FL130.'

LEFT: Plessey AR5 airways radar site at Burrington, Devon (used with the permission of and copyright of UK CAA).

Now rarely heard, the standard airways position report is a little gem of brevity dating back decades to when procedural airways control was first developed. A typical one might be as follows:

Aircraft: 'Loganair 123 Dean Cross 45 FL90 Pole Hill 10'.

This means that the aircraft was over the Dean Cross VOR, near Carlisle, at time 45, maintaining FL90 and estimating over the Pole Hill VOR, west of Leeds, at ten minutes past the next hour.

Nowadays, with comprehensive radar coverage of the airways system, a pilot may be instructed to omit position reports when flying in certain areas, his progress being monitored by the SSR read-out. This reduces the R/T loading considerably.

Certain phrases concerning the operation of transponders are listed below. SSR in the United Kingdom was once confined almost exclusively to the ACCs, but most approach control units now have the capability. The use of the word 'squawk', by the way, seems to have been inspired by the wartime instruction to operate IFF (Identification, Friend or Foe – an early form of transponder), 'Make your cockerel crow' and the pilot's confirmation that the IFF equipment was switched off after landing 'Cockerel strangled'.

Phrase	Meaning
Squawk (code)	Set the code as instructed
Confirm squawk	Confirm the code set on the transponder
Reset squawk	Reselect assigned code
Squawk ident	Operate the special position identification feature
Squawk Mayday	Select emergency code
Squawk stand-by	Select the stand-by feature
Squawk Charlie	Select altitude reporting feature
Stop squawk Charlie	Deselect altitude feature
Confirm level	Check and confirm your level (used to verify the accuracy of the Mode C derived level information displayed to the controller)

Reduced Vertical Separation Minima (RVSM) is now in operation over most of Europe. Until technology came up with radio altimeters, altimeter systems have been less accurate in the higher levels, and above Flight Level 290 the standard vertical separation of 1,000ft has traditionally been doubled to 2,000ft to allow a greater margin of error. An intensive programme monitoring height-keeping performance proved that RVSM could safely be applied. It has produced a very significant increase in airspace capacity. Special R/T phraseology has been introduced for RVSM operations to ascertain the equipment status of an aircraft and various other conditions. RVSM ops are mandatory in all UK airspace above FL290 so the phraseology will be used only by military aircraft which have a non-RVSM dispensation. Non-compliant civilian aircraft will have to remain below FL290.

Examples:

ATC: '(call-sign) Confirm RVSM approved'
Aircraft: 'Negative (or Affirm) RVSM'
Aircraft: 'Unable RVSM due turbulence' or 'Unable RVSM due equipment' or 'Ready to resume
              RVSM'

Standing Agreements
A Standing Agreement is an agreement between two sectors about how they will present certain flights to each other. Telephone co-ordination only needs to be done if a flight cannot

be presented in the agreed manner for whatever reason, or if the conditions of the standing agreement do not apply to a particular flight. Standing agreements often have conditions attached, for example, once an aircraft has been transferred to a particular sector, that sector may immediately climb, descend or turn that aircraft even if it has not yet reached their airspace. It is not uncommon for an aircraft to be transferred up to about thirty miles before it has left a particular sector, because the present sector needs to do nothing else with it and because controllers can see at least that far beyond the bounds of their sector. These provisions can be quite detailed; an agreement may allow turns to the right but not to the left; descents but not climbs.

If an aircraft does not qualify for the conditions of a standing agreement it must be individually co-ordinated. The next sector is warned that the flight is on its way, and an agreement made with them about how it will be 'presented': ie the aircraft's altitude, the approximate time it will enter the next sector and its heading (if applicable). Such a warning usually takes the form of a phone call. Normally, these calls are made between the 'Planner' or 'Co-ordinator'. His or her colleague who actually talks to the aircraft is known as the 'Tactical' controller. If all goes well, the aircraft will be accepted as is. If not, it may have to be climbed or descended to a new cruising level before reaching the next sector or maybe put on a heading.

Standing Agreements enable a massive through-put of traffic without all the hassle of individual co-ordination between sectors. Just one example in the Woodley/Compton area: London TMA outbounds to west will climb to FL130; London TMA inbounds from west will descend to FL140.

Chapter 6

Approach Control

AN ARRIVING AIRCRAFT is transferred from Area to Approach Control at a specified release point. This is not obvious from R/T transmissions because it is passed by land line between controllers shortly before the aircraft comes on to the approach frequency. It may be a position, time or level. The transfer of control is made deliberately flexible to react to differences in the flow of traffic. For example, if the release is 'Leaving FL50' the Approach Controller may not alter the heading of the aircraft until he has received a 'passing FL50' report. The reason for this is that Area Control may have been separating the inbound aircraft from other traffic above FL50.

Ideally, the arriving aircraft should be released in plenty of time to enable it to carry out a straight-in approach and at the same time to lose height. However, should a busy traffic situation exist, it might be necessary to put it into a holding pattern based upon a radio beacon. The release would then be at a specified level in the holding stack. The holding patterns are a standard oval 'racetrack', the direction of turn and headings being published in navigational charts or approach plates.

A holding pattern for IFR aircraft is based on a holding fix. This fix can be a radio beacon such as an NDB or VOR. The fix is the start of the first turn of the racetrack pattern. Aircraft will fly towards the fix, and once there will enter a predefined racetrack pattern. A standard holding pattern uses right-hand turns and takes approximately four minutes to complete (one minute for each 180 degree turn, and two one-minute straight ahead sections). In the absence of a radio beacon, the holding fix can be any fixed point in the air, and can be created using two crossing VOR radials, or it can be at a specific distance from a VOR using a coupled DME. When DME is used, the inbound turn of the racetrack may be permanently defined by distance limits rather than in minutes.

At airfields without radar, traffic is separated by procedural methods, the first aircraft making an instrument approach from, say, 3,000ft, aircraft continuing to hold above at 1,000ft vertical intervals. As soon as the first aircraft reports visual with the ground or approach lights, and there is a reasonable likelihood of a successful landing, the second aircraft is cleared for the approach and so on. If the aircraft carries out a missed approach prior to becoming visual, it must climb to the safe terrain clearance altitude, in this instance 3,000ft. Hence it is not hard to see why this altitude is left vacant at the beacon until the first aircraft breaks cloud.

The Decision Height is the level at which the pilot on a precision approach must carry out a missed approach if he fails to achieve the required visual reference to continue the approach to a landing. A precision approach is defined as being provided by an ILS, MLS or PAR facility.

RIGHT: Standard Terminal Arrival Chart for London/Heathrow via Lambourne (used with the permission of and copyright of UK CAA).

STANDARD ARRIVAL CHART - INSTRUMENT (STAR) - ICAO

DISTANCES IN NAUTICAL MILES
BEARINGS, TRACKS AND RADIALS ARE MAGNETIC
ALTITUDES AND ELEVATIONS ARE IN FEET

LONDON HEATHROW via LAMBOURNE

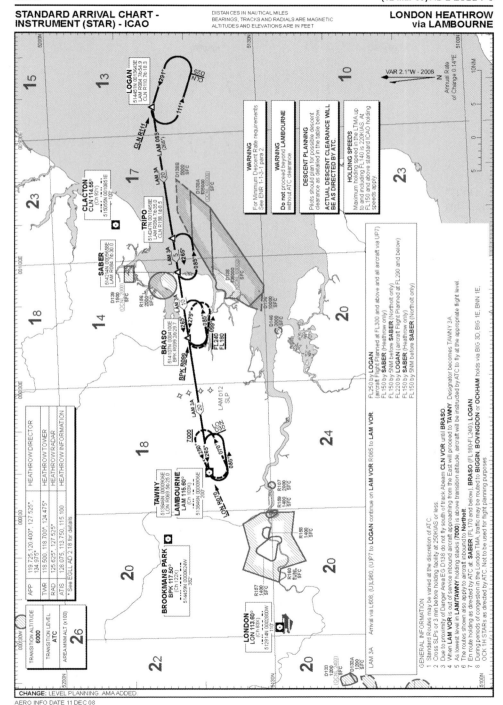

VAR 2.1°W - 2008
Annual Rate of Change 0.14°E

WARNING
For Minimum Descent Rate requirements
See ENR 1-1-3-1 para 2

WARNING
Do not proceed beyond LAMBOURNE
without ATC clearance

DESCENT PLANNING
Pilots should plan for possible descent
clearance as detailed in the table below
**ACTUAL DESCENT CLEARANCE WILL
BE AS DIRECTED BY ATC.**

HOLDING SPEEDS
Maximum holding speed in the LTMA up
to and including FL140 is 230KIAS. At
FL150 and above standard ICAO holding
speeds apply

FL250 by **LOGAN**
(aircraft Flight Planned at FL300 and above and all aircraft via UP7)
FL150 by **SABER** (Heathrow only)
FL150 by 5NM before **SABER** (Northolt only)
FL220 by **LOGAN** (aircraft Flight Planned at FL390 and below)
FL150 by **SABER** (Heathrow only)
FL150 by 5NM before **SABER** (Northolt only)

GENERAL INFORMATION

1 Standard Routes may be varied at the discretion of ATC.
2 Cross SLPs or 3 min before holding facility at 250KIAS or less.
3 Due to proximity of Danger Area EG D138 do not fly south of track Abeam **CLN VOR** until **BRASO**.
4 When **LAM VOR** is out of service inbound aircraft approaching from the East will proceed to **TAWNY**. Designator becomes TAWNY 3A.
5 As lowest level in **LAM/TAWNY** holding stacks (**7000**) is above transition altitude, aircraft will be instructed by ATC to fly at the appropriate flight level
6 The routes shown also apply to aircraft inbound to **Northolt**.
7 En route holding as directed by ATC at **SABER** (FL180-FL240), **LOGAN** (FL180+FL240 and below), **BRASO** (FL170 and below), **LOGAN** (FL180-FL240). Traffic may be routed to **BIGGIN**, **BOVINGDON** or **OCKHAM** holds via BIG 3D, BIG 1E, BNN 1E,
8 During periods of congestion in the London TMA, traffic may be routed to **BIGGIN**, **BOVINGDON** or **OCKHAM** holds via BIG 3D, BIG 1E, BNN 1E,
OCK 1H STARs as directed by ATC. Not to be used for flight planning purposes

TRANSITION ALTITUDE	6000		
TRANSITION LEVEL	ATC		
AREA MINIM ALT (x100)	26		

APP	119.725, 120.400*, 127.525*, 134.975*	HEATHROW DIRECTOR
TWR	118.500, 118.700*, 124.475*	HEATHROW TOWER
RAD	125.625*, 127.525*	HEATHROW RADAR
ATIS	128.075, 113.750, 115.100	HEATHROW INFORMATION

* See EGLL AD 2.18 for details

All other procedures, including SRAs and Localiser/DME approaches are non-precision and the term Minimum Descent Height is used instead.

Obstacle Clearance Height is the minimum safe height to which an aircraft may descend either on an instrument approach or in the event of a missed approach. This is published on the approach charts for each airfield, aircraft being divided into five speed-related categories, resulting in a reduction of the Obstacle Clearance Heights for the more manoeuverable types.

The obstacle clearance criteria are, of course, tied in with company minima for visibility and cloud base, below which a public transport flight is not allowed even to attempt an approach. There are also statutory provisions for non-public transport flights whereby recommended minima are published for the approach aids at each airfield for the guidance of pilots.

The term Expected Approach Time can be heard at non-radar equipped airports. This indicates to a pilot that if he has a radio failure he must not commence an instrument approach until this specific time to allow preceding aircraft to descend and land. 'No delay expected' means that a pilot can begin his approach as soon as he reaches the beacon. If his estimate for the beacon is 12, the next aircraft's EAT will be 19, the third's 26 and so on.

A standard seven minutes is assumed to complete the let-down procedure and three minutes will be added to this if an aircraft arrives from certain points of the compass and has to realign itself in the correct direction for the descent. The controller will calculate the figures and update them as necessary. Note that EATs are not issued in busy TMAs when the delay is likely to be less than 20 minutes. If it is likely to be more, inbound aircraft are given a general statement about anticipated delay and EATs are issued as necessary.

Pilots' interpretations of instrument let-downs vary enormously, the seven minute standard ranging from five to ten or more, depending upon wind strength, aircraft performance and other factors. One other phrase used in connection with EATs is the rarely heard 'delay not determined'. This is used to meet certain eventualities, such as a blocked runway, when it is not known how long an aircraft may have to hold.

Where Approach Radar is in use, as well as giving a release, the ACC also transfers radar identity in what is called a handover (a 'handoff' to the Americans). The Approach Controller is thus certain that the aircraft he is directing is the correct blip. The object is to pass headings (vectors) to the pilot to enable him to lock on to the ILS beam by the shortest practicable route commensurate with losing height. If there is no ILS, a Surveillance Radar Approach (SRA) will be given or, when the weather is suitable, radar positioning to a visual final.

In effect a radar-directed circuit is flown, the terms 'downwind', 'base leg' and 'final' (see page 63) all being used where necessary, although the area of sky covered is far bigger than in the normal visual traffic pattern. A closing heading of about 30° is recommended so that when the aircraft intercepts the ILS only a gentle turn is necessary to lock on. The aim is to intercept the standard 3° glide path at approximately 7 to 8 miles out on the extended centreline of the runway. As a 3° glide path is roughly equal to 300ft of descent per mile, the aircraft should be between 2,000ft and 2,500ft at this point.

Subsequent landing aircraft are vectored not less than 5 miles behind, or further depending upon the wake turbulence category of the preceding traffic (see Chapter 13). Bigger gaps may also be built in to give space for departing traffic at single-runway airports. At Heathrow, under certain conditions, reduction of the separation to 2.5 miles is authorised to ensure maximum utilisation of the arrival runway. The wake turbulence separation rules still apply of course. Sometimes an aircraft may be instructed to make a complete turn (known as an orbit or a 360 degree turn) for delaying purposes or to achieve a required spacing behind preceding traffic. For example 'GCD delaying action, orbit left for sequencing.'

It requires great skill to arrange traffic in line astern with the correct spacing, particularly at Heathrow where four holding stacks serve the airport. Speed control is also used extensively to even out the flow, a minimum of 170kt being permissible for jets and 160kt for large propeller-driven aircraft. Within the TMAs during the intermediate stages of the approach, a speed limit of 250kt is imposed on all traffic to make the radar controller's task a little easier. The same speed limit applies to outbound traffic, but the controller can lift it by using the phrase 'No ATC speed restriction', often abbreviated to 'No ATC speed'. I once heard a Shorts 360 pilot respond with 'Would that it made any difference!'

Other examples of phraseology relating to speed are: 'Report airspeed/Mach number.' 'Maintain present speed.' 'Maintain X knots.' 'Maintain X knots or greater.' 'Do not exceed X knots.' 'Increase/reduce speed to Mach X.' 'Increase/reduce speed to X knots.' 'Maintain X knots until 4-mile final.' 'Resume normal speed.'

The Approach Controller passes an 8-mile check on intercom to his colleague in the tower who will already have details of the arriving aircraft. If there are no pending departures at the runway holding point, a landing clearance may be given at this point but it is more usual to give it at the 4-mile range. Alternatively, once the pilot reports established on the ILS, Approach may tell him to contact the Tower who will give landing clearance when available. Where the tower controller has an ATM (Air Traffic Monitor) display, approach will routinely transfer aircraft to his frequency with no prior warning.

Pilots expect to receive a landing clearance at around 4 miles on final approach, but this is not always possible owing to departing traffic or a previous landing aircraft being slow to vacate the runway. Two miles is the absolute minimum for large transport aircraft because a go-around is a fairly major operation. The phrase 'expect late landing clearance' is sometimes heard because spacing has got a little tight in the final stages of the approach and the first aircraft is not yet off the runway. On other occasions, departing traffic may be slower to get airborne than expected.

A busy moment on a Boeing 737-800 flightdeck.

For a runway not equipped with ILS the radar controller is normally able to offer a Surveillance Radar Approach. If the weather is poor this can be down to half a mile from touchdown, assuming that the radar is approved for this purpose. With certain types of radar, approaches to two miles only may be allowed. This ensures a reasonable chance of seeing the approach lights and making a successful landing in all but the worst weather.

Where only one Approach Controller is on duty and the ILS fails, he may be unable to offer a half-mile SRA because of the necessity for continuous transmissions during the last 4 miles of the approach. This of course means that any other traffic cannot communicate with him until the talkdown is complete. If a second controller is available, the first can do a half-mile SRA on a discrete frequency while his colleague continues to sequence traffic on to long final for handover as soon as the preceding aircraft has completed its approach.

SRAs to 2 miles, however, do not require continuous transmissions and the controller can talk to other traffic as necessary, although he must time his calls so that range checks and the associated advisory heights are passed at the correct intervals. The advisory heights are based upon a glide path of 3°, therefore at 6½ miles the aircraft should be at a height of 2,000ft. Descent on a 3° glide path is equivalent to about 300ft per mile. Some airfields have non-standard glide path angles because of local obstructions and other considerations, the advisory heights being adjusted accordingly. It is assumed that the aircraft is flying on QFE, but if the pilot advises that he is using QNH, the runway threshold elevation is added to the advisory heights and rounded up to the next 25ft, the term 'altitude' being used in place of 'height'.

Phraseology for Surveillance Radar Approaches
This includes the following:

During the Intermediate Procedure
'This will be a Surveillance Radar Approach, terminating at X miles from touchdown. Check your minima, stepdown fixes and missed approach point.'

Azimuth information
'Turn left/right X degrees, heading XXX. Closing (final approach) track (rate of closure eg slowly, quickly) from the left/right. Heading of XXX is good. On track. Slightly left/right of track.'

Descent information
'Approaching X miles from touchdown, commence descent now to maintain an X degree glide path. X miles from touchdown – height should be X feet. Do not acknowledge further instructions. Check minimum descent height. Check gear.'

Completion
On track, half a mile from touchdown. Approach completed. Out.'

General Approach Control phraseology
Since all major airports now use radar to direct their traffic, I shall deal with this aspect first. An aircraft must be identified before it can receive a radar control or advisory service, in other words, the controller must be sure that one particular blip on his screen is the aircraft he is directing. This is simple with a radar handover from another ATC unit or by means of SSR, but at airfields outside controlled airspace, where aircraft may approach from random directions with no prior notification, a standard procedure is observed if SSR is not an option.

ATC: 'GVM report heading and level.'
Aircraft: 'GVM heading 140 at 2,500ft.'
ATC: 'GVM for identification turn left heading 110 degrees.'

The identification turn must be at least 30° different from the original heading. When the pilot reports steady on the new heading, and the controller is sure that he has related a specific blip on his display with the aircraft, he transmits: 'GVM identified 12 miles south of (airfield)'. The service to be given is then added.

ATC: 'Vectoring for an ILS approach runway (designation).'

The weather and altimeter pressure settings are then passed as a separate transmission.

If in the initial call the aircraft makes the turn requested and is still not observed on radar, perhaps because it is out of range, in weather clutter, or below cover, the controller will say 'GVM not identified. Resume own navigation'. D/F will then be used to home the aircraft towards the airfield for eventual radar pick-up. When identified, the aircraft will be vectored, that is given headings to steer to fit it into the approach sequence or, if traffic is light, direct to final approach. Outside controlled airspace the aircraft may be vectored around unidentified traffic. Information will be given by use of the 12 hour clock, 12 o'clock being straight ahead, 3 o'clock over the pilot's right shoulder and so on. The distance and relative direction of movement is also given, together with any information on speed, type of aircraft if known, etc. Typical traffic information is passed in this form:

'ABC123 unknown traffic 10 o'clock, 5 miles crossing left to right, fast moving.'

If the pilot does not have the traffic in sight he may request avoiding action. This may, in any case, be initiated by the controller if he considers it necessary. Sometimes rapid action is required to avert the risk of collision:

'ABC123 avoiding action turn left immediately heading 110 degrees'.

A few incidents have occurred where, by using a too relaxed tone of voice, the controller failed to convey to the pilot the urgency of the required action and the pilot's more leisurely response led to an awkward situation which might have been averted. The CAA eventually instructed all controllers to ensure that their tone of voice does not lull pilots into a false sense of security on these occasions!

At locations with no radar, procedural methods are used. The same applies when radar is normally available but unserviceable or seriously affected by weather clutter, or if the pilot wishes to carry out a procedural approach for training purposes. On transfer from the ACC, the first call will go something like this:

Aircraft: 'Inverness Approach GBC descending FL60, estimating INS at 42.'
ATC: 'GBC cleared for VOR/DME approach Runway 06 descend to altitude 3,500ft QNH 1021. Report beacon outbound.'

Subsequent reports will be made when 'base turn complete' and, if the beacon is several miles out on final approach, a 'beacon inbound' call will be made as well. These standard calls help the tower controller to plan his traffic, bearing in mind that there is no radar to give him ranges from touchdown.

Where the airport is equipped with ILS, permission to make a procedural approach is given thus:

'GMB cleared for ILS approach Runway 27, report beacon outbound QNH 1008'.

Subsequent exchanges would be:

Aircraft: 'GMB beacon outbound.'
ATC: 'GMB report established inbound.' (The phrase 'report procedure turn complete' may
          be substituted.)
Aircraft: 'GMB established ILS inbound.'
ATC: 'GMB report outer marker' (or 'Report 4 DME').
Aircraft: 'GMB outer marker' (or '4 DME').
ATC: 'GMB contact Tower 118.1.'

In good weather, by day or night, even though nominally flying IFR, a pilot may request permission to make a visual approach. This may be granted subject to certain provisos, the most important of which is that the pilot must have visual reference to the surface, ie the ground or water, and a reasonable assurance exists that he will be able to complete the landing visually. Standard separation continues to be applied between this aircraft and other arriving and departing traffic unless the pilot states that he can see an aircraft ahead in the approach sequence and follow it down to the runway. During daylight hours only, IFR flights may be cleared to approach maintaining VMC and their own separation, if met reports indicate that this is possible.

Inbound VFR traffic will be cleared into a control zone via a Visual Reference Point (VRP), which ensures that it remains well away from the flight paths of arriving and departing IFR traffic. An altitude restriction will also be imposed for the same reason, as well as a clearance limit in the vicinity of the airfield. This will be an easily identifiable ground feature over which the aircraft can hold until it can be fitted into the traffic pattern.

QGH and VDF

Mention should be made of QGH, a military procedure that is only available at a handful of civil airfields, usually where a University Air Squadron is based. The QGH dates back to the Second World War but is nevertheless highly effective in bringing aircraft safely down to a position from which an approach can be continued visually. This particular Q-Code meant 'Controlled descent through cloud' and today uses a cathode ray tube VDF to home the aircraft to the overhead at a safe altitude. Subsequent bearings bring it down a safety lane on to final approach. During the procedure, the pilot's replies are used to obtain D/F bearings and additional transmissions may be requested using the words 'Transmit for D/F.' Immediately the aircraft has passed overhead the VDF aerial, turn instructions are given to get it on to the outbound track:

ATC: 'V91 D/F indicates that you have passed overhead. Turn left heading 120 degrees.
          Report steady.'

On completion of the overhead turn and when bearings indicate that the aircraft is outbound, heading corrections derived from a series of bearings are given by the controller as required to make good the outbound track. Descent instructions and the appropriate pressure are also given at this point:

'V91 descend to 1,000ft QNH 1006, report level.'

The controller times the outbound leg with a stopwatch (usually three minutes) and then gives the aircraft a turn on to a heading to intercept the final approach track. Further D/F checks ensure that it remains within the safety lane and the pilot is told to continue down to Minimum Descent Height and report airfield in sight.

The civilian counterpart of the QGH is the VDF Approach which is virtually the direct opposite, in that the pilot interprets the QDM information, rather than the controller. VDF approaches are uncommon these days, reflecting the greater availability of radar and ILS. Apart from this they require a lot of practice by the pilot to perfect them and were never very popular! QDMs, by the way, are passed as three digits, eg 355. The class of accuracy is passed with the initial bearing, depending on the CAA's approval of the equipment in use, and also with any subsequent bearings which show unusual fluctuations. Class A is accurate to within plus or minus 2°, B to within plus or minus 5°, C to within plus or minus 10°, and D represents an accuracy less than Class C. The phrase 'no bearing' indicates to the pilot that he is now overhead the D/F station and can begin his letdown.

GPS Approaches

The first approved RNAV Global Navigation Satellite System (GNSS) non-precision approach for General Aviation in the UK, which uses the Global Positioning System (GPS), was introduced at Shoreham Airport in November 2008. The introduction of the Shoreham GPS approach was a significant development in the ongoing project to make GNSS non-precision approaches available to UK GA pilots. CAA has also confirmed the requirements for airfields wishing to introduce similar approaches for general aviation in the UK. The requirements state that an airfield must have a CAA licence and a runway meeting the physical characteristics required for an instrument runway – this covers the runway strip width, its cleared and graded area, surface markings, holding points and lighting (if used at night). The runway is not required to have an instrument approach system already in place. The airfield must also have an air traffic control service – not Flight Information Service or air–ground operator.

The requirements for pilots and aircraft are that pilots flying the approach must have a current Instrument Rating (IR) or an Instrument Meteorological Conditions Rating (IMCR). The aircraft navigation system installation based upon GNSS receiver equipment must meet certain requirements and be approved for the purpose. Any airfield meeting the requirements and wishing to add a non-precision RNAV (GNSS) approach will also need to work with the CAA on the design of the approach, the development of a safety plan and a validation flight.

Chapter 7

Aerodrome Control

THE TERM 'AERODROME' dates from World War 1 and is derived from the ancient Greek meaning 'aerial racecourse'. Surprisingly, it is still official ICAO terminology. The Aerodrome Controller's basic function is defined as the issuing of information and instructions to aircraft to achieve a safe, orderly and expeditious flow of traffic and to assist pilots in preventing collisions between:

(a) Aircraft flying in, and in the vicinity of the aerodrome traffic zone
(b) Aircraft taking off and landing
(c) Aircraft moving on the apron
(d) Aircraft and vehicles, obstructions and other aircraft on the manoeuvring area (ie the runways and taxiways)

The apron may also come under the jurisdiction of the marshaller, who makes sure that aircraft are parked in the required places. This is particularly important at airports where all or part of the apron is out of sight of the tower. At larger airports, self-manoeuvring markings are painted on the tarmac to guide pilots to the stand which has been allocated on R/T, thus obviating the need for 'the man with the bats'. Major airports have docking guidance systems using lights and symbols. It would be impossible to control all the service vehicles moving about the apron so these are confined, as far as possible, to outline-painted lanes.

Airfield fire and maintenance vehicles that need to go on the runways and taxiways are controlled on a UHF domestic frequency. These are not published but can be found in the range 455–461MHz (NFM). Most operate on a split frequency where the base station transmits on, for example, 455.6375 MHz and the mobile on 460.9375. Sometimes the VHF tower or GMC frequency is re-broadcast on the UHF channel so that vehicle drivers can be aware of aircraft movement. At some airfields the tower VHF frequency is used for controlling vehicles. Standard phraseology is in use (aircraft 'taxi', vehicles 'proceed' or 'tow') and vehicles have self-explanatory call-signs such as 'Sweeper One', 'Works 36', 'Security 22', 'Fire Six,' etc.

To smooth the running of the larger airports, it may be necessary to split the duties of Aerodrome Control into Air Control and Ground Movement Control (referred to as GMC). The latter's responsibility covers aircraft moving on the apron and aircraft and vehicles on the manoeuvring area, except on runways and their access points. Major airports have a Surface Monitoring Radar to follow aircraft and vehicle movements in bad visibility. R/T loading at some locations, including Heathrow, Gatwick and Manchester, necessitates a further sub-division of GMC known as Ground Movement Planning (GMP), call-sign 'Delivery', on which start-up and route clearances are passed.

Until quite recently the Tower Controller had few aids apart from the 'Mark 1 eyeball' and a pair of binoculars. Now many Visual Control Rooms (VCRs) are equipped with an Air Traffic Monitor (ATM). This is a daylight-viewing, colour radar showing the local area out to a radius

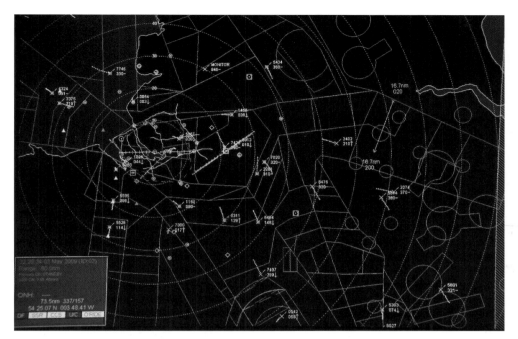

*Liverpool's Approach Radar display covering Wales and north-west England. The straight lines
are Liverpool, Manchester and Hawarden final approaches.*

of about 15 miles. At airports with only one runway and a high movement rate it is invaluable
in judging whether there is sufficient room to clear a departing aircraft to take off or to give
priority to an aircraft on final approach. It also serves to confirm the turn on to track of a
preceding aircraft so that a second aircraft can be permitted to depart. If an ATM is not
available, the Radar Controller is required to give an 8-mile check for traffic on final approach
to his colleague in the tower, using intercom. The aim is to confirm landing clearance at about
4 miles but normally at not less than 2 miles.

Runway occupancy is governed by the following rules:

(a) An aircraft shall not be permitted to begin take-off until the preceding departing aircraft is
    seen to be airborne or has reported 'airborne' by R/T and all preceding landing aircraft
    have vacated the runway in use
(b) A landing aircraft will not be permitted to cross the beginning of the runway on its final
    approach until a preceding departing aircraft is airborne

There is, however, a phrase 'land after' which seems to puzzle some inexperienced pilots who
probably think it is a place in Wales! Its purpose is to increase runway utilisation by permitting
a landing aircraft to touch down before a preceding aircraft which has landed is clear of the
runway. The onus for ensuring adequate separation is transferred from controller to pilot. The
provisos are:

(a) The runway is long enough to allow safe separation between the two aircraft and there is
    no evidence to indicate that braking may be adversely affected
(b) It is during daylight hours

(c) The preceding landing aircraft is not required to backtrack in order to vacate the runway
(d) The controller is satisfied that the landing aircraft will be able to see the preceding aircraft which has landed, clearly and continuously until it has vacated the runway
(e) The pilot of the following aircraft is warned

There is one other runway procedure which is authorised only at Heathrow and Gatwick where arriving aircraft are 'cleared to land after' (the phrase also being unique). Certain conditions must be met and the procedure is also allowed behind departing traffic. The aim is to achieve an increase in runway capacity.

At some airfields the Tower and Approach function may be combined on one frequency. This is perfectly satisfactory with light to medium traffic flows, but on busy weekends the R/T congestion can be serious, pilots having difficulty in getting a word in edgeways.

Airfields outside controlled airspace possess an Aerodrome Traffic Zone, through which flight is prohibited without a clearance. The circuit direction is a standard left hand, although this may vary for different runways to avoid overflying built-up areas, hospitals and the like. The reason for the left-hand pattern is said to date back to the First World War when aircraft like the Sopwith Camel turned much more easily to the left than the right, owing to the torque effect of the rotary engine. When larger aircraft with side-by-side seating were introduced, the pilot sat on the left and this has become traditional. In helicopters, however, this is reversed! Circuit height is normally 1,000ft above ground level (QFE), but at airfields such as Manchester-Barton it is 800ft, which sometimes leads to confusion when trainee pilots land elsewhere.

The circuit is divided into four legs: crosswind, downwind, base and final approach. The first aircraft to report downwind will be told to 'report final'. ('Number One' may be added to this.) The second will be told 'Report final number two to the Cherokee on base leg', and so on. New pilots should note that it is 'final' singular, not 'finals'! If the circuit is very busy the

Fokker 50 flightdeck.

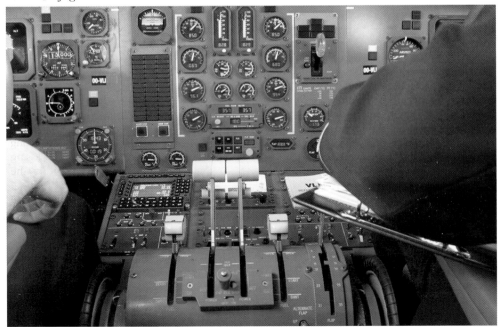

1 Downwind
2 Base Leg
3 Final
4 Long Final

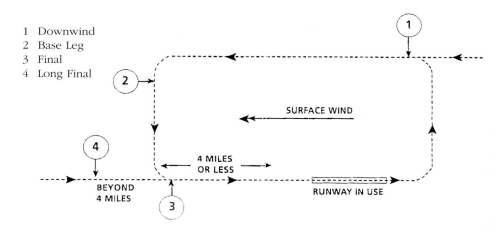

Critical positions in the aerodrome traffic circuit.

tower may instruct a pilot to 'report before turning base, four aircraft ahead'. When he does this he will be given an update on his position in traffic, there perhaps being only two ahead by this time.

The standard circuit-joining procedure is to arrive overhead the field at 2,000ft, descend on the dead side, ie the one opposite the live downwind leg and let down to 1,000ft. Whilst watching for departing traffic, the pilot then joins the crosswind leg over the upwind end of the active runway. (Wags should note that there is a cemetery under the dead side at Cambridge Airport.) This should ensure that a joining aircraft does not conflict with one just airborne, as there have been numerous cases in the past of collisions because of careless rejoins a mile or so off the end of the runway. Of course a high performance aircraft can easily be at 1,000ft by the time it reaches the end of a longish runway, so it is up to the tower to make sure that a joining aircraft does not cross its path. At many controlled airports the standard join is not used, aircraft being authorised to join directly on to final, base or downwind.

Aircraft flying under IFR are usually fed straight into the final approach, which can sometimes be tricky. One way to achieve this safely if there is circuit traffic, is to instruct the training traffic to continue downwind until he has the arriving aircraft in sight and then follow it. A warning about wake turbulence and the recommended spacing to avoid it is passed if necessary. The other solution is an orbit – 360° turn – always away from the final approach, to be continued until the traffic is sighted. The first method has the disadvantage that a strong tailwind may carry the aircraft into the next county, with perhaps an inexperienced pilot losing sight of the aerodrome. An orbit may be impracticable because of following traffic in the circuit. There is a limit to the number of aeroplanes you can orbit safely in a circuit!

If things are particularly congested and large aircraft are expected, trainers can always be told to land and taxi back to the holding point to await further take-off clearance. Another complication is wake turbulence, a phenomenon once referred to as slipstream or propwash, but now known to be a rapidly revolving cylinder of air from each wingtip. This can be so violent that it can overcome the control forces of a following aircraft and roll it over. Aircraft in the United Kingdom are placed in four categories depending upon maximum total weight at take-off. They are Heavy, Medium (divided into Upper and Lower), Small and Light. More details are to be found below.

Helicopter operations are less of a problem than might be imagined, the main one being crossing the active runway. However, they can clear it quickly and can thus be slotted between

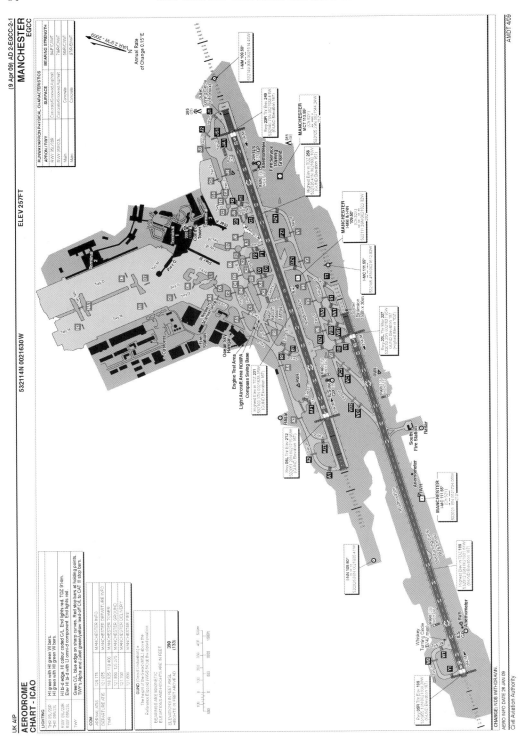

arriving and departing aircraft, remaining below 500ft until clear of the traffic zone. The same applies to their arrival. At some locations helicopters are required to use a runway for take-offs and landings. Some small helicopters have skids rather than wheels so the phrase 'air taxi' will be used instead of 'taxi'. Overflying helicopters are treated like any other crossing traffic, either cleared overhead above 2,000ft if the circuit is busy, or asked to report a few miles away and given traffic information so that they can fly through the pattern without conflict.

The Aerodrome Controller is, of course, pre-warned of arriving traffic by Approach or at some places he handles both functions on the same frequency. Similarly, for departing IFR traffic he will have the flight progress strips on his pending board, made up when the flight plan was filed with ATC.

At certain busy airports pilots on VFR flights, local, landing away or circuits, are required to 'book out' over the telephone with ATC, giving brief details. This is particularly important with circuit training as the tower controller may refuse to accept more than a certain number, or none at all, dependent upon weather conditions, scheduled traffic, existing congestion and other factors. At smaller airfields, pilots merely call for taxi clearance from the parking area stating their requirements. Training flights are often referred to by the word 'detail' as in 'Coventry Tower GAXVW request taxi clearance, two on board circuit detail.' This is a throwback to military jargon, as is the term 'fanstop' for a practice engine failure after take-off.

Aircraft on IFR flight plans should first request permission to start engines so that ATC can warn of any likely delays and thus minimise fuel wastage. If there is no delay, 'Start up approved' is passed, together with the outside air temperature in degrees Celsius. The QNH, QFE, runway in use and wind information may also be given in the same transmission, although this is optional. The alternative is to pass them when taxi clearance is given. In practice, pilots often call in advance for this 'airfield data', acknowledge it and say 'call you again for start'. Busier airfields will have an information broadcast referred to as an ATIS (see page 92).

Traffic on the congested holiday routes to the Mediterranean and other parts of Europe is subject to complex rules known as Departure Flow Regulation. They require the aircraft to take off at a specified time, ATC being allowed a small margin before and after this to cover any taxying delays or short waits for landing traffic. These Calculated Take-off Times (See-Tots) were formerly known as slot times and this terminology is still in use. Further details will be found on page 104. Busier airports are allowed longer tolerances.

Other domestic traffic within the UK is also regulated at peak periods. For example, the Channel Islands airports become very busy during the summer and flow control is employed to reduce congestion. On occasion, routes over the Irish Sea and Scotland are also subject to flow management. A time band, normally of 10 minutes, within which an aircraft must cross a specified point, is used as an alternative to an ADT. On fairly rare occasions, the parent ACC may impose a Minimum Departure Interval (MDI) between take-offs for a specified period of time. This is normally because of traffic congestion in the vicinity and is totally unrelated to slot times.

Air band listeners may wonder about the precise meaning of a 'ready message'. The phrase is often heard when an aircraft is subject to a departure slot time and the pilots are hoping to get an earlier one. Once the passengers are all on board and the aircraft is ready to start, a Ready Message may be sent by ATC or the airline's ops section to the Central Flow Management Unit (CFMU) in Brussels. The acronym MINLINEUP will not be used on R/T but it is taken into account by CFMU. It represents the minimum time needed by that flight, which has declared itself ready to depart, to start up, taxi and get airborne. If possible, CFMU will respond almost immediately with an improved slot. Otherwise, there will be silence and the

LEFT: Aerodrome chart for Manchester (used with the permission of and copyright of UK CAA).

UK AIP

(17 Jan 08) AD 2-EGPF-6-1

STANDARD DEPARTURE CHART - INSTRUMENT (SID) - ICAO

DISTANCES IN NAUTICAL MILES
BEARINGS, TRACKS AND RADIALS ARE MAGNETIC
ALTITUDES AND ELEVATIONS ARE IN FEET

GLASGOW
NEW GALLOWAY (Jet aircraft only)

D601 4000 SFC

P611 2200 SFC

AREA MNM ALT 25NM

TRANSITION ALTITUDE 6000

PERTH
PTH 110.40
562633N 0032207W

ELBAN
555717N 0043016W
GOW R343.7/b5.4
TRN R018.2/b39.7
PTH R237.2

248°

NGY 3J (11)

6000 (7.00%)

2000

XEXUS
555526N 0042010W
GOW R054.1/b4.9

GOW R054

PTH R231

TRN R012

NGY 3J (24)

NGY 3J

GOW R229

NGY 2H (20)

TRN R007 (187°)

GLASGOW
GOW 115.40°
(Ch 101X)
555214N 0042649W
37'

R504 2800 SFC

R515 2000 SFC

GOW D12 5000

GOW D14 6000 (7.00%)

NORBO
553545N 0044543W
TRN R007.0/b17.0

QDM 146°

WARNING
Do not climb above **6000**
until instructed by ATC.

5530N

25NM

5530N

VAR 4.7°W 2007

N
Annual Rate
of Change 0.17°E

TURNBERRY
TRN 117.50°
(Ch 122X)
551848N 0044702W
600'

NGY 2H 3J (32)

AVERAGE
TRACK MILEAGE
TO NGY NDB

NGY 2H 52
NGY 3J 72

ATIS*	129.575	ARRIVAL/DEPARTURE INFORMATION
ACC	124.825	SCOTTISH CONTROL
TWR	118.800*	GLASGOW TOWER
RAD	119.100, 119.300*, 121.300*	GLASGOW RADAR
* See EGPF AD 2.18 for full details		

NEW GALLOWAY
NGY 399
551039N 0041007W

6000

| 5 | 0 | 5 | 10 | 15NM |

| NGY 2H RWY 23 | Climb straight ahead to intercept **GOW VOR** R229. Cross **GOW** D12 **5000** or above. Cross **GOW** D14 at **6000** then turn left onto **TRN VOR** R007 to **NORBO**. At **NORBO** (**TRN VOR** R007 D17), turn left onto **NGY NDB** QDM 146° to cross **NGY NDB** at **6000**. | N615, N57, N864. |

OBSTACLE CLEARANCE - RWY 23: Maintain minimum 3.8% climb to **1200**.

| NGY 3J RWY 05 | Climb straight ahead to intercept **GOW VOR** R054. Cross **GOW** D4.9 (**XEXUS**) **2000** or above then turn left onto track 248° to **ELBAN** (**TRN VOR** R018), crossing **ELBAN** at **6000** (7%), to intercept **PTH VOR** R237. At **TRN VOR** R012 turn left onto **TRN VOR** R007 to **NORBO**. At **NORBO** (**TRN VOR** R007 D17), turn left onto **NGY NDB** QDM 146° to cross **NGY NDB** at **6000**. | N615, N57, N864 |

OBSTACLE CLEARANCE - RWY 05: Maintain minimum 4.5% climb to **1500**.

GENERAL INFORMATION
1. SIDs reflect Noise Preferential Routeings. See EGPF AD 2.21 for Noise Abatement Procedures.
2. Initial climb straight ahead to **526** QNH (**500** QFE).
3. Climb gradients greater than 3.3% are required for obstacle clearance purposes, as indicated. In addition climb gradients greater than those necessary for obstacle clearance are required for ATC and airspace requirements as indicated.
4. En-route cruising levels will be issued after take-off by 'Scottish Control'. Report callsign, SID designator, current altitude and cleared altitude on first contact with 'Scottish Control'.
5. Maximum IAS 250KT below FL100 unless otherwise authorised.

CHANGE: CALLSIGN CORRECTED

AERO INFO DATE 30 OCT 07

Civil Aviation Authority

AMDT 1/08

original slot will apply, to the crew's disappointment! Much of the tower controller's workload – and that of his assistant – can consist of haggling over slots. At bigger airports, this job is handled by Clearance Delivery or GMC.

The CFMU computer in Brussels knows the theoretical capacity of every bit of airspace and every runway in Europe. If it states that a certain sector can take 45 aircraft per hour at certain levels, but 50 are flight-planned into it, five of those have to be shunted into the next hour to accommodate them. Hence a departure slot is issued to delay them. There are other factors as well. For example, if a certain airport has a major weather problem that reduces arrival rate, or has staffing or equipment problems, they notify CFMU of the reduced acceptance rate. Flights inbound to the airport then get delayed so that the rate is adhered to. Note that Runway Slots at major airports are a totally different game, and one way that airports make their money by auctioning them to the highest bidding airline.

If there are no problems, taxi instructions will be given to the appropriate runway. In the meantime, ATC will have obtained an airways clearance from the parent ACC by land line and this is passed to the aircraft at a convenient moment, assuming that this has not been done earlier. Now that NATS has introduced Electronic Flight Data Display Systems at some of its airports, suitably equipped aircraft may request and receive their ATC route clearance via datalink. Enthusiasts with a commercially available decoder will be able to monitor these messages.

Datalink Departure Clearance may be requested from EOBT (Estimated Off Blocks Time, ie the time the aircraft starts moving) minus 25 minutes until EOBT plus 10 minutes. The request will be processed by the same controller who is also carrying out the voice clearances and will normally be returned to the aircraft within a short period of time. Once a clearance has been requested, one member of crew should remain available to acknowledge the returned clearance.

If receipt of the clearance has not been acknowledged within five minutes, the system will consider an error has occurred. Under these circumstances, or when any messaging error occurs, a message requiring the crew to 'revert to voice' will be sent and the datalink clearance cancelled. No further pilot or system generated departure datalink requests should be made once a successful clearance has been received. The system cannot be used for re-clearance or checking for any updates. Once the aircraft is ready to depart, voice contact should be established stating 'With datalink clearance', the aircraft type and series and the QNH.

Local procedures vary from one airport to another and it may be necessary to contact the ACC again as the subject nears the runway for permission to let it take off. This is known as a 'release'. On occasion, Approach Radar will have to separate it from inbound conflicting traffic. It will then be given a suitable radar heading to fly after departure and/or a level restriction. An example is: 'After departure, climb straight ahead to maintain altitude 3,000ft.' As soon as it is airborne the aircraft will be transferred to the Approach frequency and it will only be handed over to the Area Control Centre when the confliction has been resolved ('Clean' in ATC slang).

Where no local restrictions are applied, the tower will put the aircraft over to the ACC immediately after take-off. The departure time may also be passed to the ACC by telephone to be fed into the computer. At the busiest UK airports, including Heathrow, Gatwick and Manchester, the flow of arrivals and departures is designed so that the two do not conflict. The ideal is a 'conveyor belt' system but, although in practice this is virtually impossible to achieve, it comes quite near to being so. Of necessity the other lesser airfields in a TMA, for example Liverpool in the case of Manchester, are somewhat subservient. Their traffic flows are

LEFT: Glasgow New Galloway SID for jet aircraft only (used with the permission of and copyright of UK CAA).

very much subject to those of their busier neighbours although, on the credit side, sometimes more flexible.

By agreement with the parent ACC, some towers with SSR capability validate the SSR squawk by checking it has been set correctly and verify the Mode C by asking for an altitude check on the initial climb-out. If this is within 200ft either side of the height label on the controller's display, it is considered acceptable. Funny how often pilots set their slot time on the transponder instead of the SSR squawk!

If the weather is good, pilots of GA aircraft on IFR flight plans may elect to go VFR. This saves en route navigation charges and it is also a way to avoid delays at busy periods when an airways clearance is not immediately forthcoming from the ACC. However, pilots who try to beat the system and rejoin controlled airspace further down the airway will not get much sympathy and are likely to suffer further delay as a result! A typical ATC acknowledgement of a request to go VFR is: 'Atlantic 991 roger, IFR flight plan cancelled at 36'.

The SSR code, or 'squawk' as it is known, is allocated according to a predetermined system. The UK participates in the internationally agreed Originating Region Code Assignment Method (ORCAM). This was developed by Eurocontrol and endorsed by ICAO. Since there are insufficient code blocks to develop a worldwide system it has been necessary to group certain countries into Participating Areas. The ICAO EUR region is divided into five of these areas, the United Kingdom falling into PA West.

ORCAM is designed to reduce R/T and cockpit workload by allocating an SSR code which will be retained by the aircraft from take-off to touchdown. This helps controllers in forward planning, particularly in areas of radar data processing. Each ACC is allocated two blocks of codes, one for internal flights (Domestic) and the other (ORCAM) for international flights. The ACC with jurisdiction over the airspace first entered by an aircraft will assign a discrete code from one of its blocks. The code will depend on the destination and will be retained throughout the flight within the Participating Area, being transferred from control centre to centre along the route. (See Appendix 7).

SSR Mode S will solve the problem of the very limited number of codes available (4064). Mode S transponders employ a unique 'address' for each individual aircraft, 16 million being available worldwide. Unfortunately, the ground interrogator system has its own limitations at present which severely offset the airborne advantages. Approach Control units with SSR capability have their own small block of codes which they can allocate to traffic operating in their area, provided of course that the aircraft is transponder-equipped. Fortunately nowadays most private aircraft can comply with this. Mention of the special squawk 7000 is often made on R/T. Pilots flying outside controlled airspace and Aerodrome Traffic Zones and who are not receiving a radar service are advised to set 7000, the conspicuity code, on the transponder. As the name implies, this makes the aircraft show up better on radar as well as indicating its altitude if Mode C is fitted. Above FL110, 7000 is mandatory.

Aerodrome Control Phraseology

Aircraft: 'Liverpool Tower Easy 163D Airbus 319 request start. Information Bravo QNH 1008.'
ATC: 'Easy 163D start approved. Information Bravo is current.'

The phrase 'Start-up at your discretion', together with an expected departure time, may be used so that the onus is on the crew to start engines at a convenient time. Note that the words 'at your discretion' are used by controllers to imply that any traffic delays, getting stuck in soft ground and other misfortunes will henceforth be the pilot's fault! Controllers have very definite responsibilities and they are understandably reluctant to take on any extra ones.

Aircraft: 'Heathrow Ground Alitalia 235 Stand E3 request pushback and start.'
ATC: 'Alitalia 235 pushback and start approved.'

Controllers at work in Liverpool VCR, air controller in the foreground, GMC beyond, with their assistant to the left.

Most airports now have nose-in parking at the terminal to save apron space and to facilitate passenger handling. Aircraft have to be pushed backwards by a tractor into a position from which they can taxi for departure. A variation is the 'powerback' in which a turbo-prop aircraft reverses under its own power.

Aircraft: 'Liverpool Tower GLFSA at Kilo request taxi for local.'
ATC: 'GSA taxi Charlie hold Runway 09 via Alpha, Information Bravo is current, QNH 1001.'

Taxi instructions must always specify a clearance limit, which is the point at which an aircraft must halt and ask for further permission to proceed. The limit is normally the holding point of the runway-in-use but it may also be an intermediate position, perhaps short of another runway which is in intermittent use. To maintain a smooth operation, controllers try to anticipate calls from taxying aircraft so that they do not actually have to stop at intermediate points. Some UK airports have complex taxiway systems and each significant section is given an identifying letter (two in some cases). Holding points are allocated a number as a suffix to the taxiway designation, eg Alpha One.

The ideal is to establish a circular flow of taxying aircraft so that the ones just landed do not get in the way of those moving towards the holding point. Alas, some airports have inadequate taxiway systems with two-way flows and bottlenecks. A refusal to give crossing clearance of an active runway is passed in the form: 'GVW hold short Runway 23'. Permission to continue is: 'GVW cross Runway 23, report vacated'.

Many types of aircraft, mainly piston-engined, carry out engine run-up checks prior to departure and are not always ready for take-off when they reach the holding point so the controller may say 'GVW report ready for departure'. When ready for take-off, permission is sought from the tower. If the runway is occupied by traffic which has just landed, the aircraft will be told to 'line-up and wait'. The American phrase 'taxi into position' is sometimes tried when a foreign pilot seems to have difficulty in understanding what is meant. (Controllers always have something up their sleeves to break the language barrier and we have all had to resort to plain speech to convey our meaning to some uncomprehending student pilot!)

If there is traffic on final, the aircraft at the holding point may be told: 'After the Cherokee on short final, line up'. Care must be taken that there is no possibility of confusion with another aircraft which may have just landed. Where a preceding aircraft is beginning its take-off roll, the second aircraft may be told: 'After the departing Cessna, line up and wait'. The use of the words 'cleared immediate take-off' means that the aircraft must go without delay to leave the runway free for landing traffic. It is only to be used where there is actual urgency so that its specific meaning is not debased.

For reasons of expedition, a controller may wish to line up an aircraft on the runway for departure before conditions allow take-off. 'Speedbird 342 via holding point Alpha One line up and wait Runway 27, one aircraft to depart before you from holding point Alpha Two.' The aircraft should reply: 'Via holding point Alpha One line up and wait number two for departure. Speedbird 342'.

When line-up will take place at a position other than for a full-length runway departure, the intermediate holding point designator will be included in the line-up instruction. Controllers may include the designator in any other line-up instruction when considered appropriate. 'GCD ready for departure.' ATC: 'GCD via Charlie Two line up Runway 28.'

The circuit joining procedure has already been covered, so a few examples of phraseology will suffice:

Aircraft: 'Coventry Tower GAYMN at Ansty for landing.'
ATC: 'GMN join right hand downwind Runway 05, QFE 1004'; or 'GMN join straight-in approach Runway 23, QFE 1004.'
Aircraft: 'GMN downwind.'
ATC: 'GMN Number 2, follow the Cessna 150 on base.'
Aircraft: 'GMN Number 2, traffic in sight.'
ATC: 'GMN extend downwind, number 2 to a Cessna 150 4 miles final on radar approach.'
Aircraft: 'GMN wilco.'

Having already explained the criteria for issuing landing and take-off clearances, it only remains for me to mention a few extra points. Aircraft on what used to be known as 'circuits and bumps' may wish to do a 'touch and go' landing; in other words, the aircraft lands, continues rolling and takes off again without a pause. The wording 'cleared touch and go' is the only one approved officially but pilots may ask for a 'roller', the military equivalent. (Somebody did once read back to me 'cleared for a hit and run' but such levity is not encouraged!) Instructions to carry out a missed approach may be given to avert an unsafe situation, such as when one aircraft is too close behind another on final. 'GTE go around, I say again, go around. Acknowledge.' Sometimes an aircraft on a practice instrument approach with an intended go-around will be instructed to do this not below 400ft because the runway is temporarily obstructed by an essential maintenance vehicle.

Depending on local procedures, a departing aircraft will be retained on the tower frequency until it is clear of the circuit or changed to Approach immediately. Airways flights will of course be transferred to the ACC just after take-off or as soon as they have been separated

In the departure queue at London City Airport.

from any conflicting traffic. When the landing roll is complete, the arriving aircraft will be told to vacate the runway in the following manner:

ATC: 'GMN vacate left', or ' GMN taxi to the end, report runway vacated', or 'GMN take next right. When vacated contact Ground 121.7.'

The appropriate taxying instructions are then passed. Airborne and landing times may be passed by the tower, although there is no official requirement for this.

Strangely enough, controllers are not responsible for reminding pilots to put their wheels down on final, except when a radar approach is being provided. However, if an aircraft landed wheels-up in broad daylight, the controller would no doubt suffer some criticism, apart from the dent to his professional pride! Fortunately it is a rare occurrence these days but I once earned a pint from a Cessna 337 pilot whom I reminded just in time. (Cheap at the price – the saving in repairs would have paid my year's salary!)

One last point is defined as 'Essential Aerodrome Information'. It refers to any obstruction or unserviceability that is likely to affect operations. It is always prefixed 'caution', examples being 'Caution work in progress ahead just north of taxiway.' 'Caution PAPI Runway 27 unserviceable.' 'Caution large flock of birds north of Runway 27 threshold.'

Chapter 8

ATC at London's airports

THE ENTIRE LONDON area ATC operation is a very difficult and challenging one and the controllers who make it work it are, arguably, the world's best. Because of its intensity, traffic in the London TMA is handled rather differently from that of other British airports. London ATCC Terminal Control (TC) is designed to maximise traffic flows. TC is responsible for a number of en-route sectors in the lower levels of airspace immediately outside and on top of the TMA. These are controlled from TC because they mainly feed traffic into and out of the main London airports. They are grouped as TC East (four sectors), TC Midlands (four sectors) and TC Capital (two sectors). TC East's airspace adjoins the international boundary with Amsterdam and Brussels airspace.

The TMA itself is divided into sectors, each sector controller being responsible for a defined segment. Traffic flows predominantly in the same direction to minimise points of conflict and the need for co-ordination between controllers is kept to a minimum. Approach Control services for Heathrow, Gatwick, Stansted and Luton have been moved to Swanwick. TC's airspace extends up to FL155, above which are London Middle and Upper Sectors which mainly handle overflying traffic.

TC airspace is split into two groups or banks: TC North and TC South. North is further split into North East (three sectors) and North West (two sectors). TC South is split into South East (three sectors) and South West (three sectors). All sectors have the RT callsign 'London Control'. Arrivals for the London airports are handed over from LACC or the TC en-route sectors, usually following Standard Terminal Arrival Routes (STAR) and are descended against the departing traffic, sorted out into different levels, then routed to various holds, where they will remain until the approach controllers are ready to position them into an approach sequence to land.

Aircraft inbound to Heathrow are directed by LATCC to one of four VORs located at Bovingdon, Lambourne, Biggin and Ockham. If traffic is light they may not actually route overhead these beacons but are vectored by radar directly to intercept the ILS for the landing runway. As the traffic flow increases, aircraft may arrive at the beacons faster than the airport is able to receive them, allowing for the requisite separation on approach. Hence the term 'stacking' (in ATC more usually referred to as 'holding').

The incredible potential of enhanced Mode S transponders in aircraft is not generally known. Currently in the UK, only the London Terminal Control Centre (LTCC) has the capability of downlinking the information, but the London Area Centre is due to follow. The parameters include the current Flight Level or altitude from the autopilot, the current Indicated Airspeed from the Airspeed Indicator, the current heading, and the current rate of

RIGHT: Aerodrome chart for London/Heathrow (used with the permission of and copyright of UK CAA).

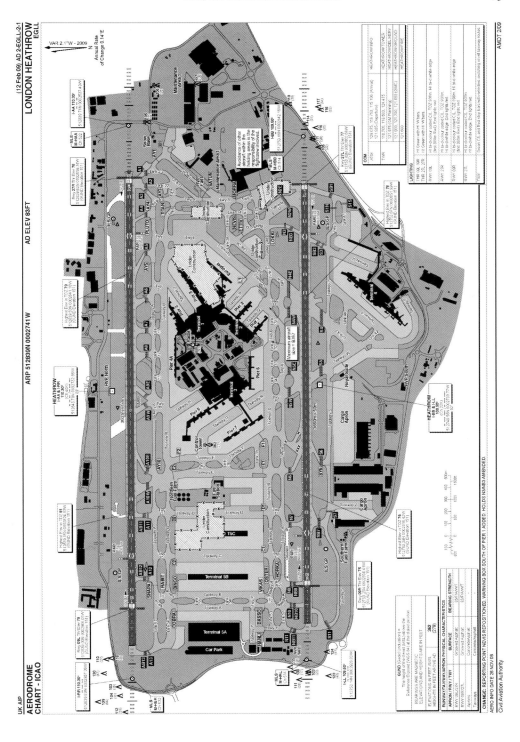

climb or descent. LTCC also use Mode S to see into the holding stacks when aircraft identity labels overlap and 'garble', the information being visible on a separate vertical stack list. The controller can even monitor the altitude selections made by a pilot on his Flight Management Computer (FMC) and alert him if a wrong selection is made. It is no exaggeration to say that this is the most significant improvement in ATC safety since the introduction of SSR.

During busy periods, when the flow of arriving traffic exceeds the immediate system capacity, the Terminal Holding Stacks form a 'reservoir' of queuing aircraft from which the approach radar controllers (known as Directors) arrange the optimum sequence. The radar technique is very deliberate, using upwind legs where possible so that the timing of the turn downwind can be controlled. This enables the length of the final approach to be fine-tuned so that it is kept at the optimum 15nm. Establishing on final at this distance enables rigid speed control to be applied to adjust any vectoring errors. The result is that the aircraft get as close as possible to minimum spacing (2.5nm) as they cross 4 miles DME from touchdown. Both the runways operate at saturation level for most of the day.

At busy times, six controllers work as a team. They consist of a North Intermediate Director and his support controller, a South Intermediate Director again with a support controller, a Final Director and a Special VFR Controller. Each Director controls the traffic from either Bovingdon and Lambourne in the north or from Ockham and Biggin in the south. As the aircraft nears one of these VOR beacons TC releases it to Heathrow Approach. On contact the pilot is told to enter the hold or, if there is no delay, vectored directly into the landing sequence. The frequencies in use are 119.725, 120.4, 127.525 and 134.975. The Special VFR Controller operates on 125.625.

The Directors work closely together, instructing pilots to adjust their height, speed and heading so that two orderly streams of aircraft, one from the north, the other from the south, are brought on to the approach path. Aircraft in these two streams are handed over to the Final Director so that he can integrate them into a single stream of aircraft approaching the runway.

At this stage a correct landing interval must be established and the Final Director ensures that all aircraft are correctly separated, depending on the prevailing weather conditions and type of aircraft involved. The wake turbulence separations are explained in Chapter 13 but there are other considerations. For example, a Boeing 737 following a small turbo-prop will obviously have no problem with turbulence but will catch up rapidly if this is not allowed for. Similarly, if visibility is on limits an aircraft may be slow to clear the runway and the 'land after' procedure cannot be applied, resulting in a go-around if the next aircraft is too close behind.

When traffic is heavy and the holding stacks are filling up, the North Director takes on the title of Master Director and decides the overall landing order. Generally this will be on a first-come, first-served basis but as soon as traffic starts to build the order will be manipulated at the earliest opportunity. The aim is to group similar aircraft types so as to maximise the landing rate. For example, if four Boeing 737s and four 747s arrived at the same time, the best landing rate would be achieved by positioning the 737s on final one behind another, followed by the 747s.

Another operational feature of London's airports that is being adopted at other UK sites is the Continuous Descent Approach Procedure (CDA). The aim is to provide pilots with the assistance necessary for them to achieve a continuous descent during intermediate and final approach, at speeds which require minimum use of flaps and speed brakes. This has significant benefits in terms of noise produced beneath the approach area and in reduction of fuel used. CDA requires ATC to apply specific, or minimum speeds to inbound aircraft and to pass adequate 'range from touchdown' information. In a nutshell, low power, low drag, less noise.

The Special VFR Controller is responsible for helicopters and light aircraft which wish to land within or merely transit the London Control Zone within the levels for which Heathrow Approach is responsible. Inbound aircraft are fitted into the approach pattern to cause as little inconvenience as possible to the main commercial traffic. Helicopters are required to follow special routes in the London area, designed where possible to keep them over the River Thames and the most thinly populated areas. The usual destination is the London Heliport at Battersea. All inbound helicopters have to route via the Thames, initially routeing to Kew Bridge, Barnes or London Bridge, depending on the direction from which they are approaching. There are numerous compulsory and on-request reporting points and helicopters may be held at a number of positions to await onward clearance. They are all located at easily recognisable places such as Hampton Court, Sunbury Lock and Hanworth.

When the two streams of approaching aircraft are satisfactorily merged into one, and as each aircraft is established on the ILS at a distance of six to eight miles from touchdown, control is transferred to Air Arrivals Control in the tower. Like any other tower controller, he or she issues landing clearances, passes wind checks and details of surface conditions where appropriate. The frequency is 118.7, 124.475 being available as a standby. If there are no wake turbulence separation requirements, the spacing used on final approach is 3nm and under certain conditions this can be reduced to 2.5nm. In LVP conditions, the spacing will be increased to 6nm, giving a landing rate of about 28 per hour.

Heathrow currently handles about 1,300 movements per day. In ideal conditions the controllers can do up to 48 arrivals per hour but more typically it is 42. Departures are normally about 45 per hour but if the traffic mix is good it can be up to 50. To make things easier (a relative term!), all aircraft are instructed to fly at the same speeds. This is usually 220kt off the stack, 180kt on base leg and, when correctly spaced on final approach, 160kt which will be maintained until 4 miles from touchdown. Tactically Enhanced Arrival Mode (TEAM) is an agreement that during very busy periods, especially 0700–0900, Terminal Control may request the use of the departure runway for some inbound traffic in order to increase the overall landing rate and thus reduce inbound delays. This is the so-called mixed mode.

After the aircraft has landed and vacated the runway it will be transferred to the Ground Movement Controller who directs it to the parking stand. He continues to monitor its progress and co-ordinates its movements with those of other aircraft and vehicles. Any airport has its quota of operational vehicles but Heathrow inevitably has more than most. There is, for example, a full-time mobile bird control unit, radio call-sign 'Seagull'. 'Checker' is the airport surface and lighting inspection vehicle, 'Pixie' the ATC vehicle.

The maintenance of runways and taxiways and their associated lighting is one of the biggest problems for Ground Movement Control. It seems that there is almost always some part of the airport being dug up or resurfaced. Each controller has an airport plan on which he notes the current unserviceable areas before taking over watch in the tower. Heathrow has an A-SMGCS – Advanced Surface Movement Guidance and Control System. Without going into too much technical detail, A-SMGCS is a surface movement radar system that displays aircraft call-signs and allocated stand numbers on the ground radar display. When a pilot switches on his Mode S transponder with the Mode A code selected, the Mode A code is transmitted via Mode S, and a label is generated which is derived from the code/call-sign database. Another feature of the system is the RIMCAS – Runway Incursion Monitoring and Collision Avoidance System. It provides audible and visual warnings in the event of runway incursions.

Heathrow ATIS includes a request for pilots to leave their transponders on Mode S after landing, without appropriate Mode 3A set. The transponder is to be left on until parked on stand and selected with the allocated code during pushback. The aim is a marked improvement in the service pilots receive from Tower and GMC in the dark and during Low Visibility Operations. From what I understand, the Mode S 'squitter' transmits the aircraft's call-sign once per second and it is this that the system uses.

Final approach to London City on the standard high glidepath angle to reduce noise.

Flight deck view of London City's cramped apron.

At night aircraft are assisted by green centreline and red stop bar lights set flush with the taxiways. These can be illuminated in sections to ensure that no two aircraft are in or crossing the same section at any one time. This complex lighting system is operated by an ATC assistant on instructions from the Ground Movement Controller. The lighting control panel is a mimic diagram, ie it is designed in the form of an airport plan with switches which directly operate the lighting in the corresponding section of the airport.

When an aircraft is ready for departure, the pilot, having noted the data on the continuous broadcast on the ATIS, and obtained his airways clearance, calls the Ground Movement Planner on 121.975 (call-sign 'Delivery') for permission to push back and start engines. He is then told to contact GMC (call-sign 'Ground') or given a likely start time to minimise ground delays and thus save fuel. Also taken into consideration are the number of other aircraft which have already started, air route congestion and ADTs issued by LATCC. GMC is responsible for issuing push-back clearance from the stand by a tractor. Guidance is then given to the runway-in-use, and as this is approached, the aircraft is handed over to the Air Departures Controller on 118.5 who arranges the aircraft in a departure sequence to achieve the maximum use of the runway. A large pan at the holding point provides sufficient space to 'shuffle' the order of departures.

The basic rule of thumb is to alternate the departures between straight ahead, left and right. For example, when two aircraft of a similar type are departing in succession, one for a destination to the north followed by one to the south, they are allowed to leave one minute apart. However, due to the variety of aircraft types using Heathrow, this time interval may have to be increased depending on wake turbulence categories and specific departure route. To minimise runway occupancy time, on receipt of line-up clearance pilots are expected to taxi on to the runway as soon as the preceding aircraft has started its take-off roll. Again, once receiving take-off clearance, they are required to roll immediately.

Aircraft departing Heathrow, Gatwick, Luton and Stansted mostly depart on a free-flow principle. This means that the radar controllers do not release each individual flight for departure, they just receive a pre-note via a computer system that the flight is pending. This cuts down on inter-unit co-ordination and allows the tower controller at the airport to decide the most efficient departure order. In many cases the aircraft's Standard Instrument Departure (SID) routeing does not conflict with the approach sequence of aircraft arriving at the airport, so the airport's approach control does not need to handle the aircraft and it is transferred straight to the TMA controller on departure. The TMA controllers then climb the departures through the arrivals to the airports that they are also working.

The pair of westerly (27) runways at Heathrow tend to be used most frequently because of prevailing winds. One is normally used for landings and the other for departures, but a local agreement ensures a change from one to the other at around 1500 hours local time each day in order to spread the noise more evenly. When the tailwind component is no greater than 5kt on Runways 27 Right and Left, they will be used in preference to Runways 09 Right and Left, provided the runway surface is dry.

ATC at Gatwick is somewhat less complex because of the single runway operation and has two holding stacks known as WILLO and TIMBA, to the SW and SE of the airport respectively. WILLO takes traffic from the north, west and south-west plus all Atlantic and some Spanish traffic. TIMBA covers all other traffic from Europe. The parallel Runway 08 Left/26 Right is a non-instrument runway and is used only when 08 Right/26 Left is temporarily non-operational by reason of maintenance or accident. Simultaneous operations are not permitted as the runways are too close together.

London Stansted has two stacks at LOREL and ABBOT both to the north. LOREL also serves arrivals for London Luton. Its approach control unit uses the call-sign 'Essex Radar' for initial vectoring, followed by handover to 'Stansted Director'. For Gatwick and Stansted there is normally a single Intermediate Radar Director followed by the Final Director. Traffic from and to London/City Airport is handled by a facility known as Thames Radar which is co-located with Heathrow Approach. Because of its proximity to London/City, Biggin Hill's IFR traffic is also co-ordinated by Thames Radar.

London TMA Frequencies

120.175	Inbounds via LUMBA, TIMBA
120.475	Inbounds via WILLO and deps via Midhurst and Worthing
121.225	Inbounds via Lambourne
121.275	Inbounds via Bovingdon
129.075	Inbounds via Ockham and deps via Compton and Southampton
133.175/133.975	Inbounds to London City, Biggin Hill and Southend
118.825	Deps via Brookmans Park
119.775	Deps via Bovingdon

Chapter 9

Oceanic Control and HF listening

TRAFFIC OVER THE North Atlantic communicates with ATC by means of the HF radio band, VHF being too restricted in range. However, aircraft requesting clearance to enter the Shanwick Oceanic Control Area from overhead the United Kingdom can be heard on certain VHF frequencies. ATC in the Shanwick OCA is provided by the Oceanic ACC at Prestwick, Scotland, supported by the communications station at Ballygireen, just north of Shannon Airport in Eire, hence the composite call-sign 'Shanwick Oceanic'. Jet aircraft are required to request oceanic clearance while east of 2°W (roughly a line Manchester–Bournemouth) or as early as possible when departing from a point west of 2°W. Entry clearance can in fact be requested while the aircraft is still on the ground. It is thus easy to intercept these transmissions in much of the United Kingdom.

There are no fixed air routes across the North Atlantic. Instead there is a procedure known as the Organised Track System that is used for aircraft flying between North America and Europe between Flight Levels 290 and 410 inclusive. The tracks reverse direction twice daily. In the daylight, all traffic on the tracks operates in a westbound flow. At night, the tracks flow eastbound towards Europe. This is done to accommodate traditional airline schedules, with departures from North America to Europe scheduled for departure in the evening thereby allowing passengers to arrive at their destination in the morning. Westbound departures leave Europe mid-day and arrive in North America in the late afternoon. In this manner, a single aircraft can be heavily utilised by flying to Europe at night and to North America in the day. The tracks are updated daily and their position may alter on the basis of a variety of variable factors, but predominantly due to weather systems.

Because of the concentration of the flows and the limited vertical height band that is economical for jet operations, the airspace is comparatively congested. The track system is thus designed to accommodate as many aircraft as possible on the most suitable flight paths, taking advantage of pressure systems to provide a tailwind where possible.

Prestwick OACC is responsible for the day track system and Gander in Newfoundland for the night. In each case, planners on both sides of the Atlantic consult with one another and co-ordinate as necessary with adjacent ATC agencies, both oceanic and domestic. This ensures that the system provides sufficient tracks and flight levels to satisfy anticipated traffic demand. On completion of negotiations, the OTS is sent out from the OACC concerned to all interested parties in Europe and North America. The daytime system is usually published by Prestwick between midnight and 01:00 hours. In addition, the track co-ordinates are broadcast on frequency 133.8MHz and this can be heard in many parts of the United Kingdom.

The tracks are known as Alpha, Bravo, Charlie and on to Mike, the most northerly being Alpha. For night use the tracks are designated Zulu for the most southerly, Yankee for the next one to the north, ending at November. Letters India and Oscar are not used. Although the routes can change daily, they maintain a series of entrance and exit waypoints which link into the domestic airspace systems of North America and Europe.

For aircraft not equipped with HF radio, there are several routes known as 'Blue Spruce', that follow short hops between Iceland, Greenland and Canada within VHF radio and VOR/NDB coverage. Some aircraft may wish to operate outside the organised track system, for example on flights between Europe and the Caribbean. These so-called random tracks are also handled by Shanwick.

Prior to departure, airline flight dispatchers and flight operations officers will determine the best track based on destination, aircraft weight, aircraft type, prevailing winds and ATC route charges. Once airborne, the Atlantic Track portion of the flight plan will be confirmed. The aircraft will then contact the Oceanic Centre controller before entering oceanic airspace and request the track, giving the estimated time of arrival at the entry point. The Oceanic Controllers then calculate the required separation distances between aircraft and issue clearances to the pilot. It may be that the track is not available at that altitude or time so an alternate track or altitude will be assigned.

Once the clearance is accepted by the pilot, the information is relayed to the relevant ACC and, where necessary, to adjacent OACCs. The clearance is then fed into Prestwick's computer, which prints the appropriate en route flight strips and relays the information to Gander's computer. These flight strips give all relevant flight details and computed times of arrival at specific reporting points along the track, normally at intervals of 10 degrees of longitude. The controller uses them to monitor the progress of the flight through the Oceanic Control Area. He is assisted in his task by the use of the Flight Data Processing System (FDPS), which carries out conflict prediction and detection, automatic update of flight profiles and data transfer to online adjacent ATC units.

Compared with the brief content of domestic airways clearances, these oceanic clearances are fairly long-winded because of the need to specify a number of latitude and longitude positions, although in certain circumstances they can be abbreviated. It is useful for the air band listener to record some of these messages on tape for subsequent analysis. The same applies to other ATC transmissions when an air band radio is being used for the first time.

Unique to Oceanic Control is the method by which aircraft request clearances. Irrespective of geographic location, an aircraft will always use one of two frequencies, either 123.95 or 127.65MHz. Aircraft registered west of 30°W use the first, those registered east of 30° the second. In practice this generally means that British airlines use 127.65 and American, Australian and Canadian use 123.95. Suitably equipped aircraft, which will enter Shanwick airspace along most of its eastern boundary, can obtain an oceanic clearance via datalink.

Outside VHF range, aircraft crossing the Atlantic communicate with ATC by means of HF radio. The same applies to any ocean or underdeveloped land mass where the short range of VHF radio waves would prove useless. An average of 1,300 commercial, military and general aviation flights over-fly the North Atlantic each day, all being handled by Shanwick. Thus the use of an HF receiver opens up a whole new area of interest for the enthusiast.

In Britain there are a wide variety of listening possibilities, principally the civil stations (nets) controlling traffic over the Atlantic from Polar regions to the Equator, the US Air Force's extensive network and those of the RAF and airline operators. There are nearly 140 ATC centres operating on HF around the world and, depending on the performance of one's receiver and other factors, many of them can be monitored. During the transatlantic slack periods (ie between the late morning/early afternoon westbound flights and the eastbound flights in the early hours of the morning) one can listen in to other parts of the world. For example, aircraft in the Far East in the late afternoon, Africa in the evening, and then, for an hour or so either side of midnight, the Caribbean and the eastern seaboard of the USA are very busy.

HF stations use a block of radio frequencies to circumvent the effects of atmospheric conditions. HF transmissions 'bounce off' the ionising layers which lie above the earth but, since the layers are affected by day and night conditions, a suitable range of daytime frequencies might suffer severe interference at night and vice versa. Although having very long range, HF lacks the clarity of the VHF channels and the atmospheric noises and constant chatter make it very tiring for crews to maintain a continuous listening watch.

The answer is SelCal, short for Selective Calling. By this method, crews need not monitor the frequency, but when the ground station wishes to communicate with them a tone is sent and decoded by the cockpit equipment. This unique code opens up the squelch on the HF radio when received by the unit, allowing pilots to hear only the radio calls for their aircraft. A 'bing-bong' sound can be heard on the radio and on the flight deck a chime or light signal also alerts the pilots to respond by R/T. Each aircraft with SelCal capability is allocated a four-letter code by ARINC (Aeronautical Radio Inc), an American company which acts as agent to ICAO to perform this function.

On the first contact with the controller, the SelCal will normally be checked and here is where the interest lies for anyone interested in aircraft registrations. The SelCal code remains with the aircraft as long as the 'box' does, despite changes of ownership. ARINC does not make public the registration/SelCal tie-ups but painstaking detective work by enthusiasts has tracked down most of them. SELDEC publishes an extensive list that is available from them or specialist bookshops. Unfortunately, SelCal codes do not always stay with the aircraft for life and nor is it true that one particular SelCal code is only used by one aircraft. Just about every SelCal code is shared by at least one other aircraft, although they are likely to be flying in different hemispheres.

Over the Atlantic, position reports are passed in a similar fashion to those on VHF, ie the present position and a forward estimate for the next one. The positions are given in terms of latitude and longitude, 56 North 10 West being an example, or as a reporting point or beacon when nearing a land mass. Approximately one aircraft per hour is requested by the Oceanic Control Centre to 'Send Met' and will include weather information with each position report. This consists of outside air temperature, wind speed and direction derived from INS equipment, plus any other relevant observations. A typical position report is: 'Position Swissair 100 56 N 20 W 1235 Flight Level 330 estimate 56 N 30 W 1310, next 56 N 40 W'.

The airspace between 27,500ft and 40,000ft over most of the North Atlantic is known as MNPS (Minimum Navigation Performance Specification) airspace. Aircraft flying within it are required to carry a certain scale of navigation equipment so that they can be flown accurately within the parameters of the ATC clearance. In this congested area, mostly unmonitored by radar, any deviation could be dangerous.

This is reflected in the large lateral separation between flights, vertical separation being the same as that described on page 27. Aircraft which do not meet the MNPS requirements are separated laterally by 120 nautical miles, which is reduced to 90 miles in certain designated airspace. A spacing of 60 miles is allowed for aircraft which meet the MNPS.

The same applies to supersonic aircraft operating at or above FL275. The rules for longitudinal spacing, ie one aircraft following another on the same track, are too complicated to list here but vary from 15 down to 10 minutes and sometimes less. It all depends upon speed, which is expressed as a Mach number. Satellite navigation, coupled with the replacement of HF by VHF satellite communications is likely to reduce separations considerably over the next few years.

Despite advances in navigation technology, such as GPS and LNAV, errors can and do occur. While typically not dangerous, two aircraft can violate separation requirements. With the introduction of TCAS, aircraft travelling along these tracks can monitor the relative position of other aircraft, thereby increasing the safety margin of all track users. The Strategic Lateral Offset Procedure (SLOP) is now standard. It was developed to increase the lateral separation between aircraft with very accurate navigation systems or in case of operational errors involving the ATC clearance. SLOP requires the aircraft to fly either the centreline, 1nm or 2nm right of centreline. No left offsets are permissible. Aircraft that do not have an automatic offset capability (ie one that can be programmed in the LRNS) should fly the centreline only. Pilots must return to the centreline by the Oceanic exit point.

Aircraft are not necessarily required to maintain their lateral offset but may switch between the centreline and the offsets at any time from entry point to exit point. SLOP can be used not only to mitigate against vertical separation loss. For the operator, SLOP costs nothing but is priceless in terms of safety. Contingency plans also exist within the North Atlantic Track system to account for any operational issues that occur. For example, if an aircraft can no longer maintain the speed or altitude it was assigned, it can move off the track route and fly parallel to its track, but well away from other aircraft. Also, pilots on North Atlantic Tracks are required to inform air traffic control of any deviations in altitude or speed necessitated by avoiding weather, such as thunderstorms or turbulence.

The Oceanic Controllers at Prestwick do not talk to the aircraft directly but teletype their instructions to specialised, usually ex-marine, radio operators at Ballygireen just north of Shannon Airport. The latter talk to the aircraft and teletype the responses back to Prestwick. This is not as inefficient as it sounds because HF communications can be so distorted that experienced radio operators do better than the controllers themselves and the short delay in reply is insignificant with such long distances between aircraft.

Many position reports are now made via a satellite communications datalink (CPDLC) rather than using HF. In this case, only a SelCal check has to be performed when entering the oceanic area and a second at 30° West, when transiting from Shanwick to Gander or vice versa, to ensure a working backup system in the event of a datalink failure.

NATS has recently launched a new high-technology system for controlling flights over the North Atlantic. The new system, the Shanwick Automated Air Traffic System (SAATS) has been developed in partnership with the Canadian air navigation service provider Nav Canada. It covers 630,000 square miles of the North Atlantic and is based at the Oceanic Operations Room of the present Scottish Centre. This ground-breaking system provides NATS oceanic controllers – for the first time – with a computer-generated 'picture' of aircraft positions whilst in flight across the ocean, beyond the reach of land-based radar. SAATS also provides fully electronic flight progress strips and a conflict prediction facility to help controllers plan the optimum safe track for individual flights. It also automatically forwards flight data to adjoining ATC centres for aircraft about to leave oceanic airspace.

New procedures have also been introduced for eastbound transatlantic traffic. The objectives of the North Atlantic European Routeing System (NERS) are to provide an organised air traffic interface between the NAT oceanic and EUR domestic airspace, to organise the fluctuating and reversing traffic flows in the most efficient manner possible, consistent with the needs of the aircraft operators and ATC, and to expedite flight planning. Eventually, once systems have been adapted to cope, it will reduce the complexity of route clearances and thereby minimise the confusion and error potential inherent in lengthy transmissions and readbacks. It will also minimise the time spent in the route clearance delivery function.

NERS is designed to accommodate airports in Europe where the volume of NAT traffic and route complexity dictate specific route management. It consists of a series of pre-planned routes from Oceanic Entry/Exit Points to one of 12 NERS 'system airports', including London Heathrow, Manchester, Brussels, Amsterdam and Frankfurt. The routes are prefixed by the letter 'E' with the numbering oriented geographically from north to south. Initially, the NERS will only be applicable to eastbound traffic and will be numbered using odd numbers. Following the number, an alpha code includes the validation code and forms part of the route identifier.

A good 99.9% of short wave aircraft communications use Single Side Band (SSB) signals. Without going into too many technicalities, the AM (Audio Modulation) method employed by VHF transmissions is built up of three components; a lower side band, a carrier, and an upper side band. By removing the carrier and one of the side bands, the power of the signal is compressed into a smaller band width which boosts reception at long range and reduces interference. However, an ordinary short wave receiver which may have the necessary frequency bands (2–28MHz) will pick up SSB as something which has been described as 'sounding like Donald Duck'. To make the signal intelligible, the carrier has to be reintroduced and this can only be done if a Beat Frequency Oscillator (BFO) or crystal-controlled carrier oscillator is fitted. Beware of short wave sets which receive only broadcast bands or else have no SSB capability. Advertisements are often misleading on these vital points, implying that the product will receive everything.

Unfortunately, a basic HF set with SSB costs considerably more than the equivalent simple VHF radio. However, for less than £200 the Sangean ATS909, also marketed by Roberts as the R861, will do the job admirably. It has digital tuning which is highly desirable with HF as there are so many operational frequencies and it obviously helps to identify them precisely for future reference. The built-in aerial is only useful for strong local signals like Shanwick, and for wider coverage a long wire aerial is needed. The longer (10 to 30 metres) and higher the better, orientated as near horizontal as you can and if possible at right angles to the direction of the station you most want to listen to, eg N/S for Atlantic traffic. Beware of short circuits in the rain from whatever tree or pole you have attached it to, not to mention lightning strikes! An aerial tuning unit (ATU) is a good investment. It tunes the aerial length electronically and matches it to the receiver to produce a peak signal.

If you are able to move up-market for higher performance, there are several choices, including the Icom, Kenwood, AOR and Yaesu ranges. Ideally, the enthusiast needs a scanner which can monitor VHF and UHF air band as well as HF air communications, but it is only recently that modern electronics have made this possible in a convenient package. Many scanners now feature HF SSB as well as VHF and UHF air band. Unfortunately, these so-called wide band scanners are inevitably a compromise between the demands of different sections of the frequency bands. A dedicated HF receiver will always outperform them. Of course, for this sort of equipment you are getting far more than the air bands. These radios are communications receivers in the fullest sense of the word. The AR-3000A at around £800 spans virtually the entire radio spectrum from long-wave broadcasts up to the limits of current usage.

We now move on to an outline of what can be heard on HF in Britain. Do not expect the quality of VHF air band and be warned that you may have to work very hard and try a lot of frequencies before you intercept anything. HF propagation conditions can fluctuate enormously. The AERAD Supplements (see page 144) and amateur radio magazines publish HF propagation forecast graphs which are very useful in narrowing down the possibilities.

The North Atlantic HF network is divided into 'families' of frequencies to obtain a balanced loading of communications on the oceanic track system. They are designated NAT-A to NAT-F. Each family uses a primary frequency with a secondary one for use when reception is poor. The frequencies are shared by several Oceanic Control Centres, including Shanwick (Shannon/ Prestwick) which serves aircraft between 45° North and 61° North and between 10 West and 30 West. The Iceland OCC at Reykjavik is responsible for traffic north of 61° North and Gander works aircraft to the west of 30° West.

Santa Maria in the Azores looks after traffic south of Shanwick's area and from 15° West to 40° West. New York OCC controls flights over a large proportion of the south-west of the North Atlantic, and with favourable reception conditions those from the Caribbean and South America can be heard as well. San Juan in Puerto Rico is responsible for aircraft south of New York's area, using the same frequencies.

Long Distance Operational Control Facilities (LDOCF) are operated by or on behalf of many airlines throughout the world for company messages similar to those heard on VHF air band. Some of these stations are equipped to provide direct voice communications between flight crews and their company operations using phone patch techniques. Alternatively, the ground radio operator will accept messages for relay over the normal telephone or telex circuits.

Since the previous edition of this book, the Speedbird London service on HF radio has been axed by BA. Company aircraft now use Stockholm Radio for relaying messages to and from their ops department. Stockholm Radio and ARINC in the USA provide similar facilities to many other airlines. Of course, many of the messages may not be in English! More information on company messages will be found in Chapter 14.

Military aircraft use HF frequencies within broadly the same range as do civil aircraft. Military radio traffic is, however, a lot more varied and much less predictable than civil. It is also difficult to find out enough background information to understand some of the things to be heard, which is perhaps just as well! Further information can be found in Chapter 17.

A fairly simple way of expanding the capabilities of an HF receiver is to use it to monitor Radio Teletype, known as 'Ritty' from its initials RTTY. A personal computer is required or alternatively a RTTY module. The radio's speaker extension is connected by lead into the PC or module and the read-out is displayed on screen and printed out if desired. The Aeradio stations around the world churn out masses of information, much of it weather reports and forecasts, but the interesting items for enthusiasts are the flight plans which are also sent by this method.

RTTY is a very specialised branch of air band 'listening' and these notes are included merely to alert readers to the possibilities. There are several frequency and reference guides available, a good source being *Radio User Magazine*'s Book Service. Suppliers of RTTY reception equipment advertise regularly in this magazine and a regular column 'Decode' covers the subject in detail. Aeronautical information is of course only a small fraction of the data sent worldwide in RTTY mode.

The Airbus A380 is now firmly established on long range routes.

A selection of HF frequencies

Do not expect to hear the distant ones routinely. Civil Air Route Regions (ICAO), frequencies and major ground stations are listed below. Virtually all frequencies listed are USB.

AFI=African; CAR=Caribbean; CEP=Central East Pacific; CWP=Central West Pacific; EUR=European; MID=Middle East; NP=North Pacific; SAM=South America; SAT= South Atlantic; SEA=South East Asia; SP=South Pacific.

NAT-A (southern tracks)	3.016 5.598 8.906 13.306 17.946	New York, Gander, Shanwick, Santa Maria
NAT-B (N/S Am-regd a/c)	2.899 5.616 8.864 13.291 17.946	Gander, Shanwick, New York
NAT-C (Eur/ Asia-regd a/c)	2.872 5.649 8.879 11.336 13.306 17.946	Gander, Shanwick, New York
NAT-D (polar routes)	2.971 4.675 8.891 11.279 13.291 17.946	Gander, Shanwick, Iceland
NAT-E (south)	2.962 6.628 8.825 11.309 13.354 17.946	
NAT-F (Mid-Atlantic)	3.476 6.622 8.831 13.291	New York, Santa Maria tracks
CAR-A	2.287 5.550 6.577 8.846 8.918 11.396 13.297 17.907	New York, Paramaribo, San Juan, Panama
MID-1	2.992 5.667 8.918 13.312	Ankara, Baghdad, Beirut, Damascus, Kuwait, Bahrain, Cairo, Jeddah
MID-2	3.467 5.601 5.658 10.018 13.288	Bahrain, Karachi, Bombay, Lahore, Delhi, Calcutta
SEA-1	3.470 6.556 10.066 13.318 17.907	Calcutta, Dhaka, Madras, Colombo, Male, Cocos, Kuala Lumpur
SEA-2	3.485 5.655 8.942 11.396 13.309	Hong Kong, Manila, Kuala Lumpur
SEA-3	3.470 6.556 11.396 13.318 13.297	Manila, Singapore, Jakarta, Darwin, Sydney, Perth
AFI-1	3.452 6.535 8.861 13.357 17.955	Casablanca, Canaries, Dakar, Abidjan, Roberts
AFI-2	3.419 5.652 8.894 13.273 13.294 17.961	Algiers, Tripoli, Niamey, Kano
AFI-3	3.467 5.658 11.018 11.300 13.288 17.961	Lagos, Brazzaville, Luanda, Windhoek, Johannesberg, Lusaka
CEP-1/2	2.869 3.413 5.547 5.574 8.843 11.282 13.261	Honolulu, San Francisco
CWP-1/2	2.998 4.666 6.532 6.562 8.903 11.384 13.300 17.904 21.985	Hong Kong, Manila, Guam, Tokyo, Honolulu, Port Moresby
SP-6/7	3.467 5.643 8.867 13.273 13.300 17.904	Sydney, Auckland, Nandi, Tahiti, Honolulu, Pascua

Base Stations

Stockholm 3.494 5.541 8.930 11.345 13.342 17.916 23.210; ARINC (New York) 3.494 6.640 8.933 10.075 11.342 13.330 17.925 21.964

Volmet

RAF 4.742 6.733 9.031 11.205; Shannon 3.413 5.505 8.957 13.264; Gander/New York 3.485 6.604 10.051 13.270; St John's 6.754 15.034

Rescue
5.680 (primary) 3.023 3.085 5.695 8.364 (international distress)

UK Defence Global HF System (TASCOMM)
3.146 4.742 6.733 9.031 11.205 13.257

UK Air Defence Radar Air Surveillance and Control System
Boulmer ('Hotspur')/Scampton ('Black Dog') 3.915 4.706 4.709 4.739 5.178 6.748

US HF-GCS (call-sign 'Croughton'/'Ascension'/'Incirlik'/'Lajes' etc)
4.724 4.742 5.703 6.712 6.739 8.992 11.175 11.244 13.200 15.016 17.975

Canadian Forces
St John's Military/Halifax Military: 4.739 5.684 5.714 5.850 6.694 6.751

NASA
3.860 14.295 21.395 (Re-broadcast space shuttle commentary but rarely heard in UK)

The decimal point is normally omitted when frequencies are referred to during communications.

Chapter 10

Flight information services

AN ATC SERVICE can be provided only by licensed controllers, but at certain small airfields an Aerodrome Flight Information Service is in operation. The AFIS Officers or AFISOs for short, are also required to be licensed, and many of them are flying instructors doing this ground job on a part-time basis. Air band listeners will notice considerable differences in the R/T phraseology used by AFISOs, reflecting the fact that their instructions are of an advisory nature only. The service provided by an AFISO is to give information useful for the safe and efficient conduct of flights in the Aerodrome Traffic Zone. From the information received pilots will be able to decide the appropriate course of action to be taken to ensure the safety of flight. Generally, the AFISO is not permitted to issue instructions or advice to pilots of his own volition.

However, AFISOs are permitted to pass instructions to vehicles and personnel operating on the manoeuvring area and information and instructions to aircraft moving on the apron and specific parts of the manoeuvring area. Elsewhere on the manoeuvring area, and at all times in the air, information only is passed to pilots. Further details on the passing of instructions by AFISOs at aerodromes are contained in CAP 410 Manual of Flight Information Services, available for download online from the CAA website.

An air–ground service is provided from Caernarfon Airport's tower.

AFISOs are also permitted to pass messages on behalf of other agencies and instructions from the aerodrome operator. If they do so, they will include the name of the agency so that pilots will be aware that the message comes from a legitimate source, eg 'London Control clears you to join...'. AFISOs must ensure that the information given to pilots is distinct and unambiguous, as pilots will use this information for the safe and efficient conduct of their flights. An AFISO may request pilots to make position reports, eg downwind, final etc. These requests do not have the status of instructions, although it is expected that most pilots will comply.

Phraseology examples
AFISO: 'G-CD, Traffic is a Cessna 172 base leg, take off at your discretion, surface wind 270 15.'

or: 'G-CD, Via C2 take-off at your discretion, surface wind 270 15.'

Aircraft: 'G-CD, Taking off.'

AFISO: 'G-CD, Land at your discretion, surface wind 050 10 knots.'

The Aerodrome Air/Ground service is a rudimentary one, but persons providing it must possess a CAA 'Certificate of Competence', gained after passing an examination and an RT practical test. It is often encountered at club and private aerodromes, Bourn in Cambridgeshire and Full Sutton in Yorkshire being examples. Basic information is passed to pilots, including wind direction and confirmation that the runway is clear. The call-signs for AFIS and A/G are 'Information' and 'Radio' respectively.

It should be noted that the phraseology used by Air/Ground Communication Service (AGCS) operators is different from that used by controllers and AFISOs. An AGCS radio station operator is not necessarily able to view any part of the aerodrome or surrounding airspace. Traffic information provided by an AGCS radio station operator is therefore based primarily on reports made by other pilots. Information provided by an AGCS radio station operator may be used to assist a pilot in making decisions, however the safe conduct of the flight remains the pilot's responsibility.

Radio operators must ensure that the full call-sign, including the suffix 'Radio', is used in response to the initial call from an aircraft and on any other occasion that there is doubt. Personnel providing an Air/Ground Communication Service must ensure that they do not pass a message which could be construed to be either an air traffic control instruction or an instruction issued by AFISOs for specific situations. Air ground operators must not use the expression 'at your discretion' as this is associated with the service provided by AFISOs and is likely to cause confusion to pilots.

'G-CD downwind.'

'G-CD roger no reported traffic.'

'G-CD final.'

'G-CD roger surface wind 220 15. Traffic is a Cessna 172 reported lining up to depart.'

'G-CD ready for departure.'

'G-CD roger. No reported traffic, surface wind 230 degrees 10 knots.'

'Roger, taking off G-CD.'

or,

'G-CD traffic is a Cherokee reported final, surface wind 230 degrees 10.'

'Roger, taking off G-CD.'

or,

'Roger holding position G-CD.'

Once the Cherokee has landed and vacated:

'G-CD lining-up and taking off.'

'G-CD roger surface wind 230 degrees 10 knots.'

A common frequency (135.475MHz) known as SAFETYCOM is made available at airfields where no other frequency is allocated, to enable pilots to broadcast their intentions to other aircraft that may be operating on, or in the vicinity of, the aerodrome. At some UK airfields, aircraft movements may take place outside the published hours of watch of the ATC unit. In the interests of safety, pilots should broadcast their intentions to other aircraft that may be operating on or around the airfield. All transmissions in these circumstances are addressed to '(Aerodrome name) Traffic.' Since this is a common frequency, use of the airfield location is essential to avoid confusion.

Aeronautical radio stations located offshore on oil rigs, platforms and vessels provide an offshore communication Service (OCS) to helicopters operating in the vicinity. The radio operator must be able to volunteer information that may affect the safety of helicopter operations, for example: 'Caution flare venting,' or: 'I am shipping light/heavy spray on deck.'

RIGHT: Wind direction and speed is shown on the tower controller's anemometer display. The average for the last two minutes near the Runway 27 threshold is selected. The maximum and minimum winds are also shown at the top.

BELOW: Tower controller's weather display.

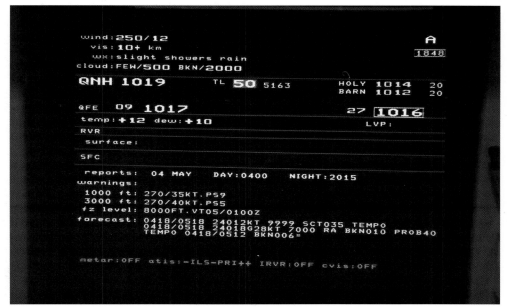

The Flight Information service provided by licensed controllers at Area Control Centres on a 24-hour basis is completely different and requires further explanation. The London FIR outside controlled airspace is divided into three, with a separate radio frequency for each, as is the Scottish FIR. The FIR controller is able to offer the following services: weather information, changes of serviceability of radio navigation aids, aerodrome conditions, proximity to other aircraft warnings and much other information pertinent to flight safety. Because of the multiplicity of possible reporting points in the FIR, ranging from disused airfields to towns and coastal features, it is difficult to assess the possibility of collision and therefore no positive control or separation can be provided. The other problem is that of civil and military aircraft flying random tracks and for whom there is no requirement to contact the FIR controller.

The Radar Advisory and Radar Information Services described in previous editions of this book have just been superseded by new procedures. A review of Air Traffic Services Outside Controlled Airspace (ATSOCA) was initiated as a direct response to Air Accidents Investigation Branch and AIRPROX reports, which raised concerns about the lack of standardisation of service delivery and the confusion that this caused. Outside controlled airspace, ie within Class F and G Airspace, it is not mandatory for a pilot to be in receipt of an air traffic service. This principle generates an unknown traffic environment, where pilots are ultimately responsible for collision avoidance and terrain/obstacle clearance.

There are now four distinct services: Basic Service, Traffic Service, Deconfliction Service, and Procedural Service. Controllers should make all reasonable endeavours to provide the service that a pilot requests, although this obviously depends on existing workload. Acknowledgement by a controller and pilot of the service being provided establishes an 'accord' whereby both parties will follow the terms of the service. If a pilot subsequently requires a different service, a new accord must be negotiated.

The Basic Service is intended to offer the pilot maximum autonomy and the avoidance of other traffic is solely his responsibility. A Traffic Service provides the pilot with radar-derived traffic information on conflicting aircraft. No deconfliction advice is passed and the pilot is responsible for collision avoidance. A Deconfliction Service provides the pilot with traffic information and deconfliction advice on conflicting traffic. However, the avoidance of other aircraft is ultimately the pilot's responsibility. A Procedural Service is a non-radar service in which instructions are provided which, if complied with, will achieve separation from other aircraft in receipt of a Procedural Service from the same controller. The avoidance of other aircraft is the pilot's responsibility. The above is merely a summary of a very lengthy document with all sorts of other conditions attaching to the different services. Whether it will make things any safer in the free-for-all outside controlled airspace remains to be seen.

Military ATC radar units provide a Lower Airspace Radar Advisory Service (LARS) to any aircraft outside controlled airspace that requests it. The lower limit is 3,000ft and the upper limit is, with certain exceptions, FL95, the service being given within about 30 miles of each participating unit. From FL95 up to FL245 a similar Middle Airspace Advisory Service is provided. Whenever possible aircraft will be handed over from one controller to the next and pilots told to contact the adjacent unit.

FIR frequencies

London Information: 124.75 (Wales and England west of a line roughly Manchester to Worthing) 124.6 (East of England from Manchester southwards) 125.475 (Northern England to Scottish Border)

Scottish Information: 121.325 127.275 129.225 134.775 133.675

Note that you may be able to hear aircraft at great distances as their messages on FIR may be cross-coupled and re-transmitted. This is so that other pilots will be aware of them and thus not interrupt.

Chapter 11

Weather and Air Traffic Control

MET OBSERVATIONS AT the larger airports are made every 30 minutes, at 20 minutes past and 10 minutes to each hour. At the less busy airports they are made once in each hour. Special observations, known as SPECIs (pronounced 'Spessys') must be made within these times if certain changes are observed, eg at the onset or cessation of hail or thunderstorms. If there is a Met Office available, the observations will be done by met staff who are all employees of the Ministry of Defence. Otherwise they are made by ATC personnel who are required to hold a Met Observer Certificate, gained after a short course at the Met College in Exeter.

There is a standard format which is passed to aircraft, consisting of the wind direction in degrees True and its average speed in knots with a note of any significant gusts. This is, however, normally read by the controller in degrees Magnetic direct from the instruments in front of him so that it can be related by the pilot to the magnetic heading of the runway. The visibility is passed in metres and kilometres in increments of 100m when 5,000m or less and in whole kilometres when greater than 5,000m. The distance is determined from the known ranges of conspicuous landmarks visible in the locality. The next item is the weather, eg drizzle, fog, rain and so on.

Cloud base is measured by means of a cloud base recorder which scans the sky overhead with a laser beam. Unfortunately, it may give inaccurate low readings when haze, mist or smoke is present. At less well-equipped airfields, cloud base is found by estimation, with experience a surprisingly accurate method. Pilot reports can be requested to confirm the base. At night estimation is difficult so a vertical searchlight is often used. The angle of the 'spot' on the cloud can then be found by sighting with a simple instrument known as an alidade. Trigonometry from a pre-calculated table enables it to be converted quickly to cloud height.

A third method, a small hydrogen or helium-filled balloon of about 2ft diameter, can be used to measure a lowish base in daylight. The balloon rises at a known rate and can thus be timed with a stopwatch until it disappears into the cloud. It is, however, time-consuming and necessitates heavy, and in the case of hydrogen, highly inflammable, gas cylinders being stored adjacent to the tower, so it is doubtful if any UK airfields still use it today.

Cloud amount is measured in oktas, ie eighths, and height in feet up to and including 5,000ft. Cloud above this level in the UK is of academic interest only to aircrew so is not reported. Not more than three layers are reported, the exception being when cumulo-nimbus cloud, known as Cb or Charlie Bravo, is present. If necessary this can be reported as a fourth group. Cloud amounts are now referred to simply as scattered (1–4 oktas), broken (5–7 oktas) or overcast (8 oktas).

Air temperature is passed in degrees Celsius, together with the dew point if the two figures are significantly close, indicating that fog may be about to form. The QNH and QFE (Threshold QFE at certain airfields) is given in millibars. These units may one day become hectopascals in the United Kingdom and are already referred to as such in most European ATC systems. American aircraft occasionally ask for the pressure settings in inches of mercury so a table is kept handy in the tower for a quick conversion.

MINIMUM WEATHER CONDITIONS

SURFACE VISIBILITY		COLOUR	BASE OF LOWEST CLOUD LAYER
RN/RAF Km (nm)	USAFE★ Km (Stm)		RN/RAF - of ⅜ or more USAFE★ - of ⅝ or more
8(4·3)	8(5)	Blue	2500ft AGL
5(2·7)	5(3)	White	1500ft AGL
3·7(2)	3·7(2·3)	Green	700ft AGL
1·8(1)	1·6(1)	Yellow	300ft AGL
0·9(0·5)	0·8(0·5)	Amber	200ft AGL
Less than 0·9(0·5)	0·8(0·5)	Red	Below 200ft AGL
Black A/D not usable for reasons other than cloud or visibility minima. Black will precede actual colour code.			

RAF colour codes for aerodrome availability/weather state.

Where the weather conditions meet particular criteria – visibility of 10km or more, no precipitation, no thunderstorm or shallow fog, no cloud below a level of 5,000ft above aerodrome elevation and no Cb at any level – the visibility and cloud groups are omitted and the word 'CAVOK' (pronounced 'Cav OK') is passed.

At most UK airports the current met observation is transmitted continuously on the appropriate Terminal VOR or Information frequency by means of a pre-recorded tape. The information is typed in and software converts it into a synthesised voice message. A transcript of a typical broadcast for London/Heathrow is as follows:

'This is Heathrow Arrival Information Juliet 0855 hours weather. Landing Runway 27 Left 250 degrees 12 knots. Slight rain, scattered at 800ft, overcast at 2500ft. Temperature plus 10 Dew Point plus 6, QNH 1002 millibars. Report aircraft type and acknowledge information Juliet on first contact with Heathrow.'

The significance of Juliet is that each observation is given a code letter, beginning with Alpha and working through the alphabet, starting once more when Zulu is reached. The controller is thus sure that the pilot has copied the latest observation. These automatic transmissions are very useful in reducing R/T loading as crews can monitor them at their leisure and the controller does not have to pass repeated weather information. Datalink-ATIS (D-ATIS) is even better because it enables a crew to download a copy of the current weather. D-ATIS is available at the major London airports and Manchester. An example of a flightdeck printout at Manchester is:

EGCC ARR ATIS Z 0850Z
LANDING RWY 24R
28010KT 20KM FEW 020 09/07 Q1017
QFE 1008

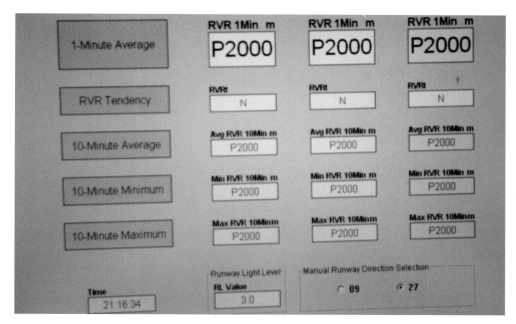

IRVR (Instrumented Runway Visual Range) showing RVR in excess of 2000m. The values (from left) are Stop End, Mid-point and Touchdown Zone.

RWY SFC WET WET WET
LINK G IS CLOSED
ACKNOWLEDGE RECEIPT OF INFORMATION Z
AND ADVISE AIRCRAFT TYPE ON FIRST CONTACT

Runway Visual Range, or RVR as it is normally referred to, makes available a more localised assessment of how far the pilot is likely to be able to see along the runway. Measurement only begins when the official met report gives a general visibility of 1,500m or less and it is essential to enable the pilot to decide whether or not it is within the limits of what are known as 'company minima' for landing or take-off. RVR is measured in 25m steps from zero up to 400m, then 50m from 400m to 800m and 100m from 800m to 1500m.

RVR is calculated by either the human observer method or by means of electronic equipment. The former requires a person, usually an airport fireman, to stand on a vehicle adjacent to the runway threshold at a specified height to simulate pilot eye-level. He then counts the number of lights or, at some locations, marker boards, that he can see down one side of the runway. The total is passed by radio to the tower and the RVR read off a pre-computed table.

The Instrument RVR system, called IRVR, measures the opacity of the atmosphere and gives a constant read-out in the tower of the RVR at three fixed points along the runway, referred to as touchdown, mid-point and stop end. If the runway lights are switched to the opposite end, the IRVR will switch automatically.

The term 'Sigmet' (Significant Meteorological Conditions) is sometimes heard on R/T, this being a warning of such hazardous phenomena as thunderstorms, severe turbulence and severe airframe icing. Another jargon word is 'Nosig', short for No Significant Change, and sometimes appended to aerodrome forecasts when passed on the radio. The term 'trend' is employed to indicate the way the weather is likely to go, codes like 'tempo' for a temporary change being added as appropriate.

Wind shear can be a very serious hazard to aircraft and pilots can often be heard reporting its presence to the tower so that following aircraft can be warned. Briefly, wind shear is a change of windspeed and/or direction between two points in the atmosphere. By such a definition it is almost always present and normally does not cause undue difficulty to the pilot. However, on take-off and especially landing what amounts to an instantaneous change in headwind can be dangerous. A sudden decrease in headwind on the approach will tend to increase the rate of descent and an instantaneous increase in headwind will tend to decrease it. In both cases the pilot is faced with a rapid change in airspeed, coupled with a departure from the glide path and either a 'hot and long' landing or an undershoot become likely. A flight deck automatic voice warning 'Wind shear, wind shear' will almost certainly result in a go around.

Horizontal wind shears are generally outflows from the bases of Cb clouds or are caused by the passage of active weather fronts. Local topographical features, both natural and artificial, can also cause shear. Buildings and other large structures close to runways can spark off turbulence and rotor effects, with marked differences in wind direction. Since wind shear is obviously invisible, much experimental work is being carried out with Doppler radar, acoustic Dopplers and optical lasers to try to detect and measure it. Heathrow is unique in the United Kingdom in having a wind shear alerting service. Certain weather criteria are used to assess its possible presence and this is backed up by pilot reports. The alert message is inserted in the arrival and departure ATIS broadcasts.

Another major hazard to aircraft is fortunately easier to measure. This is braking action when the runway is icy. It is determined by a sophisticated device known as a Grip Tester. Its forerunner, the mumeter, is still in operation but is not as accurate. The equipment consists of a runway friction measuring trailer towed by a vehicle travelling at 40mph. It provides an automatic print-out of the mean coefficient of friction at three equidistant points along the runway. When manual mode is selected, further readings can be obtained as required. The lower the figure the worse the braking action, eg something like 0.25 would indicate a very icy surface, 0.85 would be a dry runway.

The only problem with these devices is that their measurements are unreliable in slushy conditions. Slush was defined many years ago as 'a water-saturated snow which, with a heel and toe slap down action with the foot against the ground, will be displaced with a splatter'. This has caused amusement for several generations of student controllers but the description is very accurate!

The word 'Snowtam' refers to an ingenious system of describing and tabulating runway conditions under snow, slush or ice and the degree to which they are cleared or about to be cleared. Braking action as determined above is also included. A series of letters and figures, each referring to a specific detail, can easily be decoded on receipt. The word 'SNOCLO' used on R/T and in Snowtams means that the airfield is closed because of runway contamination. In the meantime attempts will be made to clear the snow.

Each airport has a Snow Plan detailing the priorities for snow clearance, the runways obviously taking first place, followed by taxiways and apron. As a general guide, the object is to clear the snow to a 'black top' surface. This can be achieved on most occasions by using snow sweepers, as long as clearing is commenced as soon as snow or slush begins to lie. Aircraft operations may continue but may be delayed while the sweeper finishes a run. Backup, if required, is provided by snow ploughs and snow blowers. For best effect, sweepers work in echelon, sweeping one full length of the runway, working outwards from the centreline. If conditions continue to deteriorate beyond those acceptable for aircraft operations, the runway will be closed to afford maximum priority to snow clearance.

In normal conditions, runway state messages on ATIS will divide the runway into three sequential sections, hence 'Runway damp/damp/damp' or 'Runway wet/wet/wet' or 'Runway wet/damp/wet'. Reports that the runway is dry are not normally passed to pilots. Hence, if no runway surface report is passed, the runway can be assumed to be dry. The reports are originated by the aerodrome authority based on regular runway inspections. Definitions are:

Damp: The surface shows a change of colour due to moisture. If there is sufficient moisture to produce a surface film or the surface appears reflective, the runway will be reported as wet.
Wet: The surface is soaked but no significant patches of standing water are visible. Standing water is considered to exist when water on the runway surface is deeper than 3mm. Patches of standing water covering more than 25% of the assessed area will be reported as water patches.
Water patches: Significant patches of standing water are visible. Water patches will be reported when more than 25% of the assessed area is covered by water more than 3mm deep.
Flooded: Extensive patches of standing water are visible. Flooded will be reported when more than 50% of the assessed area is covered by water more than 3mm deep.

Finally, in many parts of the country it is possible to pick up the broadcasts of the London and Scottish Volmet Services, the 'Vol' part of the title being derived from the French word for flight. Weather conditions in a standardised form are transmitted continuously for the main UK and selected European airports. Pilots can thus monitor Volmet whilst en route and note the current conditions at their destination and suitable alternatives without having to make specific calls for the information. If their destination is a smaller airfield not on the Volmet they can either call it direct or request the information via London or Scottish Flight Information who will obtain it by telephone.

There are four separate broadcasts on different VHF frequencies:

London Volmet North, 126.6MHz
London Volmet South: 128.6MHz
London Volmet Main: 135.375MHz
Scottish Volmet: 125.725MHz

The rather mechanical speech is due to the fact that the message is made up from a store of individual words and short phrases on tape, which are selected by a computer and then joined to form the required sentences. (ATIS is usually broadcast in this form as well.)

The presentation of the information is as described above but where significant changes are expected, one of the following will be heard:

Gradu   The change is expected at a constant rate
Rapid   The change is expected in a short period of less than 30 minutes
Tempo The change is expected to last for less than one hour
Inter   Frequent changes are expected, fluctuating almost constantly
Trend   A change is anticipated but it is expected to occur slowly throughout the period

As with ATIS described above, pilots can download Volmet via datalink.

ATIS via telephone, examples:
   Birmingham: 0121 780 0910
   Bristol: 01275 473 666
   Carlisle: 01228 574123
   Edinburgh: 0131 333 6216
   Glasgow: 0141 887 7449
   Manchester: 0161 499 2324
   Stansted: 01279 669 325
   Wick: 01955 607596

Much more information can be found on the Met Office website GETMET, including how to decode aviation weather reports and forecasts.

Chapter 12

Airfield visual aids

AIRFIELD LIGHTING RANGES from the basic edge lights found at many smaller locations to the complex and impressive systems to be seen at major airports. The paraffin flares from an earlier era, known as 'goosenecks', were retained at a few small airfields as emergency lighting, but have almost certainly been replaced by now with portable battery lamps which are easier to handle but no more effective.

On certain instrument runways the caution zone, ie the last 600m, may have yellow rather than white lights. In addition, the centreline is usually delineated by flush-fitting lights for the whole length. These are colour-coded to give an indication of the distance remaining in poor visibility. The lights are coloured red over the final 300m and alternately red and white between 900m and 300m from the runway end.

As well as centreline lighting, all runways which comply with Precision Approach Category 2 and 3 lighting standard are provided with Touchdown Zone lights (TDZs). These consist of many flush-fitting white lights set into each side of the centreline in the first 900m of the runway. A row of green threshold lights marks the beginning of the paved surface and a similar line of red ones marks the stop end. Approach lighting is usually non-existent at small aerodromes and at others varies in standard, depending upon the approach aids and type of traffic handled.

The approach lights at major airports begin at an average distance of 300m out from the threshold and extend for a further 900m out on the approach. They consist of a centreline and up to five cross-bars in white lights. Where Category 2 and 3 lighting standard is required, red supplementary approach lighting is provided within the basic system for the inner 300m as an extra aid for landing in marginal weather conditions. All lighting is controlled in intensity from the tower, the criteria being laid down clearly for differing met conditions.

The lights are displayed all the time at busy airports but the normal requirement for them to be on in daylight hours is whenever the visibility is less than six kilometres and/or the cloud base less than 700ft. At night when traffic is light at some places, the lights are turned on 15 minutes before an ETA and left on until 15 minutes after an aircraft has departed.

Taxiway lights are standardised as green for the centreline and blue for the edges. The latter are used only to delineate apron edges and as an extra guide for bends in taxiways. The lights are 15m apart which is reduced to 7m for Category 3 systems. Red stop bars mark holding points, mainly those at runway entrances. There may also be traffic lights for airfield vehicles. Both can be operated from the tower and the stop bars normally have a short time delay so that they revert to red after an aircraft has passed. London Heathrow has a particularly elaborate system of lighting for the control of taxiways. Taxiways at all airports are now designated by a letter of the alphabet, excluding Oscar, India and X-Ray. Where there are more taxiways than letters of the alphabet, double letters are used to designate some of them. Double letters may also be used to identify short taxiway stubs between a runway and an adjacent taxiway.

Fast turn-offs, now known as rapid exit taxiways, only have their centreline lights lit from the runway direction. The lights in the opposite direction are blanked off to prevent inadvertent infringement of an active runway. This was yet another result of the enquiry into the Tenerife collision.

Runway guard lights, consisting of a pair of alternately flashing lights and known colloquially as 'wig-wags', may be located on both sides of holding positions. The purpose of these yellow lights is to improve the conspicuousness of holding points and to warn pilots of the proximity of an active runway.

Once a pilot on approach is within sight of the runway, visual guidance is provided by the Precision Approach Path Indicator (PAPI). Four PAPI lights are placed in line to the left of the runway threshold. They are arranged so that when the pilot is on the correct approach path two appear white and the other two are red. When a third light shows red, the pilot knows he is getting slightly low, when all four are red he is significantly below the glide path. Conversely, four white indicators tell him he is too high.

A number of smaller airfields have an installation called LITAS (Low Intensity Two Colour Slope System). It is basically similar to the obsolete VASI system described in previous editions of this book but has lights of lower intensity placed generally on the left-hand side of the runway only. Although designed for use at night, the system has been found to give assistance by day in anything other than bright sunlight.

The other major visual aids on airports are the painted markings on the manoeuvring area. All runways in regular use will have centreline and threshold markings, the latter varying from the designator number alone to separate 'piano keys' and designator, depending upon the importance of the runway and its associated instrument aids. Whilst threshold markings are usually at the end of the runway, they sometimes need to be displaced upwind if, for example, there are obstacles like a public road on the approach. Arrows then indicate that the first portion of the runway is sterile for landing.

PAPI and how it is interpreted by the pilot (used with the permission of and copyright of UK CAA).

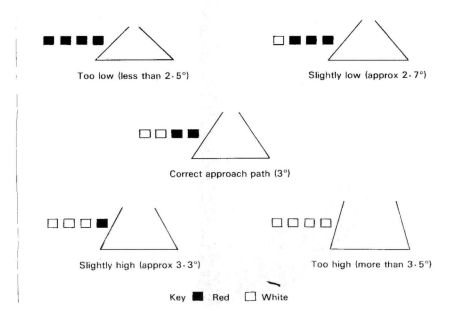

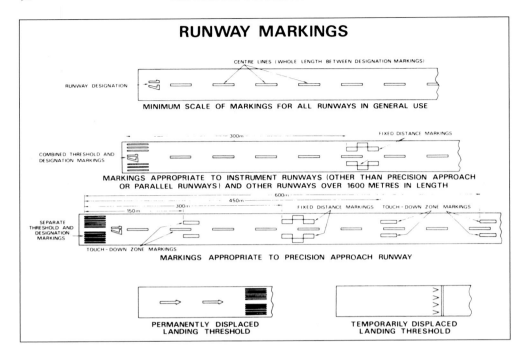

Standard runway markings (used with the permission of and copyright of UK CAA).

All runways more than 1,600m long without PAPI, and all precision instrument runways, will have an additional symbol 300m from the landing threshold known as the 'fixed distance marker'. The apparent distance between this and the threshold marking, seen from the approach, should aid pilots in judging their angle of descent and the two markings also bracket the optimum Touchdown Zone on the runway.

Touchdown Zone markings, extending for a distance of at least 600m from the threshold, will be provided on precision approach runways equipped with such aids as ILS. These are intended to give added texture by day and, except in fog, added texture by night in the light of landing lamps. Yellow lines delineate the centres of taxiways and at certain airports self-manoeuvring stand markings enable aircraft to be taxied to the correct parking position without the aid of a marshaller. There are several systems, including AGNIS (Azimuth Guidance for Nose-in Stand) and Safegate, all coming under the collective title of Visual Docking Guidance Systems. They use ingenious systems of coloured lights and words on a dot matrix display to align the aircraft and enable it to stop in the correct position.

At airfields which accept non-radio equipped aircraft, ground signals will be displayed for guidance. They are normally to be found in front of the control tower, but not always, which gives rise to a funny story. One day a pilot who had suffered a radio failure landed at Blackpool. On reporting to the tower, he complained that he could not make any sense from the ground signals. Further conversation revealed that he had been trying to interpret the strange shapes on the Crazy Golf Course adjacent to the airport's public viewing area!

Obviously not all the following ground signals can be seen at any one airfield but they cover all those to be seen at UK civil locations. This list does not include signs peculiar to military airfields:

Lined up on Runway 27 at Liverpool: TDZs, centrelines and edgelights, with PAPI to left.

Airfield lighting mimic panel showing the settings selected.

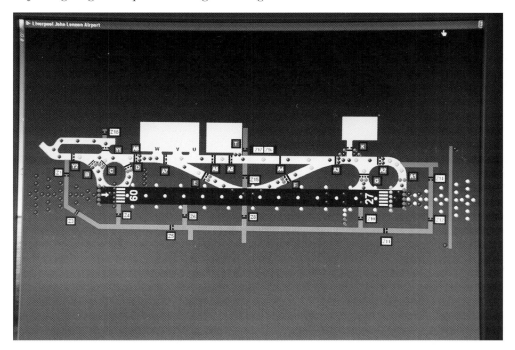

(a) Direction for landing or take-off: A large white 'T' signifies that aircraft will land or take off in a direction parallel to the 'T' and towards the cross-arm. A white disc above the cross-arm of the 'T' indicates that the direction of landing and take-off do not necessarily coincide.

(b) A white 'dumb-bell' means that aircraft movement on the airfield is confined to paved surfaces only. A black strip across each disc of the dumb-bell at right angles to the shaft signifies that aircraft taking off and landing shall do so on a runway but that ground movement is not confined to paved surfaces. A red letter 'L' superimposed on the dumb-bell signifies that light aircraft are permitted to take off and land either on a runway or on the area designated by a further 'L' (painted white) elsewhere on the aerodrome.

(c) A red and yellow striped arrow indicates that a right hand circuit is in force. This can also be shown by a rectangular green flag flown from a mast.

(d) A red square with one yellow diagonal bar warns that the state of the manoeuvring area is poor and pilots must exercise special care.

(e) A red square with a yellow cross superimposed along the diagonals declares that the airfield is unsafe for the movement of aircraft and that landing is prohibited. (Usually found at grass airfields that are water-logged in the winter months!)

(f) A white letter 'H' marks the helicopter landing area.

(g) A double white cross signifies that glider flying is in progress. (A yellow cross indicates the tow-rope dropping area on the airfield.)

(h) 'Aerodrome Control in operation' is shown by a red and yellow checkered flag or board. (Aircraft may only move on the manoeuvring area with ATC permission.) A black letter 'C' on a yellow board indicates the position at which a pilot can report to the ATC unit or to the person in charge of the aerodrome.

(i) On grass aerodromes areas of 'bad ground' are marked by triangular orange and white markers (colloquially known as 'Toblerones'), alternating with orange and white flags. Similar coloured markers outline the aerodrome boundary.

Airfield lighting panel at Manchester.

Chapter 13

Airport operations and procedures

Wake turbulence

THIS WAS KNOWN previously in the UK as vortex wake but has been changed recently to conform with ICAO terminology. Behind each wingtip of an aircraft in flight and, in the case of a helicopter, the tip of each rotor blade, a trailing cylinder of rapidly rotating air is created, known as a vortex. The heavier the aircraft, the more intense the effect, which is quite capable of throwing a following aircraft out of control if it gets too close. These hazardous wake vortices begin to be generated when the nose wheel lifts off the runway on take-off and continue until it touches down on landing. To minimise the danger, controllers apply a system of spacing which is outlined below.

In the United Kingdom, aircraft types are divided into five categories for approach and four categories for departure, according to their maximum total weight at take-off:

Heavy	162,000kg or greater
Medium	40,000kg to 162,000kg
Upper Medium	104,000 to 162,000kg
Lower Medium	40,000kg to 104,000kg
Small	17,000kg to 40,000kg
Light	17,000kg or less

There are, however, a few exceptions to this. Helicopters generate more intense vortices from their rotors than fixed-wing aircraft of the same weight, therefore AS-332 Super Pumas and larger types are included in the Small category. Several aircraft types have been grouped into wake turbulence categories which do not conform to those listed above. For example, the Boeing 707, DC-8, VC-10 and IL-62 series have been classified as Medium, (Upper Medium on approach), as experience has shown that the characteristics of these types conform more to that group.

The Medium category embraces aircraft in the Airbus A320/Boeing 737 class, together with propeller aircraft such as the Hercules and Electra. The Small category includes the Fokker 50 and Dash-8, and Light anything from executive jets downwards. The Airbus A380, whilst falling within the Heavy category, has some additional spacing applied as shown below.

A change in wake turbulence criteria would also give benefits. It is known that prescribed separations between some aircraft types are over-cautious and that vortices decay rapidly in certain wind conditions. A method of increasing peak period departure capacity is on trial at Heathrow – the reduction by half of take-off separation minima for certain types of aircraft. This means that a narrow body, a Boeing 737 for example, following a 767, is allowed to depart one minute behind rather than the current two. The decision to take off with reduced separation depends upon pilots' and controllers' discretion, usually when a crosswind is likely to disperse vortices quickly. It can be requested by any appropriate aircraft type but only

British Midland and BA crews are being asked to report any adverse affects for further analysis.

The fact that a cross wind will blow the vortices out of the way very quickly could enable a theoretical reduction in spacing, but there is no way of proving this at present. The answer is laser radar – or Lidar – developed by the Defence Evaluation Research Agency at Malvern. The laser can 'see' the vortex trails behind the aircraft and show the direction in which they are moving. The result is a predicted increase in runway capacity of up to 15% but it remains to be seen how soon the equipment becomes operational and also if pilots and controllers accept it.

The heavier the aircraft, the greater the turbulence it generates. In layman's terms, the cause of wake turbulence is really quite simple: the higher pressure under the wing results in the air spilling over the wingtip. This forms a spiral flow, or vortex, rotating back in towards the fuselage. In order for this to happen, lift needs to be generated to create the pressure difference. Thus, during the take-off roll, turbulence gradually increases and becomes significant once the nose wheel lifts from the ground. In flight, the slower the speed, or higher the angle of attack, ie the angle at which the wing enters the airflow, the more severe the vortex.

The behaviour of the vortices after they have left the wingtips depends on several factors. They are separated by approximately three-quarters of the aircraft's wingspan and will gradually descend below its flightpath, typically for a height of 900ft. However, when the aircraft is close to the ground, the vortices will descend, then move outwards from the aircraft's track at a speed of around 5kt. In completely calm conditions, this should leave a funnel through which, at a reasonable distance, it is safe to fly. Unfortunately, it is rarely completely calm and therefore, if there is a crosswind of just a few knots, it will quickly move the downwind vortex away from the runway but will hold the upwind vortex on, or near to, the runway.

Arriving flights

Where flights are operating visually (IFR flights operating under the reduced minima in the vicinity of aerodromes, VFR flights, or a mixture of the two), pilots are to be informed of the recommended spacing.

For other flights the spacing listed below is to be applied between successive aircraft on final approach:

Leading aircraft	Following aircraft	Minimum distance
Heavy	Heavy	4 miles
	Medium	5 miles
	Small	6 miles
	Light	8 miles
Medium	Medium	3 miles*
	Small	4 miles
	Light	6 miles
Small	Medium or Small	3 miles
	Light	4 miles

* Where the leading aircraft is a B757, the minimum distance is increased to 4 miles

Aerodrome operations

The minimum spacing listed below is applied between successive aircraft, both IFR and VFR flights.

(a) Aircraft departing from the same runway or from parallel runways less than 760m apart (including grass strips):

Leading aircraft	Following aircraft	Minimum spacing at time aircraft are airborne	
Heavy	Medium, Small and Light	departing from the same take-off position	2 minutes
Medium or Small	Light	departing from the same take-off position	2 minutes
Heavy (full-length take-off)	Medium, Small and Light	departing from an intermediate take-off point	3 minutes
Medium or Small	Light	departing from an intermediate take-off point	3 minutes

(b) Operations on a runway with a displaced landing threshold if the projected flight paths are expected to cross:

Leading aircraft	Following aircraft	Minimum spacing at time aircraft are airborne or have touched down
Heavy arrival	Medium, Small and Light departure	2 minutes
Heavy departure	Medium, Small and Light arrival	2 minutes

(c) Operations on crossing and diverging runways or on parallel runways greater than 760m apart. The following spacings are to be applied whenever the projected flight paths of the aircraft cross:

Leading aircraft	Aircraft crossing behind	Minimum distance	Time equivalent
Heavy	Heavy	4 miles	2 minutes
	Medium	5 miles	3 minutes
	Small	6 miles	3 minutes
	Light	8 miles	4 minutes
Medium	Medium	3 miles	2 minutes
	Small	4 miles	2 minutes
	Light	6 miles	3 minutes
Small	Medium or Small	3 miles	2 minutes
	Light	4 miles	2 minutes

(d) Opposite direction runway operations. A minimum of two minutes spacing is provided from the time a Heavy aircraft making a low or missed approach crosses over the take-off position of a Medium, Small or Light aircraft departing from the opposite direction runway.

En-route and intermediate approach

No special longitudinal spacings based on time are required. When a Medium, Small or Light aircraft is positioned by radar to cross behind or follow the same track as a Heavy aircraft, the minimum spacing is 5 miles.

The Airbus A380 has special vortex spacings:
Arriving aircraft

Medium behind A380	3 minutes
Small behind A380	3 minutes
Light	4 minutes

Departure flow regulation

At airports handling international traffic you will hear frequent references on the Tower or Ground Movement frequencies to Calculated Take-Off Times or CTOTs. These were known previously as 'slot times' and this term is often heard as well. During peak times some countries are unable, for a number of reasons, to cope with the extra traffic. For instance, over 50 European and 30 UK airports are currently sending aircraft to the Mediterranean. Spain has about nine airports to receive the majority of them, with Palma the most popular destination. When the number of aircraft wishing to fly outstrips the capacity of the control centres along the route or that of the destination airport, the flow of traffic has to be regulated to ensure safe separation both nationally and internationally. This means that aircraft have to be held on the ground at the departure airports until such time as they can be accepted.

Europe's Central Flow Management Unit (CFMU) is located at Brussels and provides departure times about two hours ahead for every aircraft flying on a regulated route. This ensures an organised system of queuing for all flights, as well as enabling airlines to plan aircraft and crew utilisation. The prime objective of Air Traffic Flow Management (ATFM) is to ensure that ATC sectors do not receive more traffic than they can handle. This first objective is therefore entirely safety-related, the second is to ensure that the available ATC capacity is used efficiently to the benefit of all aircraft operators. CFMU at Brussels achieves these targets in a variety of ways but ultimately where, despite all other efforts, an over-delivery is still anticipated to occur, a 'regulation' will be implemented and take-off slots issued. The principle of first-come, first-served is strictly applied in calculating the slot. All flights – apart from hospital ones – are therefore treated equally, regardless of aircraft size, passenger numbers, scheduled, unscheduled or private.

A flight that has been allocated a Calculated Take-off Time (CTOT) by CFMU is expected to present itself for pushback, start-up and taxi to the active runway in time to comply with the CTOT, better known as the slot. A window of 15 minutes (–5, +10) is available round the CTOT to provide GMC and the tower controller with the flexibility needed to integrate the departing traffic with other aircraft movements. This window is the average for smaller regional airports but is larger for the bigger and more complex ones. It is vital that the CTOT is complied with to avoid an over-delivery of aircraft into an ATC sector. An over-delivery is defined as a situation where the actual number of aircraft that enter a sector is more than 100% of the regulated capacity. A five minute extension to the slot window is usually available on request to CFMU.

The Traffic Orientation Scheme (TOS) forms the basis for the routeing of aircraft on the major traffic flows during the summer peak season. The aim is to balance the demand on Europe's air route system by confining traffic for a specified destination to a particular route with an alternative in the event of unforeseen en route congestion. Getting an aircraft airborne within its slot window can cause GMC or the Tower Controller something of a headache as extra-careful planning is often necessary to make sure that the aircraft gets away on time. The situation is not helped by pilots who taxi excruciatingly slowly or arrive at the runway threshold five minutes before the slot!

During busy periods, some airports may get short of parking stands so an aircraft may be required to taxi well before its slot and shut down on a remote holding bay. Certain airlines may request to pushback early on to an adjacent stand so that they can start later and taxi straight out. This is a ploy to enable them to claim that they left the stand at the scheduled time even though they subsequently went nowhere! In the meantime, a 'Ready message' will be sent by ATC or airline ops in the hope of bringing the slot forward.

Noise abatement

In an effort to minimise noise nuisance to local residents, most airports have their own noise abatement procedures. These are devised by the aerodrome operating authority in conjunction with airlines and local airport consultative committees. Over built-up areas Noise Preferential

Routes have been defined, which carefully route aircraft away from the more densely populated areas. Engine climb power is also reduced for the period when the aircraft must fly over certain conurbations.

At Heathrow different parallel runways are used for take-off and landing and these are alternated regularly so that noise is spread more equitably over the areas beneath the flight paths. Runways 27 Left and 27 Right are the preferred ones, provided the tail wind component does not exceed a certain figure and, in addition, flights are severely restricted at night. At Manchester the direction of approach is changed at regular intervals and at both locations noise levels are monitored. Operators whose aircraft exceed the permitted values are penalised.

Noise Preferential Routes are integrated with the lower end of Standard Instrument Departures, which are themselves designed to cause the least disturbance to those living below. Similarly, Continuous Descent Approaches have been brought into operation, particularly at Heathrow, to reduce noise and, as a bonus, to speed up the arrival rate. On receipt of descent clearance the pilot descends at the rate he judges to be best suited to achieve continuous descent. The object is to join the glide path at the appropriate height for the distance without recourse to level flight.

The procedure requires that aircraft fly at 210kt during the intermediate approach phase. ATC may request speed reductions to within the band 160kt to 180kt on, or shortly before, the closing heading to the ILS, and 160kt when established on the ILS. Aircraft unable to conform to these speeds are expected to inform ATC and state which speeds they are able to use. Since wheels and flaps remain retracted until the final stages, less engine power is needed, which results in a much quieter approach.

Standard Instrument Departures (SIDs) and Standard Terminal Arrival Routes (STARs)

SIDs have been developed for the main runways of major airports, the routes terminating at an airway, advisory route or at a radio navigational fix. Noise Preferential Routeing is also built in. All aircraft departing from an airport under IFR are required to follow the appropriate SID, unless and until authorised to do otherwise by the relevant ATC unit. Each SID has a designator which incorporates the name of the radio beacon or fix on which it is based. An example is the Wallasey Two Tango from Runway 27 at Liverpool, for traffic joining Lima 975 or Lima 10 westbound. Subsequent changes to SIDs result in a new number up to nine, then back to one again. The suffix letter indicates the runway.

STARs are virtually the reverse of SIDs, an example being the WILLO 3A for Gatwick traffic arriving from the west: Goodwood VOR-HOLLY-WILLO. Aircraft are expected to cross Speed Limit Points (SLPs) at or below 250kt indicated air speed.

VOR/DME holding procedures

An example is DAYNE, south of Manchester Airport, an 'offset' holding pattern for traffic inbound to Manchester. Its axis is aligned on Trent VOR Radial 313, its position between Trent DME 13 and 17 miles. The aircraft flies towards the VOR/DME on this designated inbound radial and on reaching the holding fix position carries out a procedure turn on to the reciprocal outbound track. This outbound track is flown until the limiting DME is attained and the aircraft then turns to intercept the inbound VOR radial back to the holding fix position.

In the event of a ground equipment failure at the VOR/DME installation, a standby procedure is published, based on an alternative VOR/DME or other radio beacon. In the case of DAYNE, the holding pattern is defined additionally by a radial and distance from the Manchester VOR/DME.

Aircraft type and airfield designators

For flight planning and flight progress strip presentation, aircraft types have been allocated by ICAO a designator of not more than four characters. Where possible this conforms to the

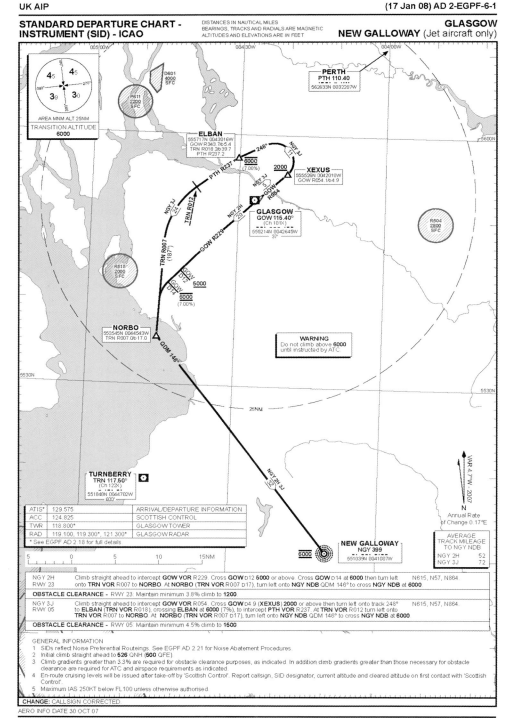

**STANDARD DEPARTURE CHART -
INSTRUMENT (SID) - ICAO**

DISTANCES IN NAUTICAL MILES
BEARINGS, TRACKS AND RADIALS ARE MAGNETIC
ALTITUDES AND ELEVATIONS ARE IN FEET

**GLASGOW
NEW GALLOWAY** (Jet aircraft only)

ATIS*	129.575	ARRIVAL/DEPARTURE INFORMATION	
ACC	124.825	SCOTTISH CONTROL	
TWR	118.800*	GLASGOW TOWER	
RAD	119.100, 119.300*, 121.300*	GLASGOW RADAR	

* See EGPF AD 2.18 for full details

NGY 2H RWY 23	Climb straight ahead to intercept **GOW VOR** R229. Cross **GOW** D12 **5000** or above. Cross **GOW** D14 at **6000** then turn left onto **TRN VOR** R007 to **NORBO**. At **NORBO** (**TRN VOR** R007 D17), turn left onto **NGY NDB** QDM 146° to cross **NGY NDB** at **6000**		N615, N57, N864.	

OBSTACLE CLEARANCE - RWY 23: Maintain minimum 3.8% climb to **1200**

NGY 3J RWY 05	Climb straight ahead to intercept **GOW VOR** R054. Cross **GOW** D4.9 (**XEXUS**) **2000** or above then turn left onto track 248° to **ELBAN** (**TRN VOR** R018), crossing **ELBAN** at **6000** (7%), to intercept **PTH VOR** R237. At **TRN VOR** R012 turn left onto **TRN VOR** R007 to **NORBO**. At **NORBO** (**TRN VOR** R007 D17), turn left onto **NGY NDB** QDM 146° to cross **NGY NDB** at **6000**		N615, N57, N864.	

OBSTACLE CLEARANCE - RWY 05: Maintain minimum 4.5% climb to **1500**

GENERAL INFORMATION
1 SIDs reflect Noise Preferential Routeings. See EGPF AD 2.21 for Noise Abatement Procedures.
2 Initial climb straight ahead to **526** QNH (**500** QFE).
3 Climb gradients greater than 3.3% are required for obstacle clearance purposes, as indicated. In addition climb gradients greater than those necessary for obstacle clearance are required for ATC and airspace requirements as indicated.
4 En-route cruising levels will be issued after take-off by 'Scottish Control'. Report callsign, SID designator, current altitude and cleared altitude on first contact with 'Scottish Control'.
5 Maximum IAS 250KT below FL100 unless otherwise authorised.

CHANGE: CALLSIGN CORRECTED.

AERO INFO DATE 30 OCT 07

LEFT: Standard Instrument Departure (SID) Charts for Glasgow (CAA).

manufacturer's designation, or at least to part of it. For example, Boeing 737-800, 747-400 are represented by B738 and B744, the Fokker 100 is the F100 and the Airbus family are represented by the individual number prefixed by 'A' – A319, A330 and A380 for example.

The codes are often used on R/T, most being fairly obvious, but some are obscure. Controllers occasionally ask a pilot for his aircraft type and get an answer which is not very enlightening. Space does not permit a comprehensive listing which would run into many hundreds of entries, but commonly heard designators are listed in Appendix 5.

Four-letter designators for airfields are often heard on HF R/T but rarely on VHF. They are allocated by ICAO on a worldwide basis for flight planning and telex purposes. British airfields are prefixed 'EG', hence EGLL for Heathrow, EGKK for Gatwick and EGCC for Manchester. A few European examples are EDDH (Hamburg), LFPO (Paris Orly), EBOS (Ostend), LSZH (Zurich) and LEMD (Madrid). American airports are prefixed 'K', as in KJFK (Kennedy) and KLAX (Los Angeles).

Low Visibility Procedures (LVPs)

Many commercial transport aircraft are now fitted with automatic landing equipment and thus, in theory, can land in the poorest visibility. However, lengthy gaps are required between arrivals, both to ensure that the first landing aircraft has vacated the runway and also to allow departures. A further consideration is that critical areas near ILS aerials must not be infringed by taxying and departing aircraft when an arriving flight is within a certain distance – usually

*A groundcrewman in intercom contact with an Airbus 319 crew gives the 'aircraft brakes off'
signal to the tug driver.*

four miles – from the runway threshold on final. The result is that runway capacity is drastically reduced and inbound aircraft may be required to hold for long periods, perhaps having to divert elsewhere when fuel approaches the statutory limits.

Air band listeners will be familiar with ILS but perhaps not aware of the weather minima associated with the different categories. ICAO, the International Civil Aviation Organisation, defines them as follows:

Cat I: A decision height not lower than 60 metres (200ft) and with either a visibility not less than 800 metres, or a Runway Visual Range (RVR) not less than 550 metres.

Cat II: A decision height lower than 60 metres (200ft) but not lower than 30 metres (100ft) and an RVR not less than 350 metres.

Cat IIIA: Either a decision height lower than 30 metres (100ft), or with no decision height and an RVR not less than 200 metres.

Cat IIIB: Either a decision height lower than 15 metres (50ft), or with no decision height and an RVR less than 200 metres but not less than 50 metres.

Cat IIIC: No decision height and no RVR limitations.

Decision height is referenced to the runway threshold elevation and is defined as the level at which the pilot on a precision approach must carry out a missed approach if he fails to achieve the required visual reference to continue the approach to a landing. Note that a precision approach must have an electronic glidepath. Localiser/DME ILS approaches have higher limits because they are not deemed to be precision approach aids and hence no category is published for them.

Cat I, as the most basic, requires little more safeguarding than keeping ground vehicles away from the aerials while the ILS is in use for an approach. They may only cause a momentary blip on the aircraft instruments but sometimes can make the ILS 'trip', in other words switch off automatically. It can normally be reset quite quickly in the tower but in the meantime the aircraft may have wandered off the centreline and be forced to make a missed approach. All localiser and glidepath signals are monitored continuously by a receiver aerial sited in their radiation path. This is known as the far field monitor. If there is a failure or change in parameters a warning light and tone is activated on the control panel in the tower.

When we enter the realms of Cat II and III there are a number of vital conditions. First, the ILS approach and runway lights must be run directly from a standby generator so that in the event of a failure the system will revert instantaneously to mains power. Since the generator is a diesel truck engine, it takes several seconds to start and run up after a mains failure and a landing aircraft could be left with no outside indications for an unacceptable period. Protection of ILS signals during Cat II and III operations may dictate that pre-take-off holding positions are more distant from the runway than the holding points used during good weather. Such holding points will display signs reading 'CAT II/III HOLD' on one or both sides of the taxi way and there will also be a stop bar of red lights. For aircraft taxying off the runway during LVPs, white flashing lights are sometimes provided at designated runway exits to enable the aircraft to report that it has vacated the runway. They are located at the boundary of the ILS sensitive area, the Obstacle Free Zone or OFZ. For practice Cat II or III approaches in good weather the safeguarding procedures are not normally imposed in order to avoid undue disruption to other traffic and essential ground vehicle movement.

Although most modern ILSs are Cat II and III capable, they will not be approved for anything other than Cat I ops unless the airfield lighting is upgraded. The extra lights required include high intensity centreline, colour-coded to warn the pilot he is approaching the end of the runway. White centreline lights extend from the threshold to 900 metres from the end of the runway, the following 600 metres are lit with alternate red and white lights and the final

300 metres have red only. Touchdown Zone lighting (TDZs) is embedded in the runway in order to give 'texture' to the surface in the landing area. The additional lights extend from the threshold for 900 metres along the runway. Other important visual clues are given by supplementary approach lights. One system is known as SHINGALS – Supplementary High Intensity Narrow Gauge Approach Lighting System – and is superimposed on the normal approach light pattern and only switched on when RVR and/or cloudbase go below specified limits.

Landing in zero conditions is not much use if you then can't find your way to the apron. At major UK airports, the exits from the runway have colour-coded alternate yellow/green centre-lines. When established on the normal green centreline the pilot must report 'Runway vacated'. ATC rely heavily on these ground position reports when visibility is bad and ground movement radar is not available. The utmost care is necessary on the part of all involved and this is a further reason why operations are slowed down so much in foggy conditions.

As another aid to ground movement in fog, a taxiway guidance system may be installed. It operates by selective switching of the taxiway centreline lights so that individual sections or routes, each terminating at a lighted stop bar, are illuminated in order to show the way ahead. The stop bar is extinguished as the next section of centreline lights is selected, indicating to the pilot that he may continue taxying. At some less well equipped airports a vehicle with an illuminated 'FOLLOW ME' sign is often used to lead aircraft to and from the runway in fog. It is a piece of World War 2 technology which is just as effective today! A further precaution is the runway guard light, colloquially known as a 'wig-wag'. They are pairs of alternately flashing yellow lights located on each side of the taxiway outboard of the holding sign. On Rapid Exit Taxiways, the green centreline lights are masked on the side approaching the runway to discourage accidental entry. (This was one of the contributory factors in the Tenerife disaster and the reason why the masking was introduced.)

The other major element in Low Visibility Procedures is of course RVR measurement. RVR is the distance the pilot of an aircraft on the runway centreline can expect to see along it. For Cat I and II the automatic or human observer systems are acceptable but for Cat III only the automatic is authorised. The manned system requires an observer near the runway threshold to count the number of runway edge lights he can see along the far side. The figure is passed to the tower by radio and a table is used to convert it into metres. The automatic IRVR (Instrumented RVR) method provides a continuous read-out of the RVR at three points on the runway known as the Touchdown, Mid-Point and Stop End.

Changes in the RVR must be passed to pilots immediately to avoid them infringing their company minima. In the case of IRVR the readings are recorded automatically on paper and, by regulation, sent to the CAA for checking against aircraft movement records. Any 'busting' of minima is rapidly picked up to the embarrassment or worse of those concerned.

Associated with LVPs is the so-called RVR Barrier imposed for intended landings at Heathrow and Gatwick. If the figure is below a certain limit, non-Cat II or III equipped aircraft are not permitted to depart from UK airfields for Heathrow or Gatwick. The aim is to prevent Cat I aircraft from taking up holding pattern capacity while waiting for a possible weather improvement. An additional procedure at Heathrow is intended to sequence aircraft ground movements for take-offs in low visibility. (RVR minima apply also to departures.) For example, if the aircraft's take-off minimum is 200 metres, the pilot is asked not to request start-up until the actual RVR is reported as equal to or greater than 150 metres. There is then a reasonable chance that the extra 50 metres may be achieved by the time he reaches the holding point. Most of the UK's regional airports have Cat I ILS. Those with Cat II are currently East Midlands, Liverpool and Newcastle. The following have Cat III: Belfast/Aldergrove, Birmingham, Edinburgh, Gatwick, Glasgow, Heathrow, Luton, Manchester and Stansted. Liverpool is currently having its lighting improved and will achieve Cat III status in the near future.

Before LVPs actually come into force, a number of conditions have to be met. They may vary with the complexity of the airport but the following are typical of the requirements. All non-essential vehicles are removed from the runways and taxiways, work-in-progress will be suspended, stand-by generators powering the ILS, airfield lighting and other vital services will be switched on, airfield and approach lighting will be checked for serviceability, a perimeter security check will be carried out and barriers placed where necessary at points where vehicles may inadvertently enter the manoeuvring area. The Airport Fire Service is also placed on Weather Standby. Once these conditions are met, the phrase 'Low Visibility Procedures are in force" will be added to the ATIS broadcast and the airport is ready to handle traffic again. LVPs are imposed in two or more phases, depending on the current touchdown RVR. When it is apparent that the visibility is dropping below, say 2,000m and forecast to get worse, airport ops are warned and everyone concerned can begin their duties.

Surface Movement Radars (SMR) at major airports are specifically designed to detect all principal features on the surface of an airport, including aircraft and vehicular traffic, and to present the entire image on a display in the tower. A-SMGCS (Advanced Surface Movement Guidance and Control System) is currently the ultimate SMR and implementation is ongoing at London Heathrow.

Apron control

Totally separate from ATC, they allocate parking stands (gates) for aircraft and communicate this information to the tower or GMC, as well as the airline handling agents. Usually this happens in advance but it is often a dynamic situation with aircraft late to taxi, meaning last-minute stand changes. It is not unknown at Heathrow for arriving aircraft to hold on taxiways for quite long periods waiting for a stand to become vacant. Apron Control is also responsible for authorising vehicle movement on the apron areas where it is likely to conflict with taxying aircraft, outside painted roadway markings for example.

Pushback operations

To maximise apron space, aircraft are often parked nose in to the terminal building. This makes it necessary to push them backwards on to what is known as the taxilane for engine start. The tug crew also monitor ATC instructions to the pilot, as a safety backup to ensure that the instructions passed to them by the crew are the same as those given by ATC. At Gatwick, to cite one example, there is a series of 'standard' pushback manoeuvres, unique to each parking position, which the tug drivers have to know off by heart. This saves time on the radio for normal operations. However, sometimes these are varied by ATC, if for instance they want the aircraft to push far enough back to allow an inbound aircraft on to the same gate. Occasionally, visiting crews whose first language is not English don't fully relay all this information to the tug crews, which is where the crew listening to ATC comes in very useful. One of the tug crew plugs a headset on a long lead into a socket under the aircraft's nose so that he can talk directly to the flight crew. A steel pin is inserted into the nosewheel steering mechanism to override the aircraft's steering system and allow the tug to turn the aircraft. After the pushback is completed the groundcrewman will wave this pin and its attached red flag at the pilots to indicate that they have control over the steering once more.

Pushback is actually quite a complex process and the groundcrew not only carry out a comprehensive final walkround to ensure all hatches are secure and that nothing looks damaged or out of alignment, but they also monitor engine start, to make sure that nothing is going to get jet blasted and that fuel doesn't start leaking out. Correct setting of brakes at all stages is another major issue and the ground crew are firmly in charge here. Being a part of the pushback crew is a highly responsible position and a major contribution to flight safety. Conversely, when an aircraft parks on stand the rules say that no-one is to approach it until all engines are shut down and the anti-collision lights are switched off.

Bird scaring and grass cutting

Most airports now have a dedicated bird control unit to make regular patrols, broadcasting bird distress call recordings and firing crackers to chase them away from the runways. Radio contact is maintained constantly with ATC to enable speedy reaction to any perceived hazard. Pilots must also be warned of the presence of birds when considered necessary. It has been discovered that birds prefer shortish grass because they can see predators approaching more easily. Thus most airfields keep the grass rather longer than your average lawn. The grass still needs cutting of course and the operation requires much liaison with ATC. An airport is divided into numbered areas for ease of reference and the grass cutter will request permission to operate in them. The cleared and graded strip each side of runways is a problem and the cutter may have to move off frequently when there is an aircraft movement. For light aircraft movements, by agreement, the runway length may be reduced using side markers to show the touchdown area. Grass cutting can then continue adjacent to the sterile portion. It may have to be done at night at some busy locations.

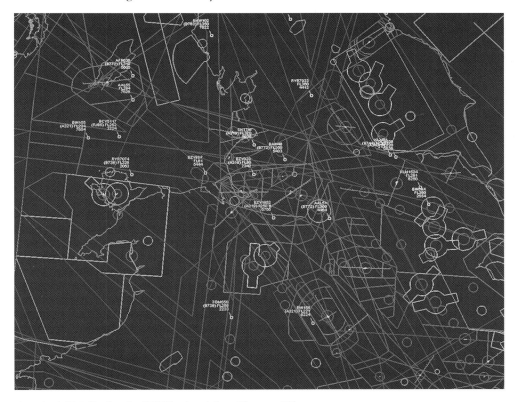

A typical SBS display for NW England (see Chapter 20).

Chapter 14

Airline company messages

INCLUDED IN THE VHF air band and listed in Appendix 3 are blocks of frequencies, generally between 129.50 and 131.975, allocated for company operational communications. They are used for the exchange of information between commercial aircraft and their ground-based operations staff or handling agents. These behind-the-scenes messages are entirely separate from air traffic control but are essential for the safe and efficient running of an airline or cargo service. Further down the scale, but no less important to their users, many flying schools have a company frequency to pass weather information to their offices and discuss flying bookings etc.

In contrast to ATC exchanges, messages on company frequencies are very informal and often resemble a telephone conversation. An exception is where one frequency is shared by several operators or by one handling agent at a number of different airports. In this case the talking is kept to a minimum. Larger airlines have their own ops channels, for example British Midland's BD Ops at East Midlands and British Airways' Speedbird Control at Heathrow. The BA Shuttle fleet has its own ops channel. Other airlines, especially foreign ones, find it uneconomical to maintain their own ops office at each airport and instead use the services of a handling agent. Best known is Servisair, a Stockport, Cheshire-based firm with offices at all the main and many regional airports. A comprehensive service is provided, including passenger and cargo handling, organising refuelling, catering requirements, aircraft cleaning, the filing of flight plans, arranging slot times, crew meals and hotel bookings.

There is no standard phraseology for company messages but the information is usually passed in a particular manner. In the initial call, the last two letters of the aircraft registration are often added as a suffix to the call-sign, eg 'Midland 85 Juliet Charlie'. Sometimes the flight number is deleted altogether as in 'Thomson Alpha Kilo'. Time 'off blocks' or 'off chocks', ie time taxying commenced, is passed first, followed by airborne time and ETA at destination. Fuelling requirements for the next sector (next leg of a series of flights or the return trip) are given in the following manner: 'In tanks X tonnes or kilos. Burn off (or burn) X tonnes or kilos. Taxi X tonnes or kilos'. Burn off is the amount of fuel estimated to be used. The term RTOW is sometimes heard. It stands for Regulated Take-Off Weight, the pre-computed weight for the aircraft plus passengers, fuel and cargo for a particular set of conditions. The latter include runway length, whether its surface is wet or dry, temperature and certain other factors.

Passenger information is usually included in various forms. The total number of fare-paying passengers is passed, followed by the number of non-fare-paying infants, eg '253 plus 2'. The infants are sometimes referred to as tenths, eg 2/10ths or as decimals ('252.2 pax'). 'No specials' indicates no special requirements. Disabled passengers may require a wheelchair for disembarkation; 'lift-off' if unable to walk, 'walk off' if able to get down the steps to the wheelchair. Other information passed via company messages is extremely varied, ranging from passengers' lost library books and special dietary requirements, to requests for the police to meet rowdy passengers on arrival. Stand or gate numbers for parking at the terminal are relayed to the aircraft by ops, having been issued by the airport's Apron Control, an entirely separate function from ATC.

Such is the computerised complexity of modern transport aircraft that technical problems are frequently passed as so-called Fault Codes. These are a series of 6- to 8-digit numbers which can be interpreted by engineering ground staff. An ADD is an Allowable Deferred Defect, in other words a minor fault which can be attended to at the end of the day's service. Also heard are references to QARs, Quick Access Recorders. The Flight Data Recorder (FDR), familiarly known as the 'black box', records certain technical aspects of a flight which can be used to analyse accidents and incidents. Unlike the FDR, the QAR is not a legal requirement but it is now fitted to many of the world's airliners. The flight data fed into it automatically is subsequently monitored and analysed by ground staff.

As an example, a Boeing 767's equipment may record up to 1,550 different parameters, covering a large number of operating aspects from engine health and Flight Director accuracy to fuel burn efficiency and Autoland precision. Any discrepancies can be rectified promptly, often with considerable cost savings to the operator, as well as increased safety. Unfortunately the QAR cassettes are soon filled up, hence the requests for new ones on reaching destination. The solution to this disadvantage is the Optical QAR, an optical disc-based device which offers up to eight times the memory capacity of the current QAR. It is now in the final stages of development and will also have datalink capability.

Aircraft Communications and Reporting System (ACARS)

An exchange of routine ops information taking up to one minute of congested VHF air-time can be compressed by ACARS into less than a second by means of a ground computer converting a databurst into a print-out. As well as a flight deck unit for keyboard data entry, an ACARS-equipped aircraft is fitted with sensing devices that send data automatically to the ground station. This happens, for example, when the aircraft has performed certain manouevres such as pushback from the departure gate, take-off, landing and gate arrival. It is possible for the amateur to receive and decode the messages with the aid of a personal computer and equipment such as the Airmaster produced by Lowe electronics (see address on page 143). ACARS Frequencies (datalink) 136.90 136.925 136.95 136.975

The use of datalink for ops messages is increasing and will one day make company voice communications obsolete but for the moment listening to ops messages can be quite fascinating at times. They really give an insight into the intricacies of running an airline. Once again discretion is advised in discussing them but the main impression gained is how well most airlines look after their customers' individual needs.

Chapter 15

Airshows

AIRSHOW FREQUENCIES ARE generally the same as those normally used by the airfield concerned. Some may be allocated by CAA on a temporary basis for venues that are not airfields. If there is any doubt, the scanner search facility will soon locate the appropriate channels. Some receivers will search for active frequencies between pre-set upper and lower limits and automatically dump them into the memory banks. The receiver does all the work for you and at airshows the external aerial can be shortened or removed altogether so that only local frequencies will be found.

For those who prefer to plan ahead, airfield frequencies can be programmed in advance, and the search mode used to detect any non-standard ones that may be in use. If the location is a civilian airfield, the number of channels in use will be small. Military airfields normally have a much greater number of frequencies, some being secondary backup channels. On VHF, 122.1MHz is used as a standard frequency for Aerodrome Traffic Zone penetration by civil aircraft. This or another assigned frequency is almost always used for the control of military airshows so as to cater for civil participants.

Many small airfields do not have a full ATC service. A simple air/ground radio channel or a rather more formal flight information service may be provided to pass basic data to pilots. When hosting an airshow, a few volunteer controllers will be on duty with a CAA temporary local validation of their ATC licences. The Royal International Air Tattoo at Fairford, for example, relies on the same team of experienced controllers working in their spare time to handle Britain's biggest airshow.

Radio calls are kept to a minimum during airshows to avoid breaking a pilot's concentration during a complex sequence of manoeuvres. As his 'slot' nears its end, he will be given a check on minutes to go. Military display teams such as the Red Arrows have their own UHF frequency for interplane transmissions. The leader or his No 2 monitors the VHF channel and relays any ATC messages. A few display teams simply use the airshow control frequency for their air-to-air communication, although they may be in a foreign language!

An expensive scanner is not essential at an airshow, as you are close to the transmitters and even the cheapest set can perform well in those conditions. Your choice of antenna, usually so critical for quality reception, is also less restricted. Many listeners use a short length of flexible wire instead of the normal antenna, which means that the set can be stowed in a jacket pocket out of the way, with no loss of signal.

An important accessory is a pair of lightweight headphones or an earphone to overcome aircraft noise. Widely available is a police-type earpiece, costing around £9, that slips over the ear and provides comfortable listening with very little weight. Earphones offer another advantage: they increase your battery life and can make the difference between them lasting all day or dying in the middle of the show. The majority of modern receivers can use rechargeable cells, but these rarely last more than 4 to 6 hours of continuous use, so a spare set of rechargeables is needed. Don't forget to top them up the day before – the charge can drain away over a period of time!

Batteries are a very important consideration and many regular listeners use alkaline cells at an airshow. They are more expensive but will easily last 10 to 12 hours. Some modern radios can run for 20 or more hours on a set and can thus last all weekend, which is very useful if the show is a two-day event like RIAT!

If your radio has memory banks, a good tip is to programme the basic ATC frequencies into one bank for rapid scanning and place display teams' channels into another for use during the individual routines. If you have a single-frequency set, the best plan is to locate the airshow controller (normally the tower controller) and stick to this all day. It will provide almost everything you need and some teams will also use it for their air-to-air communications.

There are several less obvious benefits to be derived from using an air band radio. Airshow photography has always relied upon split-second timing to get the best shots. Tuning in to the voices of the pilots as they synchronise manoeuvres can assist in getting that special picture. Display items sometimes catch the display commentator unawares – the fast, low arrival of a fighter, for example. The pilot has to inform ATC that he is running in and, if you are listening, you can be waiting, camera at the ready.

Perhaps your interest lies with video photography. The headphone socket provides a useful link to your radio if you use a camcorder. By joining a lead between the two, you will be able to add the radio exchanges to your video soundtrack. Alternatively, you can just place your receiver near to the camcorder and the transmissions will still record quite well. It will also serve to cut out background chatter from people around you and result in a greatly enhanced video that really captures the sprit of the event.

Extensive market areas are a feature of all major airshows and attract numerous aviation suppliers. Their wares range from books and magazines to air band radios and accessories and navigation charts. The major outlets which make regular appearances include *FlyPast*

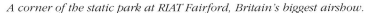

A corner of the static park at RIAT Fairford, Britain's biggest airshow.

magazine, Air Supply, Javiation, Lowe Electronics, Midland Counties Publications, Air-Britain and The Aviation Hobby Shop.

Selected display team frequencies

Black Cats:	280.475
Blue Angels:	237.8 275.35 251.6 305.5 284.25 143.6
Blue Eagles:	135.95 135.975 136.975 382.0
Patrulla Aquilla (Spain):	130.5 337.975
Asas de Portugal:	262.15
Frecce Tricolore:	307.8 140.6
Patrouille de France:	141.825 143.1 242.65 243.85
Patrouille de Suisse:	266.175 388.075
BBMF:	120.8 122.7
RAF Falcons:	255.1 256.9
Team Guinot:	118.0
Turkish Stars:	225.75 264.4 279.6
Aerostars:	123.35 122.95 122.475 124.45
Midnight Hawks (Finland):	140.625
The Blades:	136.175

Guinot Stearman with young lady wingwalker, a perennial airshow favourite.

Chapter 16

Emergencies and unusual circumstances

EMERGENCY SITUATIONS WITH aircraft are fairly common, and although the word conjures up images of catastrophic failure or fire in the air, few are very dramatic even if they may give the pilot some anxious moments. The air traffic controller is a very significant team member in the safe and successful resolution of most emergencies and the CAA's Safety Regulation Group has circulated a well-thought-out booklet entitled *Aircraft Emergencies – Considerations for Controllers*. It has been distributed to all UK controllers with the aim of increasing awareness of the effect of different types of emergencies on aircraft performance and to give guidance on ways they can assist pilots faced with emergency situations.

When flight crew are confronted with an abnormal situation whilst in flight, they will normally prioritise their immediate actions in the following order: AVIATE, NAVIGATE, COMMUNICATE. The immediate work load is likely to be high so ATC may get nothing more than a '(Call-sign) we've got a problem, standby'. The crew then follow checklists, try to diagnose the problem, discuss options and decide what to do next. A diversion or rapid descent may be necessary.

For ATC, it is vital to establish basic information as soon as possible without hassling a crew who will already be extremely busy. The facts needed are: nature of the emergency, intentions of the crew, time available, additional information. The actual degree of emergency must be established, as pilots are sometimes reluctant to use the prefix 'Pan' or 'Mayday'.

What controllers really require is a brief, preferably non-technical, description of the problem and its possible effect on the handling and performance of the aircraft. Also essential is the number of persons on board so that rescue services can account for everyone in the event of an accident.

In a critical situation such as an engine fire, an immediate landing will be required. In some incidents – an undercarriage malfunction, for example – the aircraft may have to enter a holding pattern while drills are carried out. Sometimes it may be necessary to jettison fuel to bring the aircraft down to minimum landing weight.

Types of emergency are tabulated in the booklet, including fire, loss of pressurisation, engine failure, hydraulic failure, landing gear problems, fuel shortage, control problems and icing. Crew responses and options are listed, along with controller priorities and actions. The following list attempts to highlight some of the factors that may affect the progression and outcome of particular types of emergency:

Fire: Location – engine, cabin, cargo, wheel well, extinguishable? There may be no way of using aircraft systems. Time is critical – flight crew will want to land the aircraft as quickly as possible. ATC will alert them to the nearest airfield and offer radar vectors to it. Crosswinds may cause complication on landing due to the location of the fire. Evacuation is likely.

Smoke in cockpit: Emergency descent may be necessary. Instruments may be difficult to read. Frequency changes may be impossible. Type of approach may be critical. Crew incapacitation possible.

Loss of all engines: Range (height)/endurance (electrical power reserves) available. ATC vectors to nearest airfield, maybe orbit overhead to assist in planning the glide approach. When giving turns, the rate of descent may double.

Total (or nearly total) electrics failure: Immediate diversion essential. Limited instrumentation. High cockpit workload. Navigation may be difficult. Only one radio may be available. Minimise communication to conserve batteries. Abnormal approach configuration likely. May be caused by lightning strike.

Loss of pressurisation: Emergency descent to 10,000ft or lower. Rate of descent 8/9,000ft for jet but may be much lower for turbo-prop. Descent may already be established before controller can be contacted. Possible spiral descent. Communication difficult because of high ambient noise and use of oxygen mask. Immediate diversion likely. Explosive decompression – additional technical and medical problems likely to follow.

Hydraulic failure: Very high workload with multiple system failures. Severely reduced deceleration on landing. Limited directional control. Possible runway blockage on landing, unable to manoeuvre off runway. Longer runway than normal may be required. Minimum crosswind for landing. Possibility of fire from leaking hydraulic fluid.

Engine failure on take-off: Very high workload initially – control problems and cockpit drills. Major loss of performance, larger radius of turn. Emergency return or diversion likely. The aircraft may not follow initial departure clearance – it may continue straight ahead or follow its own emergency turn procedure. Degradation of other systems can result.

Engine failure, climb, cruise or descent: Aircraft likely to drift down, crew will advise height which can be maintained. Increased turn radii. Diversion likely.

Control problems: Likely to be most serious with smaller, less sophisticated aircraft. Approach and landing possibly high speed with straight-in required. Problem may clear in warmer air if due to icing. Handling checks may be required before an approach is attempted.

Fuel shortage: Crew often reluctant to declare emergency. Either range (low quantity) or endurance (weather or traffic delays) may be a critical factor.

Icing: Predominantly a turbo-prop, piston and helicopter problem. Little or no warning – descent may already be established before controller can be contacted. Flight controls can jam. Performance of propellers, rotors and engines severely reduced, can cause engine flame-out. Descent or turn to warmer air may resolve situation.

Radio failure: Crew may be unaware of the failure. Crew may be unfamiliar with local radio failure procedures and unsure of action to take. Crew may be distracted while finding procedure. Crew may be confused initially. Other methods such as company frequency, SELCAL or ACARS can be used to contact aircraft.

Additional considerations

As the booklet comments, there is rarely a single correct way to deal with an aircraft emergency because each one is different. For example, on an occasion which I hope will remain unique, I was in the tower at Halfpenny Green Airport, near Wolverhampton, when a skydiver jumped from an Islander at 10,000ft and crashed through the roof of an accompanying Dragon Rapide. The idea was a 16-man link-up but something went very wrong.

The Rapide, with an unserviceable radio, made a rapid descent trailing torn fabric and, after it landed safely, the unexpected passenger was found to have sustained only broken wrists. The Islander pilot was moonlighting from the RAF and was anxious to keep a low profile. It was, as I remarked at the time, rather like referring to the *Titanic* as a boating accident, but we concocted a very deadpan report to the CAA and I never heard anything more about it. That was nearly 30 years ago; nowadays there would be a major investigation!

In many parts of the world a pilot has formally to declare an emergency before the safety services are alerted. A UK controller uses his or her judgment and almost always puts them on a Local Standby at the very least, working on the saying 'better safe than sorry'. There is also the possibility that a minor problem with the aircraft may distract an inexperienced pilot enough to make him misjudge the landing. For Royal Flights a Local Standby is standard procedure.

The scale of Rescue and Fire-fighting Services at a particular airport is determined by the overall length and maximum fuselage width of the largest aircraft handled on a regular basis. The lowest is the Special Category licensed solely for flying instruction to take place. Then follow Categories 1 to 10, rising from an overall length of 9m progressively up to – but not including – 90m. Bristol, a typical regional airport, is Cat 7, Heathrow Cat 10. Up to Cat 9, the category may be increased by one to cover the occasional larger aircraft, provided this does not occur more than a permitted number of times per year. At most airports by pre-arrangement much larger aircraft can be accommodated, simply by calling in off-duty personnel.

There are six standard categories of emergency beginning with the self-explanatory 'Aircraft Accident'. A 'Full Emergency' is declared when it is known that an aircraft is, or is suspected to be, in such trouble that there is a danger of an accident. The problems include the thankfully rare fire in the air, fuel shortage and the not uncommon engine failure on multi-engined aircraft. In the latter case an experienced and properly trained pilot should have no difficulty in making a safe landing as he is required to practise asymmetric flying at regular intervals and pass a check. The safety services are alerted, however, and at larger airports this usually means the outside fire services will be summoned automatically as a backup.

Next comes the 'Local Standby' which I have mentioned already and the 'Aircraft Ground Incident' which covers occurrences other than accidents. These include burst tyres, fuel spillages and bomb scares on parked aircraft. A 'Weather Standby' is instituted when 'weather conditions are such as to render a landing difficult or difficult to observe'. Bad visibility is one obvious instance, a significant crosswind component is another. The final category is 'Domestic Fire' which, as its title implies, covers such things as grass fires on and adjacent to the airfield and fires in its buildings. At major airports the rescue services have the use of a common frequency of 121.6 – call-sign (Location) Fire – to talk directly with the flight crew when necessary.

Emergencies can include the situation where a passenger on board becomes seriously ill – the Medical Emergency. A pilot is then expected to make formal declaration of this fact to ATC using the distress ('Mayday') or urgency ('Pan') prefix, depending on whether the passenger requires immediate assistance. The nature of the passenger's medical condition, diagnosed or otherwise, is included in the message. Controllers then provide the appropriate priority to such flights and inform the emergency services.

A pilot requiring immediate assistance is expected to transmit a Distress Message with the prefix 'Mayday, Mayday, Mayday'. If the situation is less serious, an Urgency Message with the prefix 'Pan, Pan, Pan' is used. Unfortunately, pilots, particularly phlegmatic British ones, are unwilling to make too much of a fuss so if you hear a 'Mayday' call, things have really reached the critical stage! The announcement of the loss of one engine – provided there are more than one – is usually delivered in a matter-of-fact tone, together with a request for diversion. This calm approach is sometimes self-defeating – a controller who would be sparked into instant action to clear a path for an aircraft that has abruptly turned into a glider in the circuit, may think he has misheard if the magic word 'Mayday' is not used, and waste time asking for a repeat.

Transmissions from an aircraft in distress have priority over all other messages. When a pilot is already in contact with an ATC unit, assistance should be sought on the frequency in use, otherwise a call should be made on 121.5MHz. On hearing a distress call, all stations must maintain radio silence on that frequency unless they themselves are required to render assistance and should continue to listen on the frequency concerned until it is evident that assistance is being provided.

The Distress Frequency 121.5MHz

The UK has two Distress and Diversion (D&D) Sections located at Swanwick and Prestwick. D&D is manned by RAF control staff, who are assisted in the provision of an emergency service on the VHF International Aeronautical Emergency Frequency of 121.5MHz and its military UHF counterpart of 243MHz by suitably equipped civil and military units and certain HM Coastguard stations.

The emergency service is available on a 24-hour basis to pilots flying within UK airspace who are in distress are or experiencing difficulties that could lead to a state of emergency. Provided the aircraft is above 3,000ft over most of the landmass to the east and south of Manchester or down to 2,000ft in the south of England, D&D has a truly amazing ability to fix an aircraft's position. This is known as Auto-Triangulation and uses 16 outstations which automatically process its radio signals and display the location to the controller on a huge map.

For pilots flying at lower altitudes, position fixing can be carried out manually using bearings from various airfields around the country, although this takes several minutes to achieve. If the aircraft is equipped with a transponder, the code 7700 can be selected to indicate an emergency. This activates an alarm at every radar station able to receive the signal and also makes the radar position symbol pulsate to attract the controller's attention.

Air band listeners monitoring 121.5 will find very little activity; the odds against hitting on anything interesting are very high! Aircraft on transatlantic flights are required to monitor 121.5 at all times, which is why it is often referred to as the Guard Frequency. There have been many occasions when a high-flying airliner has relayed messages from a much lower light aircraft on a delivery flight and alerted the rescue services. It is also used as an unofficial

An Air India aircraft dumping fuel at FL150 over north-west England prior to a diversionary landing at Heathrow with a seriously ill passenger. It had been en route from New York to Mumbai (John Locker).

means of communication between crews of the same operator. Having made contact, a terse 'Go to company' (frequency) follows, so that they can have a chat.

Careless use of 121.5 is frowned upon and the following story is claimed to be true. Above the Arabian Gulf two young American voices are discussing baseball results on 121.5. Suddenly, a typical British voice is heard, 'I say chaps, do you realise this is 121.5, the emergency channel, reserved for emergency use only?' Silence ... Then one American voice says: 'Gee! Ed, do you think it was God talking to us?'

In the UK, pilots are encouraged to make practice 'Pan' calls on 121.5, having first asked permission in case there is a real emergency in progress. The usual scenario is to simulate getting lost and request homing to destination or the nearest airfield. It is very impressive to hear how quickly D&D can fix the aircraft's position even when it is not fitted with a transponder. Not everyone agrees with this use of 121.5 for practice fixes, American airline captains especially. They can sometimes be heard complaining to the D&D controller about what they see as misuse of the frequency.

Often to be heard on 121.5 are broadcasts to alert pilots, especially military ones, to the setting up of a Temporary Danger Area around Search and Rescue (SAR) Operations. The message is usually prefixed 'Securité', Securité: Temporary Danger Area D399 established at (position in lat and long), geographical position, radius five miles, up to (X) thousand feet, SAROPS on'. The aim is to exclude all aircraft other than SAR or police-operated, thus reducing the chance of a mid-air collision.

Also associated with the Distress Frequencies are those used by the Aeronautical Rescue Co-ordination Centre at Kinloss in NE Scotland. Scene of search frequencies in use are as follows: HF – 3023kHz (civil/military night), 5680 (civil/military day), 5695 (military/day), 3085 (military night), 8364 (international intercommunication); VHF/UHF – 123.1 (civil), 156.3 (Channel 6 FM Marine), 282.8 (NATO). Other HF frequencies may be used as directed by the RCC controller. Unicom 130.425 is available for use at major emergency incidents so pilots can broadcast their intentions as they approach the area.

Fuel jettisoning
Pilots of aircraft in flight are permitted to dump fuel in emergency and may request guidance from ATC. The recommendations are that it should be carried out over the sea if at all possible or above 10,000ft agl. Exceptionally, if neither option is available, or inconsistent with safety, fuel may be jettisoned above 7,000ft in winter and above 4,000ft in summer. For fuel to be dumped below these levels the situation must be unavoidable. A vertical separation of at least 1,000ft should be maintained between aircraft. As a rough rule of thumb, aircraft dump fuel at up to two tonnes per minute, so a 747 could take anything up to an hour. Note that not all jet transport aircraft have fuel dumping capability so may have to burn off fuel to get down to minimum landing weight.

Flight plans and overdue action
When an aircraft is operating on a flight plan and fails to turn up within 30 minutes of its ETA, the controller at the destination airfield is required to confirm the ATD (actual time of departure) from the departure airfield. Other set procedures known as Preliminary Overdue Action are put into effect. After one hour, or sooner in certain cases, Full Overdue Action is taken by the parent ATCC and a search launched for the missing aircraft.

Aircraft on a flight for which a plan has not been filed have no such protection, although they are required to 'book out' with the ATC unit at the departure aerodrome, assuming one exists. The departure details – destination, time en route, fuel endurance and persons on board (sometimes referred to as 'souls on board') – are recorded but no further action need be taken, and if an aircraft goes missing it is often some time before people start asking questions, usually sparked off by anxious relatives.

Flight plans must be filed at least 30 minutes before requesting taxi clearance or start-up approval. A pilot may file one for any flight and for certain categories they are mandatory. These include all IFR flights within controlled airspace, those which cross an international boundary, and for any flight where the destination is more than 40km from the aerodrome of departure and the aircraft's maximum take-off weight exceeds 5,700kg. In addition, a pilot is advised to file a flight plan if he intends to fly over the sea more than 10 miles from the coast or over sparsely populated areas where search and rescue operation would be difficult.

For scheduled airline routes and other regularly recurring IFR flights with identical basic features, a repetitive flight plan saves operators and crews the chore of filing a separate plan each time. Often referred to as a 'stored plan', it is submitted by an operator for computer storage and repetitive use by ATC units for each individual flight.

Airprox

An Airprox Report should be made whenever a pilot or controller considers that the distance between aircraft as well as their relative positions and speed have been such that the safety of the aircraft was or may have been compromised. A sense of proportion is required for this, however, as light aircraft in traffic circuits occasionally get very close to one another, usually through inexperience and/or not keeping a good look-out.

Pilots flying under IFR in controlled airspace may well file a report if they see another aircraft that they believe is closer to them than required by the separation rules. In a radar-controlled environment this may be 4 instead of 5 miles, which a pilot flying under VFR would consider ludicrous.

All Airprox Reports are investigated, not so much to allot blame as to try to prevent a recurrence by examining the circumstances. The degree of actual risk of collision is assessed and regular summaries of the most serious ones are published for all to read. In the past, when circulation was restricted, the press had to rely on leaked reports. One they never heard about unfortunately was the large pink pig which an Army helicopter nearly rammed one hazy day over the River Thames. It was an advertising balloon that had broken away from its moorings and drifted away! Most reports make very dull reading, an exception being the celebrated Boeing 737/UFO near Manchester in 1994! (See Chapter 22.)

Level busts

A level bust is defined as 'a deviation of 300ft or more from an assigned level'. CAA has now issued an information circular setting out operational best practice specifically targeted at areas of operations relevant to level bust prevention. Most level busts occur below FL120 in busy terminal airspace and this area needs most attention in terms of Radio Telephony (RTF) discipline and the development of, and adherence to, Standard Operating Procedures (SOPs).

One way of achieving this is by incorporating these items into refresher training. Flight crew training should include altimeter setting procedures and their importance in relation to level bust prevention. SOPs should be clear on altimeter setting procedures, particularly the use of QFE and QNH. Flight crew training should emphasise the necessity, whenever possible, of having both pilots listening on the radio in use when an ATC clearance is being received and both recording the clearance. Training should also cover the procedure for setting and cross-checking the cleared level in the 'altitude select' window. Pilots should have a good understanding of the logic of autopilot level-change modes, which will increase awareness of expected autopilot performance during climb and descent monitoring.

SOPs should require that both pilots are present when the departure clearance is received; ATC clearances should only be requested when two flight crew members are available to listen. The person designated to request and read back the clearance (preferably the PM, the pilot monitoring) should also be tasked with recording it. Other flight crew members should also record the clearance provided that this does not interfere with other tasks. If necessary the pilot should ask ATC to delay transmitting the clearance ('Standby') if he can involve another flight crew member who may be off frequency at that particular moment. Adjusting the cleared altitude/level in the 'altitude select' window on the flight control panel and initiating a climb or descent should be considered as separate actions. This permits an assessment of the amount of altitude change required and highlights the risk of an autopilot and/or an aircraft high-performance induced level bust.

Flight crew training should emphasise that whenever an aircraft is climbing or descending, the PF, the pilot flying, should carefully manage the automatics and monitor the progress of the climb or descent. In particular, the PF should monitor aircraft performance within 1,000ft of the cleared altitude/level to ensure that it does not fly through the cleared altitude or flight level. All distractions should be avoided during the last 1,000ft prior to the selected altitude/ flight level so that the transition to level flight can be fully monitored.

Some level busts have been traced to the misinterpretation of flight profiles – typically Standard Instrument Departure (SID) and Standard Arrival (STAR) procedures – published in charts provided by commercial organisations. Flight crew training should include in-depth familiarisation for crews with the presentation of contents and layout of charts used by the operator. This should ensure that the layout of check altitudes, tracks, etc become 'second nature' to pilots.

Radio failure

If an aircraft suffers a radio failure there are published procedures to which the pilot is expected to adhere. A squawk of 7600 set on the transponder will alert SSR-equipped ATC to his problem. If the transponder and/or essential navigation equipment has also failed, pilots are advised as a last resort to carry out a special procedure to catch the controller's attention. The aircraft is to fly at least two triangular patterns before resuming course, as follows:

Aircraft speed	Length of leg	Transmitter failure only	Complete failure
300kt or less	2 minutes	Right-hand turns	Left-hand turns
More than 300kt	1 minute	Right-hand turns	Left-hand turns

If the controller should notice such a manoeuvre (and RAF experiments show that they often do not!) he is advised to advise D&D of the position and track and continue to plot the aircraft while it is within his radar cover. A shepherd aircraft of similar performance will then be sent out to lead it, hopefully, to a safe landing.

Quite often the failure is of the transmitter only and the controller can instruct the aircraft to make one or more turns and check if the pilot is complying. If it becomes obvious that the receiver is working, normal radar service is resumed. There are some subtle ways by which the aircraft's altitude and other information can be ascertained, such as 'After passing FL50 turn left heading 270 degrees'.

There are occasions when an aircraft receiver is working correctly but the reply transmitted is unintelligible at the ground station because the speech is badly distorted or non-existent, perhaps because the microphone is unserviceable. Military pilots are briefed on a special code which makes use of the carrier wave only. The pilot presses his transmitter button a certain number of times according to the following code:

One short transmission – Yes (or an acknowledgement)
Two short transmissions – No
Three short transmissions – Say again
Four short transmissions – Request homing
One long transmission (2 seconds) – Manoeuvre complete (eg steady on heading)
One long, two short, one long – The aircraft has developed another emergency

A controller will be alerted to the presence of an aircraft with this kind of failure if he hears, or sees on the VDF, four short carrier wave transmissions. The controller should then interrogate the pilot, using the call-sign 'Speechless Aircraft', unless he is already aware of its identity, to find out what assistance is required. He must be careful to ask questions that can be answered with a direct yes or no. The code is also recommended for use by civilian pilots as it can easily be explained by the controller in the first few transmissions.

Summary

As the CAA's *Aircraft Emergencies* booklet says: 'The controller is a very significant team member in the safe and successful resolution of most aircraft emergencies. Likewise, the controller has a variety of resources that he or she can call on to assist an aircraft. Flight crews look to the controller for direct assistance and to act as intermediaries with other ground-based services. Crews rely on controllers to provide timely and useful assistance, but not to interfere with the completion of vital checks and drills. Co-operation and co-ordination to minimise crew workload are the keys to success. Keeping procedures as close as possible to normal will assist greatly. Crews will normally want to give ATC as much information as they can, but it can take time to ascertain the full extent of the problems they face. In modern aircraft single failures are rarely significant once cockpit drills have been completed. However, some drills can be complicated and lengthy. Patience can be a virtue!'

An aircraft, in this case a Piper Navajo south of Liverpool, squawks the emergency code. The radar return also pulses to attract attention.

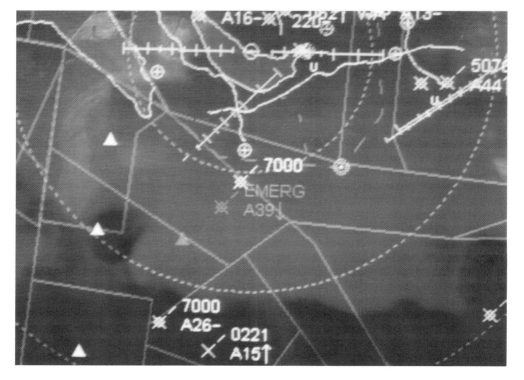

Chapter 17

Military
air band

MILITARY ATC EMPLOYS a block of frequencies between 225 and 400MHz, audio modulated (AM) as in the civil VHF air band. Although technically the Ultra High Frequency (UHF) band does not start until 300MHz, they are usually referred to as UHF and are normally spaced 25kHz apart. Theoretically this produces 7,000 separate channels and, although many are in use for airfield and area ATC, it leaves a very large number available for a variety of uses. These include in-flight refuelling, bombing and gunnery range operations, air-to-air frequencies for formation flying, satellite links and, in the case of the USAF in Britain, numerous ops and Command Post channels. Blocks of frequencies, known as TADs from the acronym for Tactical Air Directive, are allocated for air defence interception purposes by RAF radar units. Each channel has a code number such as TAD 122.

An anomaly is the use by the USAF of a few frequencies around 142MHz. To save time-consuming manual tuning, many military aircraft have pre-set radio frequencies, referred to as Studs (Button or Push to the Americans) and used in the same way as the push buttons on a car radio. For example, the current allocation for a Hawk based at RAF Valley is as follows: Stud 1: Ground Movements Control; Stud 2: Tower; Stud 3: Departures; Stud 4: Mona; Stud 5: Quiet frequency; Stud 6: Approach; Stud 7: Radar; Stud 8: Radar; Stud 9: NATO common; Stud 10: Low level; Stud 11: Air-to-air; Stud 12: Air-to-air; Stud 13: Air-to-air; Stud 14: London Mil; Stud 15: London Mil; Stud 16: Scottish Mil.

It is possible that the military could adopt 12.5kHz spacing in the UHF air band or even 8.33, as in civil aviation. This would free up a large number of frequencies but it would have to spread throughout NATO, at great cost in radio equipment modification and reorganisation. Likely channel interference would be another problem.

Military ATC in Britain is organised much the same as its civil counterpart, although the ultimate purpose of a considerable amount of military ATC is to bring aircraft together (formation join-ups, air-to-air refuelling, interceptions, etc) rather than to keep them apart. Most airfields have a Ground Movements Controller as well as a Tower Controller who is known also as the 'local' controller. The controller who sequences traffic on to final approach is the Director, the next stage being the Talkdown Controller who uses Precision Approach Radar (PAR) to bring the aircraft down to visual contact with the runway. PAR, discontinued in UK civil ATC about 25 years ago in favour of ILS, uses two radar displays. One shows the aircraft and final approach in plan view, the other the picture from the side which monitors deviations above and below the glidepath. The pilot can thus be given height as well as heading corrections.

The RAF makes considerable use of ILS installations, but few are rated more accurate than the minimum civil Category 1 (minimum of 200ft cloud base and 600 metres RVR). Efforts are being made to improve this situation to counter the planned demise of PAR, MLS being seen as the eventual replacement for both systems.

RAF rules governing runway occupancy, separation and other procedures are similar to those in civil ATC. R/T phraseology is, however, somewhat different, although it is planned to bring it into line with civilian practice as an ongoing process. Military jet circuits tend to be relatively tight and are more oval-shaped than civil practice (see page 63). Military controllers use 'two-in', 'three-in', etc for the number of aircraft present in the circuit. The 'final' call is made just before turning base leg. 'Roll' is used instead of the civil 'touch and go', and an 'overshoot' is a low approach rather than a go around. A 'run and break' is a useful method of killing excess speed by approaching the runway, pulling up sharply and turning downwind for a close-in final. USAF bases in Britain use their own style of American phraseology.

R/T exchanges are often clipped and difficult for the layman to understand; for example, two clicks on the mike button often serve as an acknowledgement. The use of oxygen mask microphones tends to depersonalise voices but it does, however, make many RAF transmissions instantly identifiable as such! Ground operations frequencies at RAF and USAF bases can be found in the 30–39, 68–69, 72–80 and 406–414MHz ranges, all NFM mode.

Military aviation thrives on initials and code words. Among the many to be heard on UHF are PD (practice diversion), RTB (return to base), Homeplate (base), Chicks (friendly fighter aircraft), Playmate (aircraft being worked with) and Pogo (switch to channel ...). The Americans have their own jargon such as Code One (a fully serviceable aircraft), RON (remain overnight), TOT (time on target), Lima Charlie (loud and clear), Victor freek (VHF frequency), and Uniform (UHF frequency).

London Air Traffic Control Centre (Military) is co-located with the civil ATCC at Swanwick to form the London Joint Area Organisation (LJAO). To meet the requirements of all airspace users, the civil controllers provide air traffic services to en route GAT (General Air Traffic) flights usually within the airways system and within fixed geographical sectors, and the military controllers give a service in a more flexible fashion to OAT (Operational Air Traffic) flights. OAT flights are generally those that cannot conform to the requirements of flights within airways and other regulated airspace. Within the airways system GAT, including military traffic operating as GAT, is normally given priority over OAT. Exceptions are made, however, for such operations as military aircraft engaged in the calibration of a radar system. Conversely, outside the airways and upper route structures OAT generally gets priority over off-route GAT.

The Initial Contact Frequencies (ICF) for each sector at what is known from its call-sign as 'London Mil' are monitored permanently using dedicated UHF and VHF frequencies. The Central (Mil) Sector is the busiest of the five sectors, the others being Northwest, West, Southwest and Southeast.

Flight Plans are vitally important for the efficient operation of the system. GAT Plans are processed in the normal way by the civil computer, while those for OAT are fed into the military Myriad computer by the RAF Air Movements Section. If any of the flight plans affect LJAO airspace the relevant flight progress strips are printed and distributed to the appropriate sectors.

As one military controller working in LJAO remarked, it soon becomes obvious that most of the aircraft based in the east of England want to exercise in the west, and those from the west want to exercise in the east! The problem is that to get to those areas the aircraft need to cross one of the busiest air route complexes in the world. In most cases the crossing is achieved with very little fuss due to constant co-ordination with the civil controllers on the spot.

Virtually all crossings of the airways are accomplished by means of a 'cleared level', which means that no aircraft under civil control will be allowed to occupy the negotiated level for the period that the military aircraft is crossing. When this is not possible owing to busy traffic situations, the military controller is permitted to use radar separation to achieve a safe crossing, a procedure known as 'taking five'. The name comes from the prescribed separation of at least five nautical miles or 5,000ft vertically from any GAT aircraft in the airway. Obviously it is easier to 'take five' with a fighter aircraft than a transport owing to the higher speed and manoeuvrability.

When this method is being employed and there is a possibility of a confliction with one particular aircraft, the controller can co-ordinate with his civil opposite number. When a course of action is agreed, the military controller is able to reduce separation against that one aircraft to the standard radar separation required, depending on its flight level, ie 5 miles horizontally or 1,000ft vertically (2,000ft above FL245). In an emergency, when neither a radar nor procedural crossing can be obtained, an airway may be crossed at an intermediate 500ft level, ie a level of 1,000ft plus 500ft. If already at a 1,000ft level, the aircraft must climb 500ft before entering the airway.

A further method of crossing airways is via the Radar Corridors that have been established at the points most frequently required to be crossed by military flights. The Lichfield RC in the north-west Midlands facilitates crossings at FL140, while the Gamston RC runs through airway L975 at FL190, being controlled by London Mil. The Daventry RC allows crossings at FL100, and the Westcott RC takes military traffic across the airways system just north of London at FL230 or FL240. Brize Radar at Brize Norton in Oxfordshire provides a service for the Swindon RC at FL230 and FL240, while Yeovilton Radar does the same for N864. These 'blocks' of airspace simplify crossing procedures, but the pilot must still request a prior clearance from the controlling authority.

Every other sector in the LJAO is similar in operation to the Central Sector, if not quite so busy. On the Clacton, Dover and Seaford Sectors, handovers are made between LJAO and foreign military agencies, chiefly Mazout Radar in France and Belga Radar in Belgium, the aircraft being transferred to the appropriate frequency when it reaches the FIR boundary. North of 55°N, roughly an east–west line through Newcastle, Scottish Mil at Prestwick operates on the same lines as London Mil. The East Anglian MTA is co-ordinated by RAF Waddington and stretches from FL245 to FL350. The North Wales MTA, under RAF Valley, has limits of FL245 and FL450. Outside the published hours of training activity MTAs revert to normal MRSA status.

Most of the UK airspace at and above FL245 up to FL660 is designated as a Mandatory Radar Service Area (MRSA) with an ATC radar unit responsible for each sector. It is compulsory for pilots intending to fly in the MRSA to call the appropriate radar unit and fly under its instructions, except when operating as civil air traffic or under air defence radars. The North Wales Military Training Area (MTA) and the east Anglian MTA are established within MRSAs to afford freedom of operation for aircraft engaged in exercises incompatible with radar control.

Aerial Tactics Areas (ATAs) reach from FL50 up to FL245 and enable high-energy combat manoeuvres to be carried out by formations of up to six aircraft. Current examples are The Wash ATA, the primary users of which are Coningsby, Cottesmore, and Wittering and the Lakenheath ATA, mainly used by Lakenheath itself. Within The Wash ATA is the ACMI Range (see page 31).

Military units also offer a Lower Airspace Radar Service (LARS) outside controlled airspace up to FL100 for both military and civil aircraft, and a similar service up to FL245 within what is termed 'Middle Airspace'. Its availability is subject to the range and cover of the particular radar in use as well as controller workload. The procedure when within approximately 30 miles of the radar unit is to establish R/T contact on the appropriate frequency using the phraseology '(ATC unit) this is . . . (aircraft call-sign) request Lower Airspace Radar Service'. Pilots may be asked to 'standby for controller'. When asked, they are to pass aircraft type, position and heading, flight level or altitude, intentions and type of service required.

Military Aerodrome Traffic Zones (MATZ) normally consist of a circle of five nautical miles radius from the aerodrome up to 3,000ft above aerodrome level, together with a 'stub' out to five miles protecting the approach path of the most used instrument runway. A MATZ Penetration Service is provided to civil aircraft, the common frequency being 122.1. Traffic information will be given along with any instructions necessary to achieve

RAF Valley tower controllers at work.

A Valley Hawk inches from touchdown, as seen from the runway caravan.

Runway controller's caravan at RAF Valley.

Valley tower controller's magnetic board to indicate aircraft positions.

separation from known or observed traffic in the zone. In some areas MATZs may overlap to form a combined zone; in this case the altimeter pressure setting will be passed to aircraft as a 'Clutch QNH'.

The RAF Distress and Diversion Cells at Swanwick and Prestwick have already been described in Chapter 15. 'London Centre', as it is known by its call-sign, has a computer-based facility which can calculate and display the position of any aircraft transmitting on the military distress frequency of 243MHz. If a crash or ditching occurs, Search and Rescue (SAR) is co-ordinated by Kinloss Aeronautical RCC in NE Scotland, call-sign 'Kinloss Rescue', and HF frequencies are employed because of their long range. The primary day frequency is 5680kHz; 3023 is used at night. Since both are worldwide common frequencies, other units such as Stavanger can be heard on them at times, as well as ground units such as Mountain Rescue Teams (RAF call-sign 'Alpine', and civilian equivalents, for example Kendal MRT 'Mintcake').

Of course the emergencies do not just involve aircraft; they may be ships in distress, climbing accidents, floods and a variety of other incidents. A Temporary Danger Area is established around the site so that SAR ops can be continued without interference from press aircraft and other non-essential intruders. When an aircraft is fitted with an ELT (Emergency Locator Transmitter) or a downed pilot activates a SARBE (SAR Beacon), the signals will be picked up by SARSAT (Search and Rescue Satellite Aided Tracking). The system is highly sensitive in detecting transmissions on 121.5, 243 and 406MHz and alerting the rescue services.

Operational control of No 32 (the Royal) Squadron is vested in the RAF. Royal Flight status is often extended to other reigning sovereigns, Prime Ministers and other Heads of State as a courtesy. Contrary to popular opinion, there are no special increased separations for Royal flights; they are treated exactly the same as any other aircraft in controlled airspace, although a higher priority is given where necessary as the Royal personage usually has to meet a tight schedule. Royal flights in fixed wing aircraft are always provided with controlled airspace to cover the entire flight path when it is within UK airspace. This coverage is obtained by the establishment of temporary controlled airspace where the route runs outside existing Class A and B airspace, and special Control Zones at the departure and destination airfields if these are not already in existence. The vertical dimensions, relevant radio frequencies, times and any other pertinent information will be detailed in the NOTAM concerning the flight.

The NOTAM is prepared by the Airspace Utilisation Section whenever a Royal flight is arranged. It is distributed to the ATCCs and airfields concerned, normally providing at least 48 hours' warning. The airspace concerned is notified as Class A, ie any aircraft within it must fly under IFR at all times. In the case of temporary Control Zones, ATC may issue Special VFR clearances to pilots unable to comply with the IFR requirements and thus ensure positive separation.

Controlled airspace is not normally established for Royal helicopter flights but a Royal Low Level Corridor, marked by a series of check-points, is promulgated. These check-points will be approximately 20 miles apart and will usually coincide with turning points on the route. Pilots flying near the Corridor are expected to keep a good look-out and maintain adequate separation from the Royal helicopter. The NOTAM will incorporate a list of nominated aerodromes from which pilots may obtain information on the progress of the flight. The person on board a Royal Flight used to be readily identifiable by the call-sign, eg Kittyhawk when HM the Queen was a passenger, Rainbow was the Duke of Edinburgh, Unicorn the Prince of Wales, and Leopard Prince Andrew. However, for various reasons only Kittyhawk and Rainbow now remain in use. Kittyhawk, followed by the number allocated to the individual pilot of The Royal Squadron, with the suffix 'R', is now used for all Royal Flights except those in helicopters; these use Rainbow. Training and positioning flights are identified by 'Kitty' and the pilot's number. 'Sparrowhawk' identifies a chartered civil aircraft.

RIGHT: The military TACAN Route System (used with the permission of and copyright of UK CAA).

UPPER AIRSPACE MILITARY TACAN ROUTE SYSTEM

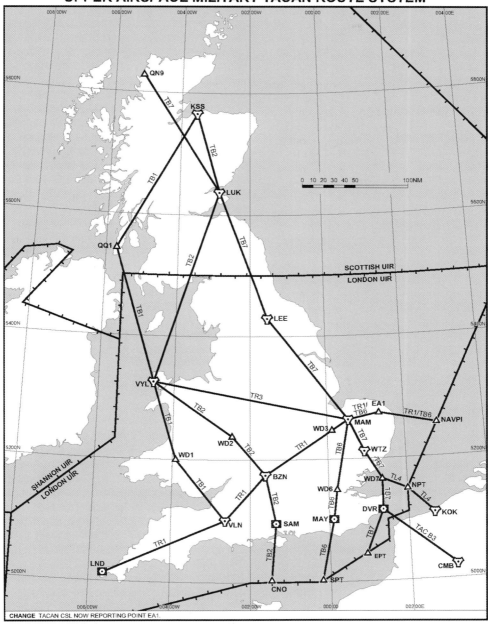

CHANGE TACAN CSL NOW REPORTING POINT EA1.

AERO INFO DATE 15 AUG 06

US Air Force operations from British bases are handled in a similar way to those of their RAF opposite numbers. They have their own controllers in the airfield towers, but approach control may be centralised and co-ordinated as at Lakenheath and nearby Mildenhall. Similar arrangements can be found at various RAF stations where a Centralised Approach Control service may be operated. There is a network of military upper airspace TACAN (Tactical Air Navigation) Routes across Britain and Europe linking TACANs, the military equivalent of the civil VOR/DME.

To preserve security, some military transmissions may employ DVP (Digital Voice Protection) techniques. The speech is electronically digitised, mixed at random and then transmitted. A compatible receiver then unscrambles the sequence and restores its intelligibility. There are several code words for this secure mode; USAF AWACS aircraft, for example, refer to it as 'in the green'. Other terms are 'going tactical' and 'going crypto'. Some NATO strike aircraft are able to engage a frequency-hopping communications system 'Have Quick', which uses eight channels in sequence to foil the eavesdropper. However, a receiver with a very fast scan rate can still monitor the messages, but a developed version is highly secure because of its ability to race through many more frequencies right across the UHF band.

Military aviation makes considerable use of the HF bands, both the RAF and the USAF having their own networks, as do the Canadian Forces. Other foreign air forces are represented as well, but since the transmissions are made in the native language they are of limited interest. The RAF's Flight Watch HF network is known as the UK Defence Global HF System with the call-sign 'Tascom', pronounced Tazcom. Its task is to handle the military equivalent of company messages, arrange telephone patches to home stations and operations centres and provide met and other information on request. It utilises the Terrestrial Air Sea Communication (TASCOM) System. Allied military and other aircraft are provided support in accordance with agreements and international protocols. Stations operate from the UK, Cyprus, Ascension and Mount Pleasant in the Falklands.

The UK Air Defence System runs a separate net providing communications between Sector Operations Centres and interceptor aircraft patrolling the UK Air Defence Regions. Friendly, Unknown and Zombie (Russian) aircraft are investigated. Positions are given by the Georef system, a worldwide RAF system of grid squares, each designated by a four-letter code. They can be found on the En Route Charts published by the RAF and available to the public. Positions in latitude and longitude are converted into a code of four letters and four numbers. In the example shown, aircraft Friendly 1234 is at 58N 02W (MKPP0000). It is thus possible to listen to interceptions and plot their progress!

The USAF equivalent to TASCOM is the High Frequency Global Communications System (HF-GCS), which divides the world into 14 Zones. The English base is at Croughton (first syllable pronounced as in 'crowd') in Northamptonshire, call-sign Croughton Global. There are no operators here now, the messages being relayed remotely from Andrews Air Force base in Maryland, USA. Its primary frequency is 11176kHz, sometimes referred to as 'Triple One Upper'. This is a common HF-GCS frequency used also by Incirlik in Turkey and Ascension Island, among others, and they too can be monitored under good reception conditions. Most frequent users are the transports of Air Mobility Command giving details of loads and unserviceabilities to their destinations or ops centres. The latter are sometimes designated by a code name such as Phantom Ops, the European Airlift Control Centre at Ramstein, Germany.

When an aircraft crew wish to call an Airlift Command Centre they often use the blanket call-sign Mainsail to alert HF-GCS stations that a phone patch is required. The ground station will respond only if the aircraft signal is reasonably strong and clear. It is not uncommon for Croughton to have several aircraft 'queuing' for phone patches, so there are a number of backup frequencies available. Many of the calls involve met information known as Metro (pronounced 'Mee-tro'). Aircrew may offer PIREPS, pilot reports of weather conditions

Georef chart as used by RAF.

encountered en route. This can be useful because the aircraft serial number and type are usually quoted as well as its tactical call-sign if one is in use. Capsule messages can also be heard, periodically updating operation instructions to transport aircraft.

HF-GCS channels are interrupted frequently by Air Combat Command 'Foxtrot' routine mission status broadcasts, known as 'Skybird' after the blanket call-sign for ACC ground stations. Part of the former Strategic Air Command (SAC) fail-safe system, now incorporated in ACC, they test communications between aircraft, ground stations and missile silos. Should the US ever have been involved in a nuclear exchange the 'go code' would have been transmitted via this network. Consisting of a string of alpha-numerics, these coded messages have been going out on HF since at least the early 1960s. The ground stations' initial call to all SAC (Strategic Air Command) aircraft, 'Skyking, Skyking, do not answer, do not answer', will be familiar to regular HF listeners. The broadcasts on HF-GCS are repeats of those going out on the former SAC's own group of frequencies which is known as Giant Talk. A basic form of security is the use of a channel designator such as 'Sierra 391', rather than the actual frequency. As with many military HF frequencies, they can be 'dead' for long periods.

Ground stations employ imaginative call-signs which are changed daily, examples being Acidman, Chipmouse, Big Daddy and Red Cedar. The other major HF network is the Canadian Military Aeronautical Communication System (MACS). Trenton in Ontario and St John's in Newfoundland can both be heard at times.

Nightwatch is an HF system used for communicating with airborne command post E-4 and E-6 aircraft, the so-called TACAMOs (TAke Charge and Move Out). Much like the old Mystic Star network now replaced by encrypted comms, the frequencies are identified by a designator such as Sierra 391, rather than the actual frequency. Much more can be found on the web about such activities. The US Navy has its own HF net which often involves aircraft as well as ships. US Coast Guard aircraft can sometimes be heard over the Eastern Seaboard of the USA talking to their bases. Other miscellaneous users of the HF band include anti-drug-running aircraft and the so-called Hurricane Hunters tracking storms.

The call-signs employed by military aircraft take many forms. Most common for RAF aircraft until recently was the tri-graph, eg ABC12. However, most first-line aircraft have adopted an alpha-numeric system usually changed every 24 hours, examples being 7NE44, a Chinook, and F5G20, a Puma. The first two characters are always a letter/number or number/letter sequence. The third character is always a letter and the three together are known as the call-sign root. The last two characters are the mission identifier and are always numbers allocated at random. If a flight of aircraft is operating the same mission, ie in formation, an additional suffix letter is used. Another style resembles the USAF tactical call-sign (Carbon Two, a Tornado). The RAF decided to fall in line with the ICAO system and registered a number of three-letter prefixes for training units, examples being VYT and CWL (Valley and Cranwell Training respectively). More are listed in Appendix 6.

RAF Air Support Command uses 'Ascot' as a prefix, the aircraft type and unit or base being identified as in the following examples, individual call-signs being numbered sequentially from the round figure quoted: 4000 – Hercules, RAF Lyneham; 5000 – Hercules, RAF Lyneham; 7500–7749 – BAe 125 of 32 Squadron, Northolt. Individual call-signs, eg Ascot 4609, are known as Task numbers.

Rafair is another prefix of long standing, used for transit purposes or overseas operations. Some RAF units have special call-signs reserved for formation flights. They include 'Cherwell' Formation (Oxford University Air Squadron) and Liver Formation (pronounced 'Lie-va') for Liverpool UAS. RAF Valley Hawks sometimes use 'Cobra' or 'Python' as well as 'Jester' and 'Mustang', the 'formation' prefix being dropped in fast jet operations. The USAF makes considerable use of so-called tactical call-signs such as Skull 20 (a B-52), the number being the pilot's personal designation. These prefixes are changed periodically but, having said that, there are many which have been retained for years, and some are included in Appendix 6.

When a formation is involved, the leader will handle all voice communications with the ground. To find out how many aircraft are in the flight, listen for a frequency change and count each aircraft checking in on the new channel. 'Shark 21 Flight, check' '2!', '3!','4!' etc. The same procedure is used for all formations, whether they be military or civil. Air Mobility Command transports generally use the aircraft serial, referred to as the 'tail number'. Alphanumeric codes are employed as well, eg Reach 7M8RH. On occasion the suffix has represented a particular exercise, eg 'FL' for 'Flintlock' and 'RF' for Reforger. The US Navy is another alpha-numeric user, Navy 6 Golf 086 for instance, the first two characters often referring to the code painted on the aircraft. Other foreign air forces use self-evident prefixes such as Danish, Saudi, etc. 'Aussie' identifies the Royal Australian Air Force and 'Kiwi' the Royal New Zealand AF; the Greeks use 'Hellenic Air Force' but the Norwegians hide behind 'Juliet Whiskey'. French Air Force transport aircraft often use 'Cotam', the initials of this arm of the Air Force, while the French Navy uses

'FMN' or sometimes France Marine. Mission and up to four figures is frequently heard in use by German military aircraft and also by aircraft of other countries, including the RAF.

Air-to-air refuelling

As an example of refuelling over the North Sea, Flamborough West flights will initially be working London Mil, perhaps on the same frequency if tanker and receiver are making their way north around the same time. London Mil may play a part in setting up and arranging the join-up, as the AR/IP (Air Refuelling Initial Point) is in their airspace. On handover to Scottish Mil, both will normally use the same frequency, with the receiver then only using the AR Primary (maybe after asking to switch to the tanker frequency). The tanker then identifies both as a 'Flight' in comms with ATC. Sometimes the receiver may stay in contact with ATC throughout. It is around this time that the join-up will be in progress with 'MARSA' being declared/accepted by the tanker, who will then be controlled by the receiver (squawking Standby) until they split. Military Accepts Responsibility for Separation of Aircraft (MARSA) applies to aircraft above FL245 that are under constant radar control. However, when aircraft join up with less than the 1,000ft minimum, then the radar unit is no longer responsible for separation and aircraft 'accept MARSA'.

Procedures and phraseology at military aerodromes

It is Ministry of Defence (MoD) policy to encourage civil use of military aerodromes where this does not conflict with military flying operations. While the same general rules and procedures apply to aircraft at all aerodromes, the specific requirements of military operations mean that the way they are applied often makes them appear quite different from those to which civilian pilots have become accustomed.

Precision approach radar (PAR) may be provided, which can be likened to a ground controlled ILS. The controller directs the pilot on to the final approach, and then gives heading directions to maintain his flight path on the runway centreline, telling him not to acknowledge such instructions unless requested. Once the aircraft reaches the glidepath the controller will tell the pilot regularly whether he is above or below it, but will not give specific rate of descent directions. The pilot is expected to make his own adjustments to follow the glideslope down to his decision height. On any instrument approach, the controller will say 'carry out cockpit checks, advise complete' before the aircraft turns on to the base leg, and 'check gear, acknowledge' during the final approach.

Civilian pilots must expect military traffic to be given priority as they tend to use a lot of fuel, and often do not carry much spare for diversion. Many military aerodromes expect visitors to carry out a standard overhead join. However, depending on the direction of your approach, ATC may direct you to join downwind, or on base leg. Circuit patterns are usually flown at heights which depend on aircraft type. For example, a turboprop trainer may fly the pattern at 1,000ft on QFE, light piston aeroplanes at 800ft, and, if traffic is mixed, fast jet traffic at 1,200 or 1,500ft. The 'military standard join' involves approaching parallel with the runway in use from an 'initial point' outside the Aerodrome Traffic Zone on the dead side of the runway centreline, at circuit height or lower. A call of 'initials' will be made at that 'initial point'. Some aircraft may approach at high speed for a 'run and break', as described above. Approximately 1–1½ minutes after calling 'initials' the aircraft will turn steeply, level or climbing to the circuit height, from the deadside to downwind, calling 'on the break' instead of the normal 'downwind' call. If the aerodrome has 'no dead side' (often when helicopters operate together with aeroplanes) the run in may take place over the runway itself. Any non-standard procedures would normally form part of the visiting aircraft brief.

Most military circuit patterns are oval. The downwind leg is flown closer than at most civilian aerodromes, because the turn after take-off, and the final turn, both involve continuous 180 degree turns. The 'downwind' call is standard, but the call of 'final' is given as the aircraft starts its final turn at the end of the downwind leg.

Intentions transmitted by military pilots are slightly different from those found in CAP 413, the civil phraseology guide. 'Roll' effectively equates to 'touch and go'. 'Land' equates to 'full stop'. The term 'overshoot' may be heard, which means a pilot will make a low approach to the runway followed by a go-around, while confusingly an instruction to 'go-around' is the same as an 'orbit'. ATC do not take responsibility for separating aircraft in the visual circuit. A visiting civilian pilot is expected to fit in with the other traffic, and if that is not possible, go-around. Priority is normally given to instrument traffic, and ATC will transmit the position of that instrument traffic with its type.

MARSA – Military Accepts Responsibility for Separation of Aircraft

The nature of some military operations prohibits compliance with certain ATC regulations. For example, clearance may be granted for a formation to enter controlled airspace provided the individual aircraft can maintain separation from each other visually or by the use of airborne radar. They must also be able to communicate with the formation leader who is in contact with the controlling authority. A formation may therefore be considered as a single unit for separation purposes provided that the formation elements are contained within one mile laterally and longitudinally and are at the same level. Standard UK military call-sign procedures apply to formations. In instances where there is any doubt, such as when working USAF or foreign aircraft whose call-sign procedures may be different, the suffix 'flight' is used to indicate on R/T and landline that the call refers to a formation.

Examples: 'Blackcat'   – denotes a UK formation
              'Blackcat 1'   – denotes a UK single element
              'Deadly 31 Flight'   – denotes a USAF formation
              'Deadly 31'   – denotes a USAF singleton

Weather colour codes

In addition to a normal TAF or METAR, military aerodromes use a colour code, which is a form of shorthand for their crews to reinforce the information in the main message. The meaning of each colour is listed below. Civilian PPL holders without instrument qualifications are advised that any code except 'blue' or 'white' may indicate serious problems, and even 'white' is no guarantee that the weather is good, even at the time of the report.

Colour	Minimum base of lowest cloud (Scattered or more)	Minimum reported visibility at aerodrome level
Blue	2500ft	8km
White	1500ft	5km
Green	700ft	3,700m
Yellow	300ft	1,600m
Amber	200ft	800m
Red	Below 200ft (or sky obscured)	Below 800m
Black	Aerodrome unavailable for reasons other than cloud or visibility	

Chapter 18

Air band radios

THE POTENTIAL PURCHASER is faced with a bewildering choice of sets from around £15 to well over £1,000. The major drawback with all the cheaper receivers is the absence of an accurate tuning facility, so you are never quite sure to which frequency you are tuned until you have listened for a while. Some radios cover the entire air band with a 1-inch scale and if, say, 124.2 is tuned, transmissions on the adjacent frequencies of 124.0, 124.05, 124.10 and 124.15, and 124.25, 124.30, 124.35 and so on, may be picked up as well. They are not usually as loud as the primary frequency being monitored, but are annoying and confusing, particularly when a powerful transmission from a nearer source swamps the aircraft in which you are interested. A longer scale makes tuning easier but has no effect on the lack of discrimination.

The answer is a scanning receiver, better known simply as a scanner. They are divided into hand-held portables and desktop sets, often referred to as base stations. A hand-held is very useful in that it can double for use at home or outdoors and will usually cost less than a base station having similar frequency coverage. Desktops are, however, usually easier to operate, as there is more room available on the front panel for additional buttons and controls, together with larger frequency and channel display. Often – but not always – in the case of budget models, base receivers give better technical performance than a hand-held in terms of their ability to receive weaker signals. A word of caution: some hand-held scanners have no keypad for entering frequencies. This is done via multi-function buttons. Younger enthusiasts, having grown up with technology, will have no difficulty coping with this, but their elders may find it unnecessarily complicated and definitely not user-friendly. It is possible, with some sets, to download frequencies from a PC.

There have been many changes in the scanner market since the previous edition of this book. Legislation has come into force throughout the EEC to cover the use of dangerous materials in solder in electrical products. Such metals as mercury, lead and cadmium have been banned on items imported to, and sold, within the community, especially in the solder of electronic products including radio scanners. As virtually all these items are made in the Far East, it meant that the manufacturers had to change dramatically the way their scanners were produced.

Some manufacturers, including Yupiteru, were not interested in implementing these changes, due to the high costs involved, and the reduced market on a worldwide basis. Sadly this meant the demise of the much-admired Yupiteru sets, including the excellent MVT 7100. Also in recent years scanners have become more 'computer friendly', incorporating technology from the cell phone market. With the exception of most sets in the lower price scanner market virtually all the others are now full VHF/UHF capable.

At the bottom end of the market, the reduced size of many sets, and the incorporation of a 'menu'-driven flexible key operation means these sets no longer incorporate an alphanumeric (numbered) keypad. They now have fewer operation keys, with a varying system controlled through a 'function' button, which operates the same way as a 'shift' key on a computer keyboard. This has reduced manufacturing costs. No longer do scanners have internal memory capacitors, or crystals. They are now fitted with the ubiquitous PC 'chip', a 'solid state' component, and therefore cheaper and more reliable. Firstly we should deal with the hand-held radios, as they are now more numerous than base sets.

The good news is that you can buy a fully operational hand-held air band scanner for well under £100. A few years ago the cheapest scanner on the market was the old WIN 108 at £149! These reasonably cheap sets only cover the civil VHF air band, but for £140 upwards all scanners cover the full VHF/UHF bands, for those wishing to monitor the military. In fact, most stretch from at least 25MHz to 1300MHz.

These sets can be divided into two types – the keypad-operated ones, and the 'menu'-driven ones. Examples are the Alinco DJ-X3 and DJ-X30, the tiny Alinco DJ-X7, the Yaesu VR120, and the Icom IC-R5. All these sets are 'computer friendly', and with the right cable connection, and PC programme acquired separately, can be used in conjunction with a computer database, which can be downloaded to the set.

One should be aware that most manufacturers no longer supply rechargeable batteries or power supply charge as standard, although there are some exceptions. When we move to the more sophisticated sets, then batteries/battery packs are usually, though not always, included in the box. Many of these top-of-the-market sets in the price band from about £200 upwards are now moving away from the familiar 'banks and channels', to 'dynamic programming' which is more complicated to use when manually entering frequencies, but a lot easier when programming from a computer.

The advantage of this type of programming is that no group/system/bank/channel is wasted. The user can have a memory as flexible as they want it, without wasting the storage capability of the set. Systems, groups, and even individual channels can be specifically named using the set's built-in menu. Programs to help with this can be downloaded from the Internet, or in many cases from the manufacturer's website. It is obvious that these sets are really for the experienced scanner user, and should be avoided by a beginner who has never used one before.

Moving on to base scanners for use at home or in the car, the range incorporating air band has drastically reduced, mainly because of the EEC restrictions previously described. The expensive AOR and ICOM ranges and Yaesu are still there, but within the purchasing power of the average enthusiast there are only two Bearcat models available for less than £300. There is now nothing below £200 unless one buys second-hand.

Scanner basics

Scan
Scan is the term used to describe the type of operation where the receiver runs through frequencies that have been pre-programmed into the equipment memory channels by the user. For example, local airport and area control frequencies. The receiver scans through these memory channels and stops when a signal is detected. The number of memories that can be scanned depends on the make of the receiver, but most offer a minimum of 20, with the facility to 'lockout' or temporarily remove from the scanning cycle those memories that are not of interest at the moment.

Search
Search is a term often confused with Scan and this is the other main feature on most receivers. If you don't know the exact frequency that a particular service operates on, but you have a rough idea, or want to monitor activity on the civil or military air bands in general, then use can be made of the search facility. The user programs into the receiver the upper and lower

frequency limits of the band to be searched and also the frequency step size that the receiver is to search with. The receiver then automatically searches over the set range and stops when a signal is detected.

Some of the more sophisticated sets offer a whole range of different signal detection systems for use in the search and scan modes. These are designed to prevent the receiver from staying on one frequency for too long if a continuous signal is present. You should decide whether you are going to make the most use of either the scan or search function and choose the receiver with the facilities to suit. The priority channel function, sometimes called the AUX or auxiliary facility, allows any one pre-set channel to be interrogated automatically every two seconds so that you won't miss anything on, say, the local tower frequency.

Frequency coverage and tuning step size

Ensure that the bands you want to listen to are present as, in general, only the so-called continuous coverage scanners will include the UHF aircraft band. Some scanners claim to cover the UHF band but miss out sections of it. The coverage you should be looking for is 108.00 to 137.00MHz and 225 to 400MHz, the civil and military air bands respectively. Another consideration is that many of the receivers on offer will only tune in multiples of 5kHz as a result of the American method of assigning channels. This can be a problem in Britain as most of the channels are allocated in multiples of 12.5, 6.25 or the new 8.33kHz VHF air band spacing. Depending on the filter fitted to the receiver, the recovered audio can, in some cases sound very distorted, as the receiver cannot tune exactly to the wanted signal. The better receivers let you select from several tuning steps. Many budget scanners offer air band coverage but don't include the UHF military air band range. Others do cover that range but some can't be switched from FM to AM bands aside from 108–137MHz.

Some scanners only allow 5, 10, 15 or 25kHz steps and although 5kHz steps will usually bring you near enough, you will find that it takes two-and-a-half-times longer to search across a given range in the inappropriate 5kHz steps rather than in 12.5kHz increments. Most en route control centre frequencies are transmitted from up to four remote locations to render the coverage as wide as possible. To eliminate the characteristic screech, known as a heterodyne, when more than one station transmits simultaneously, an offset carrier system is used. The offsets are ±5kHz for a two-carrier system, ±7.5kHz and 0kHz for a three-carrier, and ±7.5kHz and ±2.5kHz for a four-carrier system. Therefore, where the sensitivity of the receiver allows, reception may be improved by tuning the set slightly higher or lower than the published frequency.

Close Call

Certain receivers in the Uniden range incorporate a function that revolutionises scanner performance. Known as Close Call, it looks for active frequencies within range of the unit and automatically tunes them in. It is no longer necessary to have huge memory banks full of frequencies or to search frantically through the bands looking for a certain transmission. A specific waveband can be targeted, such as VHF air band when listening at an airport, so as to avoid picking up unwanted transmissions from other services. It is an amazing technical leap, and Alinco has since introduced a similar feature called Flashtune that automatically tunes the receiver to a nearby transmitter.

Antennas (aerials)

Radio waves are attenuated (weakened) by a lot of things, including buildings. If you can get the antenna that is connected to your scanner outdoors and as high as possible, you will hear very much more. A further method of improving reception is a pre-amplifier (usually abbreviated to pre-amp), which fits between the antenna and the receiver on a hand-held model or inside the case of a base station. The device boosts the received signals and feeds them into the receiver. Results can vary but it may be possible to receive, for example, the ground transmissions from a distant airport that were previously audible only as 'noise'. Better quality pre-amps have filters that can be switched in to suit the frequency range in which you are interested.

Computer interface
If you are interested in finding new frequencies or logging channel usage, then this is the option to look for. Many receivers now boast computer ports and an increasing amount of software is available, making it very easy to get a sophisticated system running. If the set has a squelch relay output, you can connect a tape recorder and monitor frequencies over a long period of time. Doing this permits you to compress several days' activity into just a few hours.

Birdies
All radios rely on internal oscillators, crystals etc in order to operate. With the extremely wide coverage offered by most modern scanners, it is inevitable that the receiver will sweep across some of its own, internally generated frequencies (and often their harmonics and mixing products). These are sometimes sufficient to stop a search when there is nothing really there! They can also block a frequency you want to listen to. Manufacturers try their best to avoid the worst by careful design, but it is impossible to eliminate them all. A good way to deal with them, once identified, is to use the lockout facility. Some manufacturers list the offending frequencies in the handbook. Good news is that on some new designs it is possible to move the birdies if they are blocking a useful frequency.

Specifications
These can be very misleading! One of the best ways to see if a receiver is up to the mark is to read the reviews, particularly where measurements have been made. This is because the manufacturer's figures are usually a minimum standard and many models are much better than the published figures.

Sensitivity
This is the ability to hear signals and should be lower than 1milliV for 12dB S/N on AM and 0.5milliV for 12dB S/N on NBFM.

Selectivity
This is the ability to reject unwanted signals on adjacent frequencies. The best choice seems to be around ±7.5 kHz at –6dB for most services in Britain, but up to ±12 kHz at –6dB is usable.

Spurious response/Image rejection
This is the ability to reject unwanted signals. The image rejection is usually a problem with older designs of receiver and can result in other transmissions interfering with the wanted signal, as is possible with the lower frequency ranges. A minimum of 50dB rejection should be expected for both image and other spurious responses. However, a lower figure is to be expected on hand-held models as a result of design economies in order to get the circuitry to fit inside the outer case.

Batteries
Hand-held radios tend to eat batteries so investment in rechargeables and a transformer for home use is obviously desirable. The former are usually supplied with the set as standard, along with a mains transformer. It is a good idea to obtain a second rechargeable battery pack so that the two can be alternated; life between charges is only a few hours.

There are a great number of features on today's radios and it is important to find out exactly what is or is not included in the purchase price. Some require separate aerials, others power supplies and battery chargers. All the specialised dealers hold stocks of accessories, such as aerials, headphones, earpieces, spare crystals and assorted plugs, leads and adaptors.

As has been stated before, VHF reception is 'quasi line-of-sight', so the higher the aerial the better the result. If the usual telescopic aerial or rubber antenna supplied with the set proves inadequate, a remote air band antenna can be purchased. A wide variety of these are available for outside or loft mounting. They can in turn be improved by attention to the coaxial cable used to connect aerial to receiver. If by re-routeing it you can shorten it, great, but if you can't get it any shorter than about 40ft (13m), consider using UR67 coaxial cable – expensive but offering much lower reception losses than cheaper cable.

For VHF air band the ground plane type of aerial can be recommended. One designed for air band use will give better performance than almost any other aerial, including wide band types intended for general use with scanners. Ideally, it should be mounted as high as possible in the clear, but is still capable of good results if left swinging from a rafter in your loft!

However, if you want to listen to military UHF as well as civil VHF, an aerial is needed that will cover the whole range from 100 to 500MHz. The professionals use a discone aerial for this purpose. Although looking like a demented hedgehog, they are the only simple aerial to work over a wide frequency range and the performance is first class. For those who want to fit an air band aerial to a vehicle, a vertical whip aerial is easy to fix and use, especially with a magnetic mount. As all signals in the VHF air band are vertically polarised, it is likely to be quite efficient.

Newcomers to air band listening may want to buy one of the more inexpensive sets first to familiarise themselves with what is being said and its meaning and perhaps move up to a more ambitious receiver later on. Second-hand models are often advertised in radio magazines and many dealers offer a good selection of trade-ins. It can also be argued that right from the start investment in a proper air band scanner is desirable. As ever, it all depends on money!

The performance of some advanced scanners can be boosted by computer control. With the aid of software they can be run from a PC via a standard serial lead. By exploiting the memory capabilities of the PC, more memory banks can be programmed and, if required, they can be uploaded to the scanner's internal memory for subsequent use without the computer. An 'activity count' mode is available where you can set the scanner searching a given bank of memory channels with the program performing a percentage count of the activity on each. This can be for virtually any period you like and a printed report is supplied at the end! This is very useful for assessing the listening possibilities of particular air band frequencies.

Those with access to the internet will find an almost infinite range of aviation information, including new frequencies and procedures discovered by enthusiasts and unusual visiting aircraft, often with advance warning of their arrival.

ATC Computer Simulations

Air band enthusiasts may want to go a stage further and learn some of the techniques themselves via a computer simulation. By far the best is the London Control ATC Simulation System, an amazingly convincing piece of computer software. It is an incredibly accurate representation of the airways, terminal areas and control zones in England and Wales. For the flying side of the operation there are several excellent flight simulations available, notably Microsoft Flight Sim. RC Simulations and Transair Pilot Shop stock a wide range of ATC and flight sim software; their addresses are on page 143.

IC-RX7 scanner.

Intek AR-109 scanner.

AOR AR-Mini scanner.

*GRE PSR-500 scanner (all via Roger Hall,
RadioUser magazine).*

A selection of air band radios currently available
Price range £60–£100
Uniden 72XLT – Hand-held scanner. VHF/UHF air band.
Uniden 30XLT – Hand-held scanner. VHF air band.
Uniden 92XLT – Hand-held scanner. VHF air band.
Maycom AR108 – Hand-held scanner. VHF air band,
Alinco DJ-X3 – Hand-held scanner. VHF/UHF air band.
Intek AR-109 – Hand-held scanner. VHF air band.

Price range £105–£150
Yaesu VR-120D – Hand-held scanner. VHF/UHF air band.
Uniden UBC 3500XLT – Hand-held scanner. VHF/UHF band.

Price range £160–£200
Yaesu VR-500 – Hand-held scanner. VHF/UHF air band.
Uniden UBC 785XLT – Desk-top scanner. VHF/UHF air band.

Price range £200–£300
ICOM IC-RX7 – Hand-held scanner. VHF/UHF air band.
Alinco DJ-X2000 – Hand-held scanner. VHF/UHF air band.
AOR AR-Mini – Hand-held scanner. VHF/UHF air band.

Price range £400–£500
AOR 8600 Mk II – Desk-top scanner. VHF/UHF air band.

Principal air band and hobby suppliers
Air Supply, www.airsupply.co.uk Tel: 0113 250 9581
AOR UK, Unit 9, Dimple Road Business Centre, Dimple Road, Matlock, Derbyshire DE4 3JX.
   Tel: 01629 581222
The Aviation Hobby Centre, Visitors' Centre, Main Terminal, Birmingham Airport B26 3QJ.
   Tel: 0121 7822112
The Aviation Shop, Terminal 1 Arrivals, Manchester Airport M90 1QX. Tel: 0161 489 2444.
   Also in Aviation Viewing Park.
Haydon Communications, Unit 1, Purfleet Industrial Estate, Off Juliette Way, Aveley, Essex
   RM15 4YA. Tel: 01708 862524.
Javiation, PO Box 708, Bradford BD2 3XA. Tel: 01274 639503.
Lowe Electronics, Sandyhill Park, Middleton, Matlock, Derbyshire DE4 4LR. Tel: 01629 820820.
ML&S Martin Lynch, Outline House, 73 Guildford Street, Chertsey, Surrey KT16 9AS.
   Tel: 0845 2300 599.
Moonraker, Cranfield Road, Woburn Sands, Bucks MK17 8UR. Tel: 01908 281705
Nevadaradio, Unit 1, Fitzherbert Spur, Portsmouth, Hants PO6 1TT. Tel: 023 9231 3090.
RC Simulations, The Hangar, Unit 6, 306 Industrial Estate, 242–244 Broomhill Road, Bristol BS4
   5RG. Tel: 0117 9715000
Short Wave Shop, 18 Fairmile Road, Christchurch, Dorset BH23 23LJ. Tel: 01202 490099
Thunderpole, 1 Hartburn Close, Crow End Ind Est, Northampton NN3 9UE. Tel 01604 402403
Transair Pilot Shop, Shoreham Airport, Shoreham-by-Sea, West Sussex BN43 5PA.
   Tel: 01273 466000. Central London Shop: 50a Cambridge Street, Victoria SW1V 4QQ.
   Tel: 020 7976 6787. Coventry Airport: CV8 3AZ. Tel: 02476 306033. 1st Floor, Aviation
   House, Gloucestershire Airport, Cheltenham GL51 6SR. Tel: 01452 856749
Waters and Stanton, Spa House, 22 Main Road, Hockley, Essex SS5 4QS. Tel: 01702 206835.
   Scottish Store: 20 Woodside Way, Glenrothes, Fife KY7 5DF. Tel: 01592 756962

Chapter 19

Charts and related documents

ALMOST AS IMPORTANT as an air band radio itself is the acquisition of a set of radio navigation charts. They are essential to build up an overall picture of the UK airways system and the positions of its beacons and reporting points.

En route charts are published by three organisations for the United Kingdom; the Royal Air Force, Aerad and Jeppesen. The US Air Force produces its own charts but these are more difficult to obtain. Obviously the information on the different charts is fundamentally the same, but the presentation differs quite considerably. There is also some variation in the areas covered. The RAF covers the UK with two charts; UK(H)2 for high altitudes and UK(L)2 for low altitudes.

Aerad charts for the UK cover high altitude (EU H/L2 and EU H/L8) at a scale of 30 miles to the inch. Low altitude over the UK and Ireland is covered by UK(L)2 to a scale of about 17 miles to the inch. Aerad also produce a wide range of other related documentation, including Standard Instrument Departure charts, Standard Arrival charts and airport and apron layouts. Aerad's other important publication, much prized by enthusiasts, is the *Europe and Middle East Supplement*, one of a set of four which cover the entire world. It is a soft-backed book packed with information on airports, including their aids, runway lengths and radio frequencies.

The other chart publisher is Jeppesen Sanderson Inc, an American firm whose main distributor in the UK is CSE Aviation at Oxford Airport. Four sheets cover the UK, two for high level (Ref E(HI)1 and 2) and two for low altitudes (Ref E(LO)1, and 3). The company also produces a wide variety of associated data, the most important of which are airport approach charts.

The CAA distributes a wide range of charts, including topographical maps, which are of only limited use to air band listeners, SIDs and STARs. The CAA is of course responsible for the UK Aeronautical Information Publication, once known as the *Air Pilot*. This is really the bible for aviators in Britain's airspace but the bulky three-volume document has now been replaced by a CD-ROM updated monthly. The AIP itself is viewable at no charge on the AIS website, www.ais.org.uk It is divided into general information such as ATC rules and procedures, details of each aerodrome and an en route section listing all air routes and sub-divisions of airspace. At the time of writing, it was announced that CAA is to hand over responsibility for its data production to NATS.

At first sight, radio navigation charts are a perplexing welter of intersecting lines, symbols and figures, but, like any other maps, there is a key and with a few minutes' study they become logical. The radio beacons are identified by name and a three- or two-letter abbreviation. The Wallasey DVOR, for example, may be referred to by ATC and aircraft as Wallasey or Whiskey Alpha Lima. The frequency of 114.1MHz on which the beacon radiates will be adjacent to its name on the chart. Also shown on the chart are the designations of airways, their bearings in both directions, the distances in nautical miles between reporting points, the heights of their bases and upper limits and the lowest available cruising levels.

Many of the charts are stocked by air band radio suppliers but they can also be purchased direct from the publishers or their agents at the addresses listed below. Out-of-date charts are sometimes advertised in the aviation press at reasonably low prices and can also be found on eBay. Provided that they are not too old, say more than 12 months, they can still be useful.

Other information sources:
CAP 413 RT Phraseology. The bible for correct UK phraseology. As with the other Civil Aviation publications listed below, it is available for free download on the CAA website.
CAP 413 Supplement. A Quick Reference Guide to UK Phraseology for Commercial Air Transport Pilots.
CAP 413 Supplement 2. A Reference Guide to UK Phraseology for Aerodrome Drivers.
CAP 493 Manual of Air Traffic Services Part 1. All you ever wanted to know about UK ATC and a lot you didn't. Student controllers will have to learn most of this in detail! Note that MATS Part 2 is not available to the public; this is the section unique to each ATC unit, whether it be airport or area control centre. It covers all local procedures in detail.
CAP 427 Flight Information Service and the FISO Licence.
CAP 410 Manual of Flight Information Services Phraseology for AFISOs.
CAP 452 Aeronautical Radio Station Operator's Guide. Phraseology for Air/Ground Operators.
CAP 745 Aircraft Emergencies: Considerations for Air Traffic Controllers.
CAP 637 Visual Aids Handbook: A compendium of visual aids intended for the guidance of pilots and personnel engaged in the handling of aircraft.
CAP 624 Rating Requirements for Air Traffic Controllers. Sub-divided into a number of parts, this details syllabus for training in each ATC discipline.
CAP 722 Unmanned Aircraft System Operations in UK Airspace.

A new easy-to-use quick-reference guide for commercial pilots on radiotelephony (RTF) phraseology has been released by the Civil Aviation Authority and NATS. The booklet follows on from the *Top Ten Tips* leaflet and the *Communication Errors* DVD, both released last year. Standard phraseology is designed to protect against communication errors and good RTF discipline is a significant factor in enhancing safety. The guide is available in both a printed ring-bound checklist format and also online as an interactive version. It provides details of the exact phraseology to be used by pilots throughout all stages of a flight from start-up to approach and landing. A separate section deals with emergency communications.

Errors of communication are known to be a significant contributory factor in incidents such as level busts and runway incursions. Clear and unambiguous communication between pilots and controllers using the standard words and phrases contained in the guides can help to reduce the risk. The documents are supplements to the official CAA radiotelephony guide, CAP413, but provide the information in a more user-friendly way and give background explanations to some of the more common situations. Further versions of the document are planned to address the needs of airside drivers and GA pilots.

SKYbrary
SKYbrary, Eurocontrol's new Wikipedia-style website. has now been online for a some time at www.skybrary.aero It aims to be the single point of reference for aviation safety knowledge and has been launched in partnership with the International Civil Aviation Organisation and the Flight Safety Foundation. Initially, SKYbrary hosted some 1,000 articles covering 15 subject areas, including safety critical issues such as level busts and runway incursions. Articles are added regularly and search words in the articles link to additional information in both SKYbrary and other external sites. The Wikipedia format means that visitors can contribute articles and information. An open discussion forum aims to enhance visitors' awareness of safety issues. Although obviously compiled for aviation professionals and often quite technical,

there is much of interest here for air band listeners, especially in the section on air–ground communication.

YouTube
There is a lot of ATC-related content on this site, most of it American.

Flight tracking sites
These include openATC, a worldwide network of ADS-B receiver stations, permitting anyone to see where aircraft were located five minutes ago. To find a specific flight, enter in the search box either its flight number or any part of the-3 letter ICAO airline code.

Suppliers of airways charts, flight guides and related material
CSE Aviation Ltd (Jeppesen Agents), Oxford Airport, Kidlington,Oxford OX5 1RA.
Royal Air Force, No 1 Aeronautical Documents Unit, RAF Northolt, West End Road, Ruislip, Middlesex HA4 6NG.
Civil Aviation Authority, Printing and Publishing, Greville House, 37 Gratton Road, Cheltenham, Gloucestershire GL50 2BN.
Air Supply, www.airsupply.co.uk.
See also the list on page 143.

Chapter 20

Virtual radar for the enthusiast

SBS-1 IS NOW established as the most exciting air band development since scanning radios were introduced in the 1970s. A truly amazing piece of kit is now within the grasp of any enthusiast with around £300 to £400 to spare. Now you can monitor aircraft on a real time virtual radar display, almost like the ATC professionals. It even has a few features that controllers using older radar equipment would love to have! Indeed, the manufacturers of the SBS-1, Kinetic Aviation Products Ltd, hope to offer it to smaller airfields as a significant aid to operations. With some development to meet CAA requirements, this type of equipment might one day supersede, or at least backup, vastly more expensive current radar systems.

The SBS-1 and its more recent competitor, the AirNav RadarBox, relies on aircraft Mode-S and/or ADS-B transponders to perform its magic. Equipped with a small antenna, it is simply connected by USB lead to a laptop or desk PC loaded with the BaseStation software provided. On launch, it immediately begins to auto-detect suitably equipped aircraft in the vicinity, the process taking between 40 and 70 seconds. Range, as with a VHF antenna, will depend on location, results in a city, for example, leaving much to be desired.

The virtual radar screen takes up most of the left side of the picture, the rest being taken up with a window listing all the aircraft displayed. This contains details of aircraft status, ie climbing, descending or in level flight, call sign, altitude, speed and several other parameters. Colour can be used to show whether an aircraft is climbing, descending or level. This window can be resized or removed and the radar display expanded to fill the whole screen if you wish. It is also possible to confine the radar picture to any required area, such as the airspace around your local airport, while retaining a separate picture over a much wider area. In other words, two active radar screens side-by-side. As with professional radars, each aircraft has a data block, but these take up a lot of space with unnecessary information such as bearing from the ground station, exact height, for example, 25,525ft. Fortunately, these data blocks can be customised as required.

Now, what makes it work? Since March 2005, the CAA has introduced Mode-S airspace initially in the London TMA. Later it will spread to the Manchester and Scottish TMAs, together with some major airways and control areas. Mode-S is a Secondary Surveillance Radar (SSR) technique currently on two levels: Elementary and Enhanced. Both provide greater integrity of data than the current system by practically eliminating false responses and garbling of data labels, particularly in busy airspace such as holding stacks. Additionally, the Enhanced level provides the capability to down-link extra data from the aircraft cockpit. Currently, the SBS-1 will 'see' only about 50% of traffic within range, another 30% may be listed but not tracked for various reasons. Light aircraft – and there is obviously no way of telling how many – may be there too but unequipped and therefore not visible. The numbers displayed on screen will obviously increase as more aircraft are equipped with Mode-S.

ADS-B is the acronym for Automatic Dependent Surveillance–Broadcast. Aircraft equipped with ADS-B broadcast their precise position in space via a digital datalink along with other data, including airspeed, altitude, and whether the aircraft is turning, climbing, or descending. ADS-B receivers that are integrated into the air traffic control system or installed aboard other aircraft provide users with an accurate depiction of real-time traffic, both in the air and on the ground. The system relies on the satellite-based global positioning system to determine an aircraft's precise location in space. It then converts the position into a digital code, which is combined with the flight details.

The digital code, containing all of this information, is updated several times a second and broadcast from the aircraft on a discrete frequency, called a datalink. Other aircraft and ground stations within about 150 miles receive the datalink broadcasts and display the information in user-friendly format on a computer screen. Pilots in the cockpit see the traffic on a Cockpit Display of Traffic Information (CDTI). Controllers on the ground can see the ADS-B targets on their regular traffic display screen, along with other radar targets. ADS-B has been in use over the Pacific and other areas outside conventional radar range for several years.

The SBS-1 has an interface mechanism for connectivity to a range of popular radio scanners, thus allowing users to watch aircraft and listen to air traffic in a single consolidated action. With two mouse clicks, an attached radio scanner will be tuned automatically to the frequencies selected. Frequencies can either be entered freehand or associated with waypoints. Another accessory is a pre-amp mounted directly behind the equipment. This will increase the receiving range quite considerably.

Software allows the user to load the equipment with the registration or call-sign to provide an audible alert when one or more particular aircraft are on the system. It can also be set up for an alert when an emergency transponder squawk is received. Another useful feature is the ability to lock on to a particular aircraft, making it the centre of the display for as long as it is in range.

A wide range of free downloads are available, most of them created by ordinary SBS users. Some of the programs have proper Windows installation routines but many are just ZIP files containing new data sets or maybe a document explaining how to change SBS settings. For the latter files it is strongly recommended that the included instructions are read carefully. If a download involves making changes you are not familiar with – such as editing an INI file in Notepad – it is wise not to attempt to make such changes until you clearly understand what is involved.

The many downloads include the UK airway system, control areas and control zones, as well as ILS runway centrelines out to ten nautical miles. Permanent Danger Areas, Prohibited and Restricted Airspace and a number of military applications, including AWACS orbit areas and Air-to-Air Refuelling Areas can be added. Waypoint and radio frequency files are available, together with the links required for the scanner interface. The default setting shows the flag of the country from which a particular aircraft originates but if you prefer the registration prefix, a downloadable file will enable this to be displayed instead.

The designers of the SBS-1 soon released a major upgrade to the system's BaseStation software. The upgrade, known as Snoopy, builds upon the previous BaseStation's virtual radar display by adding an embedded database and additional reporting and logging software to allow historical analysis of aircraft sightings. To this has been added an open database interface and data socket that together allow third-party software developers to create powerful companion applications.

When SBS-1 first appeared early in 2006 some aviation professionals voiced concern about the implications of virtual radar and wanted a ban on the general sale of these devices. They feared that people might report incidents of supposed separation losses to the press or, in an unlikely worst case scenario, an evildoer could use a transceiver to direct aircraft on collision courses by means of bogus instructions. A Sunday newspaper published a predictably alarmist article about the equipment and its supposed usefulness to terrorists. This was rapidly refuted by enthusiasts for a variety of reasons and the story sank without trace.

The SBS-1 is designed and produced in the UK, and Martin Lynch and Sons provide Radio Scanner Interface for the SBS-1 and full technical support for the product where an answer is urgently required. For more general information, the manufacturer provides comprehensive downloadable material and a user forum. There is also at least one SBS user group. It will be interesting to see how this revolution in spotting resources develops, as there seems to be no end to its possibilities. The first time I saw it up and running at a friend's house, I was astounded. The picture of North West England and the Irish Sea looked almost exactly like the professional radar I am used to, only more colourful! Truly a revolution in aircraft spotting capability.

John Locker tells me that Map Mode S is going live soon (see planeplotter.com for current status). This means that SBS-1 virtual radar users pool their map information via a hub and it is then sent back to their screens en masse, theoretically providing full UK coverage. Bearing in mind that there are lots of users near to airfields, an enthusiast in the north of England should be able to 'see' taxying traffic at Heathrow and Prestwick. Indeed almost anywhere in Europe. The downside is that the CAA is insisting on a five-minute delay, rather than viewing in real time. Meanwhile, data released by CAA shows that many pilots flying outside controlled airspace could enhance their safety by making better use of current transponder equipment fitted to their aircraft.

A relatively new procedure being undertaken by NATS allocates transponder codes to aircraft receiving an air traffic service from London Information. Although the Flight Information Service Officers providing the service have no radar, the unique code allocated can be seen by other radar controllers and tells them that the aircraft in question is currently on the London Information frequency. This enables them to pass any relevant safety information to the aircraft, such as warnings of impending airspace infringements or navigational advice and assistance if an infringement has occurred.

The CAA has introduced a new method for allocating a unique number for every UK-registered aircraft, known as the International Civil Aviation Organisation (ICAO) 24-bit aircraft address. One of the primary uses of the address is the unique identification of an aircraft via its Mode S transponder. An ICAO 24-bit aircraft address will now be allocated to every UK-registered aircraft regardless of whether the individual aircraft will ever be fitted with a Mode S transponder. The address is unique to a particular airframe for the period that the aircraft remains UK-registered.

If an aircraft is fitted with Mode S, then the address has a number of uses for ATC and other services, such as airborne collision avoidance systems. If an aircraft is fitted with an emergency locator transmitter then this can also use the same address to identify the aircraft to search and rescue services. A CAA spokesman said: 'The move to auto-allocation of 24-bit idents is designed to improve our administrative process, and removes the need for aircraft owners to apply separately for an address. Currently, owners who require an address to be allocated must make a separate application to the CAA. Under the new process, the address will be automatically allocated by the CAA's Aircraft Registration Section as part of the existing registration application process. All those aircraft currently registered that do not have an address already will have one allocated en bloc. Details of the allocated addresses will then be available via the G-INFO UK Register database, thereby eliminating the need for individual requests for allocations to be made.' The system of automatically allocating ICAO 24-bit aircraft addresses to every registered aircraft is already in use in the USA, Canada and Switzerland.

Thanks go to John Locker for explaining and demonstrating the workings and capabilities of SBS-1. John is a satellite communications consultant, broadcaster and free lance journalist and his fascinating website is at www.satcom.website.orange.co.uk

Chapter 21

Unlawful interference

THE CONTINUING POSSIBILITY of airborne terrorism means that fighter aircraft are always ready to counter it. Each state enjoys exclusive sovereignty over the airspace above its territory and territorial waters. Consequently, no aircraft may enter its airspace without prior permission or authorisation. Each state will react to an intruder according to its own interpretation of the risk being faced. A trigger could be a single event or a combination of small errors. Historically, actions resulting in a scramble of QRA (Quick Reaction Alert) aircraft have been: unauthorised deviation from the cleared flight profile; loss of radio contact, particularly if associated with a flight profile deviation; unauthorised SSR transponder code changes or extended use of the Ident feature (the aircraft position symbol will pulse on the radar display); use of non-standard phraseology by the crew or other actions that could be construed as a covert attempt to alert agencies to a situation on board; and notification of a threat from official or non-official sources.

Some nations, such as France, have a very overt reaction policy. For example, fighters are scrambled against any aircraft failing to establish two-way communication as it enters their airspace. Having scrambled, they will often complete the interception, even though communications may subsequently have been re-established. In contrast, the UK has adopted a slightly less overt threat-based Air Defence posture, which is changed constantly to meet the perceived threat to UK airspace and the homeland. Consequently, over the UK it is highly unlikely that civil aircrew will see RAF QRA aircraft at close quarters unless all other methods of confirming the integrity of the flight deck have been exhausted. Standard procedure is for the interceptor to follow in trail about a mile behind with transponder inactivated to avoid a TCAS alert.

If the airline crew are aware of the presence of an interceptor, they must inform ATC and try to contact it on 121.5MHz and/or 243.0MHz, the VHF and UHF international distress frequencies, respectively. They must then comply with all instructions. Non-compliance will obviously give the agencies on the ground cause for greater concern. If radio contact between the two aircraft is established, but communication in a common language is not possible, the following internationally agreed phrases are used to convey instructions and obtain acknowledgements:

Intercepting aircraft phrase	Meaning
Call-sign	What is your call-sign?
Follow	Follow me
Descend	Descend for landing
You land	Land at this aerodrome
Proceed	You may proceed

Intercepted aircraft phrase	Meaning
Call-sign	My call-sign is …
Wilco	Understood, will comply
Cannot	Unable to comply
Repeat	Repeat your instruction
Am lost	Position unknown
Mayday	Mayday
Hijack	I have been hijacked
Land (place name)	I request to land at (place name)
Descent	I require descent

The key recommendations for pilots and aircraft operating in UK airspace to ensure that any event is handled in the most appropriate manner are: be aware of potential situations such as loss of two-way communications or inadvertent selection of the hijack transponder code that may indicate to ATC a potential security threat to the aircraft; communicate clearly when in your opinion there is an actual security threat; volunteer information regarding the integrity of the flight deck to ATC in a timely manner; use appropriate R/T phraseology and special purpose SSR codes; comply with government instructions whether given by radio or through visual intercept signals.

Some years ago, two Dutch F-16s were scrambled when a Boeing 737 en route from Bulgaria to Belfast failed to establish radio contact with ATC. The incident caused some consternation in the Netherlands as people are not used to the military being active on weekends, let alone going supersonic in the process. As is standard practice, the Sector Supervisor at Maastricht informed his military counterpart of the apparent radio failure. This information was passed to Air Defence, who made the decision to launch the QRA flight. The aircraft was intercepted and contact soon regained. Not generally known is the fact that NATO had an AWACS in the air over Germany during the World Cup in 2006 in case a repeat of 9/11 should be attempted, so any such incident is obviously being taken very seriously.

Another incident occurred in April 2008 when a Vietnam Airlines 777 flying from Hanoi to Frankfurt narrowly escaped being shot down. It seems that the 777 flew through the airspace of the Ukraine, Poland and the Czech Republic for over an hour on the night of April 17/18 without any radio communications. As the aircraft deviated from the prescribed flight path, the Czech authorities were prepared to shoot it down, even though it was displaying the assigned transponder squawk. Two fighters were sent up to intercept it and, a few minutes after visual contact, radio communications were established.

Later the same year, on 10 August, a Delta Airlines flight from Istanbul to New York was intercepted by two Dutch F-16s over the Netherlands. The Delta flight apparently failed to contact Maastricht Eurocontrol Upper Area Centre, while flying a considerable distance. An MP3 sound file of the interception was temporarily available on the web. On it you could hear AJ33, one of the two F-16s scrambled from Twenthe, talking to Dutch Fighter Control (call-sign Bandbox) on UHF, although the ground station is not audible. Later on in the recording AJ33 is heard talking to the Delta crew on VHF guard frequency 121.5. When the situation is resolved, the F-16 pilot leaves the scene and calls 'Switches Safe'. Standard procedure, of course, but chilling to hear in the circumstances. A similar incident occurred on May 29 when two Dutch F-16s intercepted a British Mediterranean Airbus 320 inbound to Heathrow from the Middle East. It entered Dutch airspace and failed to contact Maastricht. One of the fighter pilots used hand signals to alert the crew and the situation was soon resolved. The interception was witnessed by many people on the ground who noticed the contrails of the F-16s and the airliner close together.

In response to this kind of incident, ICAO is currently developing general principles for managing the extreme situations that now threaten civil aviation. Distinctly different procedures may have to be adopted for situations involving an element of uncertainty, such as attempted or suspected hijacking. These principles would concern situations where a flight crew is still in control, or thought to be still in control, and one where the hijackers appear to be in control of the aircraft. Consideration may also need to be given to the manner in which controllers respond to circumstances of lost radio or transponder contact. While many of these situations will arise because of equipment or operational error, there is always the possibility that a communication lapse is caused by an act of unlawful interference. Either circumstance may give rise to deviation from assigned routes and levels, followed by an interception that may itself lead to a violent outcome.

Controllers, therefore, must have a ready means to differentiate between incidents attributable to genuine operational or technical causes and those potentially related to hijacking. Any delay in determining the reason for loss of radio or transponder contact should be minimised by the use of procedures that isolate the cause or by utilising technology that would resolve doubt, or by both. To this end, several projects are under way to develop better means of tracking unlawfully commandeered aircraft. In the course of a normal flight, significant periods may elapse between R/T exchanges, but one possibility for a timely alert involves the development of a transponder that cannot be reset after the emergency mode has been activated. This may involve use of a 'panic button' that, once activated, automatically transfers selection of the transponder signal to the avionics and out of reach of personnel in the cabin and on the flight deck.

Another project provides for tracking aircraft after an alert code has been automatically transmitted to the designated ground-based receiving station. Such an alert would be triggered by first securing cockpits against unauthorised access. This can be achieved through voice biometrics using a technology that indexes stored voice parameters of authorised persons. With such a system, all personnel are required to log on prior to departure, after which changes are locked out until the aircraft has arrived at its destination. During flight, if the system detects any voice other than those logged on, the alert code would be transmitted. Such a system would also display the aircraft's position derived from the Global Navigation Satellite System (GNSS).

Due Regard

Press reports of the renewed Russian Air Force Bear flights close to the UK have been predictably exaggerated. The facts are that the flights take place in international airspace where military aircraft, including those of NATO and European air arms, can and do operate as they wish. The procedure is called 'Due Regard' and is employed for situations when military aircraft are not able to accomplish the mission while complying with ICAO procedures for point-to-point and navigation flights. There are operational situations that do not lend themselves to ICAO flight procedures. They may include politically sensitive missions, military contingencies or classified missions. When operations of this type are not conducted under ICAO flight procedures, they are conducted under the 'due regard' prerogative of military aircraft. Due regard means that the aircraft commander, of a state aircraft, will operate that aircraft with 'due regard' for the safety of all air and surface traffic. Before an aircraft commander can declare due regard, there are certain conditions that must be met:

(1) Aircraft shall be operated in Visual Met Conditions (VMC); or
(2) Aircraft shall be operated within radar surveillance and radio communications of a surface radar facility; or
(3) Aircraft shall be equipped with airborne radar that is sufficient to provide separation between themselves, aircraft they may be controlling, and other aircraft; or
(4) Aircraft shall be operated outside controlled airspace and, when possible, away from high density traffic areas.

Essentially, flight under the due regard option obligates the aircraft commander to be his own ATC agency and to separate his aircraft from all other aircraft. Currently, no specific language is published for notifying a controlling agency that you are exercising the due regard option. An aircraft commander must ensure that the affected controlling agency understands his intentions. Prior co-ordination can help limit potential communication problems.

However, for civilian controllers due regard is unsatisfactory and poses a perceived danger to civil operations, despite being legal. UK sovereign airspace is not being breached, only the airspace for which the UK has civil ATC responsibility. Middle East civil air routes are being infringed continuously by USAF or RAF aircraft operating under due regard. The Bear infringements are no worse but in fact a lot less dangerous because the Bears are tracked initially by the Norwegians and the radar picture is shared. As they cross the Kola peninsula around 30 degrees east, a penetration time for the UK Air Defence Region is calculated on the assumption that they will continue south-east. This will be more than two hours ahead and the RAF's QRA takes one hour to get there, so there is no necessity for a Battle of Britain-type scramble as claimed by the newspapers! The Bears tend to cruise at around Flight level 360 and normally do not talk to ATC or file a flight plan. They stay in international airspace over international waters and do not infringe the 12-mile limit and therefore contravene no laws.

Sleeping radios

NATS has recently undertaken an investigation into the operating characteristics of air–ground communications, following a number of 'Loss of Communications' reports. A phenomenon known as 'sleeping radio' is suspected. Some of these incidents have led to airliners being intercepted by fighters as a precautionary measure. In common with many other European ATC providers, NATS uses a method of radio transmissions where the same signal is radiated simultaneously from up to five separate radio stations. This system is used to provide area coverage by extending the effective range of the operating frequency. Detail testing showed that, despite meeting the published minimum performance specifications, some aircraft radio equipment is susceptible to spontaneous receiver muting when subjected to multiple transmissions.

Operations in UK and European airspace can be subjected to localised phenomena known as the Multi-Carrier Effect. The effect is usually observed by aircrews as an apparent 'hole in coverage'. The principal defining symptom is that all ATC to pilot communication is suppressed, while pilot to ATC and pilot to pilot calls operate normally. The presence of the multi-carrier effect can often be suspected when routine RT traffic from other aircraft can be heard but any corresponding ATC instructions are inaudible. In the event of a suspected occurrence, it is suggested that aircrew should make contact with ATC via another aircraft using an air-to-air relay call.

In the 1970s a TWA Boeing 707 freighter with a crew of three overflew its Los Angeles destination westbound. Fortunately the SELCAL chimes alerting the pilots to a message on the HF frequency finally woke them before they reached a critical fuel state over the Pacific. With such incidents in mind, the Boeing 777 (and probably similar types) has a Crew Alertness Monitor linked into the FMC (Flight Management Computer) which continuously monitors switch action on associated control panels, radios and other systems. After around 15 minutes or so since the last switch action was detected, an advisory message 'PILOT RESPONSE' is displayed. If there is still no action for about five minutes after this then a caution message is displayed. A further five minutes will lead to a very loud warning wail. In the descent, these timings are much reduced. Pushing ANY monitored switch will cancel the 'PILOT RESPONSE' message. Simple, but effective.

Chapter 22

UFOs and air traffic control

HAVING BEEN AN aircraft enthusiast for more than 50 years and an air traffic controller for nearly 40, I have spent much of my time gazing up at the sky. In all that time I regret that I have never seen anything that I considered extra-terrestrial but I keep an open mind and live in hope! Aware that there is enormous interest in UFOs, I have added this chapter to describe some factual incidents. No conclusions are offered of course, but there is much food for thought.

The world of ATC is a small one and gossip soon goes the rounds. According to the grapevine, there were several incidents involving lights in the sky around Manchester Airport in the early 1990s. Nothing was seen on radar and no official reports were made, as far as I am aware. That was until January 1995 when a near-miss was reported between a Boeing 737 and a UFO about nine miles south-east of the airport. The 737 was at 4,000ft over the Pennines being radar vectored for an ILS approach by Manchester Radar. Although it was dark, visibility was good. While flying just above the tops of some ragged cumulus cloud, the crew saw a lighted object fly down the right-hand side of the aircraft at high speed from the opposite direction. The captain was able to track the object through the right-hand windscreen and side window, having it in sight for a total of about two seconds. There was no apparent sound or wake and the first officer instinctively ducked as it went by.

A brief exchange followed on the radio between pilot and controller but, as the latter could not see anything else on radar, it was inconclusive. In subsequent telephone conversations, the captain was convinced that the object was itself lit. 'Although he could not determine a definite pattern, he described it as having a number of small lights, rather like a Christmas tree.' The first officer, however, felt that the object was illuminated by their landing lights ... he was unable to assess its distance, other than to say that he involuntarily ducked, so it must have appeared to him to have been very close.

He was entirely convinced, as was the captain, that what they had seen was a solid object and not a met phenomenon, balloon or any other craft with which they were familiar, or an F-117 stealth aircraft, which he had himself seen and which he feels he would have recognised. Recordings of the radar data showed only the 737 and other aircraft being radar sequenced in the Manchester Terminal Area. There was no evidence of military activity 'from any official source'. The possibility that the object might have been a hang glider, paraglider or microlight was investigated but dismissed as extremely unlikely on a dark, windy night. Sensibly, the investigators refuse to speculate on extra-terrestrial activity, preferring to leave this 'to those whose interest lies in this field'.

UFO sightings tend to be made by well-meaning members of the public rather than oddballs but, having handled many queries to ATC over the years, I know that it is very difficult to convince them that what they saw was almost certainly the planet Venus or aircraft lights just above the horizon on a clear night.

The CAA's Manual of Air Traffic Services Part One (available online) has a section on UFO reporting. On receipt of a report from a member of the public, ATC is required to obtain the following information and telephone it *immediately* to the Distress and Diversion Cell at London Mil and forward the completed report to Ministry of Defence Sec (AS). The format of the report is as follows:

(A) Date, time and duration of sighting (local times to be quoted); (B) Description of object (number of objects, size, shape, colours, brightness, sound, smell, etc); (C) Exact position of observer (geographical location, indoors or outdoors, stationary or moving); (D) How observed (naked eye, binoculars, other optical device, still or movie camera); (E) Direction in which object was first seen (a landmark may be more useful than a badly estimated bearing); (F) Angular elevation of object (estimated heights are unreliable); (G) Distance of object from observer (by reference to a known landmark wherever possible); (H) Movements of object (changes in E, F and G may be of more use than estimates of course and speed; (J) Meteorological conditions during observations (moving clouds, haze, mist, etc); (K) Nearby objects (telephone or high-voltage lines, reservoir, lake or dam, swamp or marsh, river, high buildings, tall chimneys, steeples, spires, TV or radio masts, airfields, generating plant, factories, pits or other sites with floodlights or other lighting); (L) To whom reported (police, military organisations, the press, etc); (M) Name and address of informant; (N) Any background information on the informant that may be volunteered; (O) Other witnesses; and (P) Date and time of receipt of report.

In practice, many of the sightings can be explained immediately to the satisfaction of ATC, even if the person reporting it is not always convinced! MoD has never revealed what happens to the reports but presumably they are filed away somewhere. Of course, from certain quarters there are slightly hysterical accusations of cover-ups. I think the truth is that the authorities don't really know either and, as UFOs do not seem to pose a threat to national security, there is no point in serious investigation.

CAA published an Airprox Report of an encounter between a BAe146 and 'an unknown object'. While nowhere near as weird as the Boeing 737/black triangle UFO nearmiss described above, it still raises some interesting speculation. On 7 June 1996 a BAe146 was inbound to Stansted at Flight Level 90 between some huge towering cumulo-nimbus clouds. About two miles east of Stevenage the captain saw a military aircraft heading towards him.

He started an immediate left turn as the other aircraft flew down the right side about 2–300 yards away and 100 feet below. His first officer also saw the aircraft and, although it was only visible for a couple of seconds, followed it all the way into his four o'clock. It was 95% red with blue and white stripes. He commented later that he did not claim to be an expert in aircraft recognition but it looked to him like a Hawk and he noted the engine intakes against the fuselage sides.

The captain asked the London radar controller 'Did we have a Red Arrow pass quite close there about two minutes ago in our turn?' The controller could see no primary or secondary radar returns near the 146 and told the pilot so, asking if he wished to file a report. The pilot asked him to check it out and agreed to call him after landing. Aeronautical Information Services (Military) conducted extensive investigations to try and locate any aircraft matching the reported description that could have been in the area at the time, but without success. They also studied radar recordings from the three separate systems which cover the south-east. There was no primary or secondary return in the reported position that could be the unknown. Nor were there any intermittent returns entering or leaving the area which could be related to an aircraft passing through it. The whereabouts of all RAF and British Aerospace company Hawks were traced. This task was simplified by the incident time of 1900 local on a Friday, a time when few, if any, such aircraft would normally be airborne. The last two RAF Hawks to land were down by 1520 and the Red Arrows had not flown at all that day, nor where there any BAe company Hawks active.

The reported colour of the aircraft led AIS to check the whereabouts of all Gnats on the civil register and initially one was rumoured to have been airborne, but further investigation discounted this. In addition, all operators of ex-military jets were contacted and again none was flying at that time. In the absence of any firm evidence the investigators could only speculate that the sighting could have been something, possibly inflatable, which had been carried aloft by the convective weather conditions. Due to the 146's forward speed and close passage, it might have seemed like an aircraft going the other way. The total lack of any radar contact made the investigating board 'reasonably certain of only one thing; what had been seen was not an aeroplane'.

The incident was assessed as a confliction between the BAe146 and an unknown object, a form of words which recognised the pilots' conviction that they had definitely seen something. The report comments that there are three or four other incidents on the Airprox database of respected commercial pilots in controlled airspace reporting conflictions with aircraft which were never subsequently traced, despite intensive investigations.

By coincidence, in February 1999 the crew of another BAe146 reported an unidentified bright light below them at Flight Level 280. The position was over the North Sea, 58 miles west of Ramme VOR which is located on the west coast of Denmark. The area below the aircraft was illuminated for 10 seconds by an incandescent light which was not considered by the crew to be an aircraft landing light. They stated that three other aircraft reported seeing it moving at high speed or static. ATC were informed but they reported no other aircraft in the vicinity. Five minutes later a radar return was present (ie something was showing) at 75 miles on weather radar, although the atmosphere was reported as stable.

Another mysterious Airprox happened near Heathrow in June 1998. It involved an MD81 which had just departed for Oslo and was flying in and out of cloud at around 3,000ft. When about two miles west of Heathrow, both pilots saw an object pass in the opposite direction down their port side and slightly above. The captain described it as 'metallic grey and the size of a small aircraft with lights on'. The first officer, who saw it a fraction of a second later, described it as 'a bright light very close'. They both estimated that it passed 30–50 metres away.

Despite extensive enquiries, no explanation for this object could be found. A thorough ground search of the area was carried out by the police and the possibility of models, light aircraft, fireworks and flares was investigated. All proved negative. Radar replays also revealed nothing of the intruder. ATCO members on the Airprox Board were certain that even a small aircraft would have been detected, particularly on the Heathrow 10cm radar. With no clues as to the nature of the reported object, the Board concluded that, owing to the lack of information available to them, the incident was unassessable with regard to both cause and risk.

A few years ago, an odd encounter was reported over south-east England. A Swissair A320 inbound from Zurich to Heathrow had to take avoiding action on an unidentified aircraft. Two bright wing lights and a dark shadow in between them (like an airliner or transport aircraft shape) were spotted through the captain's left-hand window. It was flying straight towards them, except for the last one or two seconds as the lights appeared to descend and the A320 pilot banked to the right to avoid it. Both the unidentified aircraft and the A320 entered a cloud layer shortly afterwards and contact was lost. Despite a call to ATC, no contacts were observed on radar at the time or found subsequently on the video recordings. All very mysterious, unlike another story which emerged recently. Following an incident where the captain declared a full emergency due to a problem with the aircraft's ailerons, two days after the event ATC received a telephone call from a local radio station. The caller asked if it could confirm or deny that an aircraft had recently declared an emergency, having been forced to land at the aerodrome because of aliens!

Despite my scepticism, there are definitely a number of incidents on record which defy explanation, particularly where credible witnesses were involved. One has to keep an open mind on the subject and, if you are an air band radio listener, you might just be lucky enough to be able to confirm a pilot's UFO report from the ground!

Chapter 23

A career in Air Traffic Control

AN INTEREST IN aviation and a basic familiarity with ATC gained from air band monitoring may spur younger readers into the thought of taking it up as a career. Like most jobs in aviation, Air Traffic Control is very demanding and requires the highest standards. It is also a job which is associated with high levels of stress, although this depends on location and experience. You may ask what are the basic qualities required by a controller? Difficult to answer; many psychologists and other medical people have attempted to analyse the pressures of the job, so far be it for me to comment further. One source did say that controllers often speak, listen, write and think all at the same time!

To summarise the ATC system, the Tower Controller works at airports and aerodromes, co-ordinating the traffic on the runways and taxiways by using radio instructions, issuing the necessary clearances to the cockpit crew before and after landing and take-off. At very busy airports, Ground Movement and Clearance Delivery Controllers will share the Tower's workload. Most of the time, the Tower Controller works from visual reference, by keeping the aircraft in sight. Soon after take-off and for a period prior to landing, the pilot communicates with an Approach Controller or a Terminal Controller, depending on the configuration of the airspace. The Approach or Terminal Controller, using radar, directs arriving flights to the point where they are handed over to the Tower and directs departing flights to the point where control is assumed by an Area Control unit (sometimes called an En-Route unit). When 'en-route', the aircraft may transit several control areas. It maintains course with the help of radio beacons and modern airborne navigation systems but remains under constant control from controllers in an Area or En-Route Control Centre.

To act as a civilian air traffic controller in the UK, a full UK Air Traffic Controller's licence is required. Before obtaining the licence you will need successfully to complete a course of training at a CAA-approved ATC training establishment and obtain a first Certificate of Competence. Once you have successfully completed the first rating course (in most cases this will be the Aerodrome Control rating) you will be issued with a Student Air Traffic Controller's licence. This will allow you to undertake on-the-job training at a UK ATC unit. The training will form the minimum experience requirement (MER) or approved unit training plan (UTP) and should lead to the grant of a first Certificate of Competence and the issue of a full ATC licence. The MER or UTP must commence within 12 months of completing the rating course.

ASTAC at Gloucestershire Airport and BAe at Cwmbran both offer *ab initio* controller training courses, an expensive step if sponsorship is not available. The realistic option is to apply to NATS, the new name of what was previously National Air Traffic Services, for a trainee controller job. Application forms can be downloaded from the NATS website, the basic entry requirements being: You must be at least 18 and under the age of 36 at date of application, have 5 GCSEs at Grade C or above, including English and Maths, and be eligible to work in the UK. If successful, you must pass a CAA Class 1 medical examination and have security clearance. Wearing glasses is acceptable if your eyesight reaches certain standards, but colour blindness will bar you. ATCOs also have to pass a thorough medical examination every two years until they are 40, then every year after that. Detailed career information can be found on the NATS website and also on the GATCO (Guild of Air Traffic Controllers) site.

Candidates will attend a selection test day, which includes some tests to measure skills such as the ability to check information quickly and accurately, spatial visualisation, decision-making ability and short-term memory. Also questionnaires to gauge personality, learning style and motivation. If they pass this successfully, they will be invited to further interviews and tests. In preparation, it is important to familiarise oneself with the challenges and demands of the job and a thorough reading of NATS literature and its website is essential. The more you understand about the job you are applying for, the better you will feel as an applicant. A deep knowledge of aviation is neither expected nor necessary but some familiarity is obviously an advantage. The ATC section of the Professional Pilots' Rumour Network website (www.pprune.org) contains a wealth of advice from and for candidates for NATS interviews and training.

The College course lasts approximately 11 months for Area Trainees and Terminal Control Trainees, and between six and nine months for Aerodrome/Approach Trainees. This is not the end of the training and there is a period of validation training at the posted operational unit; the validation period is dependent on the unit and the individual's ability to reach the desired competency. The number of Trainees allocated to each discipline is determined by the NATS business need. The biggest requirement is for area controllers so normally the majority of trainees are streamed to the area discipline. During the Basic Course, a decision will be made on which discipline you will follow, primarily based on the skills you have demonstrated in your training. Your personal preference on which discipline you would like to pursue will be taken into account as a secondary factor in the decision.

Your progress through training is assessed continually by means of theoretical examinations, practical assessments and oral tests, and successful completion of these assessments will be required for continuation of training. The course of action following failure of an assessment is determined on a case-by-case basis taking account of all relevant factors including regulatory requirements and it could result in training being terminated. Obviously as you come towards the end of your College course you will be asked where you would prefer to be posted. Whilst NATS tries to take personal circumstances into account its operational needs must come first. You therefore must be prepared to work anywhere in the UK.

Unfortunately, the failure rate in ATC training is high, somewhere around the level of 40% it has been said. It is important to understand that a student may be dismissed at any stage of training if his or her results are unsatisfactory. They do not have to reimburse any of the costs incurred. This negative aspect should nevertheless not stop you applying. Other job and education opportunities will also carry a certain amount of difficulty and risk of failure in examinations or tests. Having said that, many of my colleagues fell by the wayside for various reasons and, with a little less pressure, became competent controllers at regional airports. Some have even returned to NATS at a later date, having proved themselves in the meantime.

New technology, new airspace, new regulations all combine to produce an ever-increasing level of complexity for controllers to cope with. There will shortly come a time – indeed many believe it has already arrived – when controllers will have to specialise, not just when they go operational but from day one of their training. The current controller training tends to follow a well-worn path of theory leading to aerodrome training, approach training (procedural followed by radar) and then finally on to area training. In today's complex airspace, the area controller rarely, if ever, draws on his aerodrome skills, so it could be argued that there is no point in learning them.

In 1949 when the forerunner of NATS College of ATC was set up in wartime huts on the edge of Hurn (now Bournemouth) Airport, the training aids were rudimentary, movements were relatively few, and controlled airspace as we know it today was non-existent. Today over 150 students per year from all over the world pass through the College at Bournemouth.

Those destined for NATS operational units will be part of a team that handles a combined total of 6,000 movements per day in complex and crowded airspace. In order to achieve a skill level commensurate with such a demanding control environment, today's students must have access to the very best teaching aids. These comprise modern classroom facilities and teaching techniques, simulators that accurately represent the airspace and traffic they will experience in real life, and lessons and training exercises that are designed to prepare them fully for all eventualities they will experience in the 'real world'.

The career of an operational controller in NATS is clearly structured and will depend on your progress in attaining and maintaining the necessary levels of proficiency and experience. If you wish, you may spend your whole career as an operational controller. As you acquire more experience and follow technical and operational developments, your progress could lead to the attainment of the grade of principal controller. You would continue to benefit from the advantages of shift-work, including flexibility of working patterns and shift-work payments on top of an already good salary. Different career development opportunities exist for those with the right abilities (operational training officer, supervisor, centre supervisor) and those who wish to progress to management responsibilities. An operational (shift-working) controller will cease active operational service at the age of 55 (which could be extended to a maximum of 57) and will receive a retirement pension calculated according to the pension rights acquired at that date. NATS currently provides the ATC service at fourteen of the UK's major airports: Heathrow, Gatwick, Stansted, Luton, London City, Manchester, Birmingham, Cardiff, Edinburgh, Glasgow, Aberdeen, Belfast International, Southampton and Farnborough, as well as the Control Centres at Swanwick and Prestwick.

The harmonised European ATC Licence, introduced at the end of 2003, is the first step towards a pan-European controller workforce. Along with the harmonised ATC Licence comes a need for harmonised ATC training, and the requirement to train to a common standard – Common Core Content – has already had an impact on ATC training providers across Europe. There are already opportunities to work in Europe because Eurocontrol, responsible for the Maastricht Upper Area Control Centre, is actively recruiting trainee controllers. This site in the Netherlands houses a multi-national team of controllers, supported by engineers, technicians

Manchester Ground Movement Controller.

and other specialists, controls traffic operating above 24,500 feet in the skies of Belgium, Luxembourg, the Netherlands and northern Germany.

Eurocontrol training lasts about 2½ years, including courses with theoretical and simulator lessons at the Eurocontrol Institute of Air Navigation Services in Luxembourg and intensive on-the-job and simulator training at the Maastricht UAC. Current entry requirements are: You must be at least 18 and less than 25 years of age; be a national of one of the 30 or so Eurocontrol Member States; have successfully completed secondary education at an advanced level; have a good knowledge of English; and be medically fit. Air Traffic Control is traditionally seen as a stressful occupation, but much depends on training, experience and temperament. A Eurocontrol document has this to say about it: 'Stress is a physiological syndrome. You feel it when put under mental or physical constraint. Stress can be a positive and necessary stimulator of action to help you work out a difficult situation. Due to its multivariate pattern, stress might also be inappropriate to solve the problems with which you are faced. Obviously, some aspects of the ATCO tasks make the mental workload rather high (monitoring and managing routine traffic, switching attention, solving conflicts, updating spatial mental picture, providing services). A high level of stress, including its physical component, might therefore be undesirable. Nevertheless, the tolerances to stress manifestation vary from one individual to another. It is thus not easy to say whether ATC is a stressing activity as such'.

The Royal Air Force, of course, employ their own controllers, recruiting within the age group 17½ to 36. Required educational qualifications are: two A-levels or three Highers or equivalent, and five GCSEs/SCEs at Grade C/3 minimum or equivalent, including English Language and Maths. Sponsorship may be available, for example if you are in the Sixth Form you can qualify for a Sixth Form Scholarship of up to £2,000. You can also apply for a University Bursary of £2,000 a year while you do your degree. In return, you are asked to become a member of the University Air Squadron (UAS) (or Air Training Corps while still at school) and to join the RAF once you finish your studies. The usual service contract is six years with option to renew. Many RAF controllers move on to civilian controlling.

The role of an Aerodrome Flight Service Officer (AFISO) is described in Chapter 10. Before a licence is issued by CAA, examinations in procedures, air law, navigation and meteorology have to be passed. After that a minimum of 40 hours' practical experience has to be completed under the supervision of a qualified AFISO. A validation will then be granted for the particular airfield after a check-out by a CAA inspector. AFISO work is not well paid but it provides valuable experience for moving on to full ATC. Much of the study syllabus is almost identical for both disciplines.

Apart from being a controller, there are several other employment opportunities in ATC. Almost all ATC units employ Air Traffic Services Assistants (ATSAs). ATSAs provide support to controllers and provide administrative functions necessary for the air traffic service system to continue working (eg flight plan acceptance and pre-flight briefing for pilots). ATC units also require engineering support (Air Traffic Engineers, ATEs) to ensure that the equipment and navigation aids are maintained and operate correctly. You should contact your local airport directly to enquire about employment prospects as an ATSA or ATE. Some ATC units may sponsor suitable ATSAs for controller courses.

In addition to ATC services, NATS provides comprehensive engineering design and maintenance for all its systems including centres, radars, communications and navaids. It trains all its engineers in technical skills for a wide range of equipment installation and maintenance, safety management, and general skills.

So there you have it; a rewarding and interesting job with constant challenges. A real buzz when you get it right. I have been lucky enough to spend most of my time in ATC working in a tower environment. As one of my enthusiast colleagues observed, you get very well paid to watch aeroplanes all day. Simplistic, maybe, but not far from the truth!

Appendix 1

Beacons and reporting points

THE CENTRELINES OF airways are marked by navigational beacons positioned at strategic intervals, such as where the airway changes direction or where two or more of them intersect. Airway beacons are mostly VORs with a co-located DME to indicate range, but some, Lichfield being a major example, are NDBs. Many small airfields have an associated NDB used as a sole aid for instrument let-downs. Larger airports generally retain an NDB as a backup in the event of ILS unserviceability. With the aid of a radio navigation chart it is easy to find the ones nearest to your home.

Many of the so-called Significant Points are not beacons at all, but hypothetical positions formed where certain radials from two VORs intersect, and are given a standard five-letter name. It may be related to a geographical feature such as the name of a nearby town, and is often a distortion of the real name to arrive at five letters. Examples are LAMMA south of Edinburgh (Lammermuir Hills), SAPCO near Sapcote in Leicestershire and REXAM near Wrexham. Others are purely artificial but often imaginative, eg children's comics (BEENO, DANDI, TOPPA); naval heroes (BENBO, HARDY, DRAKE). ROBIN in the East Midlands commemorates Robin Hood, KEGUN, used by Liverpool, refers to former footballer Kevin Keegan! Sadly, it seems that five-letter codes will in future be computer-generated, producing a pronounceable but meaningless word such as XAMAB. There are now so many and they are replaced or discontinued so often that there is little point in listing all of them.

As described in Chapter 6, each major airport has one or more terminal beacons. Well known are the LBA at Leeds, the BEL at Belfast and the GOW at Glasgow. Even if the destination is not mentioned in transmissions whilst on airways, such routeings as Pole Hill-LBA will immediately give a clue. A standard 'WILLO Arrival Runway 26 Right' will identify the destination as Gatwick. Similarly, knowledge of the runway designators at various airports will be useful. Since the trend is to a single main runway with an instrument approach at both ends, with perhaps one subsidiary for light aircraft, you can soon become familiar with those in your home area. Examples are Birmingham 15/33; Heathrow 09L and 09R, and 27L and 27R; Glasgow 05/23; and Manchester 05L and 05R, and 23L and 23R.

Beacons and reporting points

VOR frequencies are in MHz and NDBs in kHz

Name	Frequency	Code	Type	Approximate location
ABBOT				Stansted/Luton STARs
Aberdeen	114.3	ADN	VOR	Scottish East Coast
ALD	383.0		NDB	Alderney Airport
ALKIN				London City STARs
ASKEY				Stansted/Luton STARs

ASTRA				Gatwick STARs
Barkway	116.25	BKY	VOR	Nuthampstead, Herts
Barra	316.0	BRR	NDB	Western Isles
Belfast	117.2	BEL	VOR	East of Belfast City
Benbecula	114.4	BEN	VOR	Outer Hebrides
Berry Head	112.05	BHD	VOR	Near Torquay
BHX	406.0		NDB	Birmingham Airport
BIA	339		NDB	Bournemouth Airport
Biggin	115.1	BIG	VOR	SE stack for Heathrow
BIR	406.0		NDB	Birmingham Locator Beacon
Bovingdon	113.75	BNN	VOR	NW stack for Heathrow
BPL	420.0		NDB	Blackpool Airport
Brecon	117.45	BCN	VOR	South Wales
BRI	380.0		NDB	Bristol Airport
Brookmans Pk	117.5	BPK	VOR	North of London
Burnham	421.0	BUR	NDB	Berkshire
BZ	386.0		NDB	RAF Brize Norton
CAE	320.0		NDB	Caernarfon Airport
Carnane	366.5	CAR	NDB	Isle of Man
CBN	374.0		NDB	Cumbernauld airfield
CDF	388.5		NDB	Cardiff Airport
CHASE				Birmingham STARs
Chiltern	277.0	CHT	NDB	North of Heathrow
CL	328.0		NDB	Carlisle Airport
Clacton	114.55	CLN	VOR	Essex coast
Compton	114.35	CPT	VOR	Berkshire
Cork	114.6	CRK	VOR	Ireland
Costà	111.8	COA	VOR	Belgian coast
CT	363.5		NDB	Coventry Airport
CWL	423		NDB	RAF Cranwell
Daventry	116.4	DTY	VOR	South Midlands
DAYNE				Manchester STARs
Dean Cross	115.2	DCS	VOR	West of Carlisle
Detling	117.3	DET	VOR	Kent
Dieppe	115.8	DPE	VOR	French coast
DND	394.0		NDB	Dundee Airport
Dover	114.95	DVR	VOR	Near town
Dublin	114.9	DUB	VOR	North of city
EAS	391.5		NDB	Southampton Airport
EDN	341.0		NDB	Edinburgh Airport
EKN	357.5		NDB	Enniskillen Airport
EMW	393.0		NDB	East Midlands Airport
Epsom	316.0	EPM	NDB	Heathrow stack when Ockham out of service
EX	337.0		NDB	Exeter Airport
FNY	338.0		NDB	Doncaster Sheffield
Gamston	112.8	GAM	NDB	South Yorks
Glasgow	115.4	GOW	VOR	Glasgow Airport
GLG	350.0		NDB	Glasgow Airport
Goodwood	114.75	GWC	VOR	Chichester Goodwood Airport
GROVE				Birmingham STARs

GST	331.0		NDB	Gloucestershire Airport
Guernsey	109.4	GUR	VOR	Guernsey
HAV	328.0		NDB	Havefordwest Airport
HAW	340.0		NDB	Hawarden Airport
HB	420.0		NDB	Belfast/City Airport
HBR	350.5		NDB	Humberside Airport
Henton	433.5	HEN	NDB	Bucks
Honiley	113.65	HON	VOR	S of Birmingham Airport
HRW	424.0		NDB	London Heathrow
Inverness	109.2	INS	VOR	Inverness Airport
Isle of Man	112.2	IOM	VOR	Southern tip of island
Jersey	112.2	JSY	VOR	Near airport
Killiney	378.0	KLY	NDB	Near Dublin
Koksy	114.5	KOK	VOR	Belgian coast
KW	395.0		NDB	Kirkwall Airport
LA	282.0		NDB	RAF Lyneham
Lambourne	115.6	LAM	VOR	NE stack for Heathrow
LANAK				Glasgow STARs
Lands End	114.2	LND	VOR	Lands End
Lashendon	340.0	LSH	NDB	Kent
LAY	395.0		NDB	Islay Airport
LBA	402.5		NDB	Leeds-Bradford Airport
LCY	322.0		NDB	London/City Airport
Lichfield	545.0	LIC	NDB	North Midlands
London	113.6	LON	VOR	London Heathrow
LOREL				Stansted/Luton STARs
LPL	349.5		NDB	East of Liverpool Airport
LUT	345.0		NDB	Luton Airport
Lyneham	282.0	LA	NDB	Wiltshire
Macrihanish	116.0	MAC	VOR	Kintyre, Scotland
Manchester	113.55	MCT	VOR	Manchester Airport
Manston	347.0	MTN	NDB	Kent
Mayfield	117.9	MAY	VOR	Sussex
Midhurst	114.0	MID	VOR	Sussex
MIRSI				Manchester STARs
NEDUL				Bournemouth/S'ton STARs
New Galloway	399.0	NGY	NDB	South Scotland
Nicky	117.4	NIK	VOR	Belgian coast
NOT	430.0		NDB	Nottingham Airport
NT	352.0		NDB	Newcastle Airport
Ockham	115.3	OCK	VOR	SW stack for Heathrow
OLIVE				Birmingham STARs
Ottringham	113.9	OTR	VOR	Humberside
OX	367.5		NDB	Oxford Airport
OY	332.0		NDB	Belfast Aldergrove
Pampus	117.8	PAM	VOR	Holland
Perth	110.4	PTH	VOR	Central Scotland
PIGOT				East Midlands STARs
PIK	355.0		NDB	Prestwick Airport
Pole Hill	112.1	POL	VOR	N of Manchester

PY	396.5		NDB	Plymouth Airport
ROKUP				East Midlands STARs
ROSUN				Manchester STARs
St Abbs	112.5	SAB	VOR	Scottish east coast
St Inglevert	387.0	ING	NDB	French coast
Seaford	117.0	SFD	VOR	South coast
Shannon	113.3	SHA	VOR	SW Ireland
SND	362.5		NDB	Southend Airport
Southampton	113.35	SAM	VOR	Southampton Airport
SPEAR				London City STARs
Spijkerboor	113.3	SPY	VOR	Holland
STIRA				Edinburgh/Glasgow STARs
STM	321.0		NDB	St Mary's Scillies
Stornoway	115.1	STN	VOR	Outer Hebrides
Strumble	113.1	STU	VOR	Coast of SW Wales
SWN	320.5		NDB	Swansea Airport
Talla	113.8	TLA	VOR	South Scotland
TD	347.5		NDB	Durham Tees Valley
TIPOD				Liverpool STARs
Trent	115.7	TNT	VOR	North Midlands
Turnberry	117.5	TRN	VOR	S of Prestwick Airport
TWEED				Edinburgh STARs
Vesta	116.6	VES	VOR	Denmark
Wallasey	114.1	WAL	VOR	Wirral Peninsula
Westcott	335.0	WCO	NDB	South Midlands
WFD	380.0		NDB	Woodford airfield
Whitegate	368.5	WHI	NDB	Manchester TMA, SW corner
Wick	113.6	WIK	VOR	Northern Scotland
WILLO				Gatwick STARs
WL	385.0		NDB	Barrow airfield
Woodley	352.0	WOD	NDB	Berkshire
WTN	337.0		NDB	Warton airfield
YVL	343.0		NDB	Yeovil airfield

MORSE CODE AND PHONETIC ALPHABET

Letter	Morse	Word		Letter	Morse	Word
A	• —	Alfa		Q	— — • —	Quebec
B	— • • •	Bravo		R	• — •	Romeo
C	— • — •	Charlie		S	• • •	Sierra
D	— • •	Delta		T	—	Tango
E	•	Echo		U	• • —	Uniform
F	• • — •	Foxtrot		V	• • • —	Victor
G	— — •	Golf		W	• — —	Whiskey
H	• • • •	Hotel		X	— • • —	X-ray
I	• •	India		Y	— • — —	Yankee
J	• — — —	Juliett		Z	— — • •	Zulu
K	— • —	Kilo				
L	• — • •	Lima		1	• — — — —	6 — • • • •
M	— —	Mike		2	• • — — —	7 — — • • •
N	— •	November		3	• • • — —	8 — — — • •
O	— — —	Oscar		4	• • • • —	9 — — — — •
P	• — — •	Papa		5	• • • • •	0 — — — — —

Appendix 2

Airways frequency allocation

London Area Control Centre (Swanwick) Sectors and Frequencies
Lakes Sector (NW England): 132.860 133.705
Wirral Sector (Northern Irish Sea): 135.580
North Sea Sector (NE England): 126.780 128.125
Daventry Sector (Midlands): 127.105 127.880 129.205 131.130
Clacton Sector (East Anglia): 118.480 128.160 133.455
Bristol Sector (S Wales and W England): 129.375 133.6 134.75 135.255
London Middle Sector: 132.455 132.605
London Upper Sector: 127.430 132.840 135.425
Dover Sector (SE England): 128.425 134.460 134.9
Berry Head Sector (SW England and W Channel): 126.075 132.95 135.540
Seaford Sector (Sussex coast): 127.825 129.425 135.05 135.325

Scottish Area Control Centre Frequencies
119.875 123.775 124.5 124.825 125.680 126.25 126.1 126.3 127.275 129.225 132.725 133.675
134.1 134.775 135.85. Formerly Manchester Control: 118.775 119.525 128.05 128.670 133.05
133.8 134.425 136.575

Dublin Area Control Centre Frequencies
124.65 129.175 136.05 136.15

Shannon Area Control Frequencies
119.075 124.7 127.5 131.150 132.150 134.275 135.225 135.6

London Area and Terminal Control Centre and London
Military Remote Transmitter Sites and their Frequencies
Chedburgh, Suffolk: 118.480 121.225 126.6 127.105 128.125 128.160 128.7 132.605 133.455
134.425 252.975
Clee Hill, Shropshire: 124.75 126.875 128.7 132.86 133.6 133.9 134.75
Daventry, Northamptonshire: 127.105 127.80 128.6 129.205 131.130 133.3 275.475 291.8
Davidstow Moor, Cornwall: 124.75 131.2 132.6 132.95 133.3 133.6 134.175 252.875
Grantham, Lincolnshire: 123.95 124.6 127.65 128.125 131.05 135.375 275.5
Great Dun Fell, Cumbria: 125.475 126.6 128.675 277.775 251.25
Greenford, Middlesex: 127.880 128.25 129.205 133.9
Kelsall, Cheshire: 118.775 128.05 128.675 132.13 133.8 134.425
Preston, Lancashire: 118.775 128.05 128.675 131.13 133.05 134.425 136.575
Reigate, Surrey: 128.425 128.6 129.425 132.3 132.605 134.460 135.325
Rothwell, Humberside: 125.275 126.780 128.925

London Area Control Centre and London Military Transmitter Sites.

Snaefell, Isle of Man: 123.775 125.475 128.05 126.875 133.05 282.125
Swingfield, Kent: 118.480 128.160 128.425 132.455 133.45 134.9 136.6 284.7
Trimmingham, Lincolnshire: 121.325 124.6 125.275 125.475 126.780 128.125 131.225
Ventnor, Isle of Wight: 124.75 126.075 127.825 128.6 129.425 132.3 132.840 135.05 135.325 135.375 136.6
Warlingham, Surrey: 124.6 127.430 132.455 134.9 135.05 275.625
Winstone, Gloucestershire: 126.075 127.430 127.7 129.375 132.840 134.75 135.255 135.540

This list is not exhaustive. Note that some frequencies may be offset up or down by 2.5, 5 or 7.5kHz (see page 139) so it is worth experimenting if reception is poor.

Appendix 3

VHF air band frequencies

SINCE VHF TRANSMISSIONS follow approximate lines-of-sight, those from high altitudes carry many hundreds of miles. This means that a larger number of separate frequencies have to be allocated or the protection range between a single frequency shared by two Area Control Centres greatly increased. The recommended limits for contacting the larger airports are 25 nautical miles at 4,000ft for tower and 25 miles from 10,000ft for approach. Mutual interference can also arise under conditions of enhanced radio propagation even whilst operating within protected limits. Such conditions normally exist very briefly and the planning of frequency allocation takes account of all but the worst of these situations. All pilot/controller conversations are recorded automatically for use in incident and accident investigations. Radar and computer exchange data is also recorded although, since this is an ICAO recommendation only, the practice is not universal.

Frequencies of airports and airfields

Aberdeen: Tower: 118.1 GMC: 121.7 Approach/ Radar: 119.05/128.3/134.1/135.175 ATIS:121.85/114.3

Aberporth: See *West Wales (Aberporth)*

Aberporth Range: 119.65

Alderney: Tower: 125.35 GMC: 130.5 Approach (Guernsey): 128.65

Andrewsfield: A/G: 130.55

Anglia Radar (Aberdeen): 125.275 128.925

Ashcroft Farm: A/G: 122.525 (by arrangement)

Audley End: A/G: 122.35 (by arrangement)

Badminton: A/G: 123.175

Bagby: A/G: 123.25

Baldonnel/Casement: Tower: 123.5 GMC: 123.1 Approach/Radar: 122.0/122.3/122.8

Ballykelly: Ops: 130.1 DZ: 129.95

Barkston Heath: Tower: 120.425 Departures: 119.375 PAR: 123.3

Barra: AFIS: 118.075

Barrow (Walney): AFIS: 123.2

Barton: See *Manchester/Barton*

Beccles: A/G: 120.375

Belfast (Aldergrove): Tower: 118.3 GMC: 121.75 Approach/Radar: 128.5 120.9 ATIS: 128.2

Belfast City: Tower: 122.825 Approach/Radar: 130.85 134.8 ATIS: 136.625

Belle Vue (Microlights, Devon): A/G: 123.575

Bembridge, Isle of Wight: A/G: 123.25

Benbecula: Tower/AFIS/Approach: 119.2 ATIS: 113.95

Benson: Tower: 127.15 GMC: 121.8 Approach/Radar: 136.45/120.9/127.15

Beverley/Linley Hill: A/G: 123.05

Biggin Hill: Tower: 134.8 Approach: 129.4 ATIS: 121.875

Birmingham: Tower: 118.3 GMP: 121.925 GMC: 121.8 Approach/Radar: 118.05 131.0 131.325 ATIS: 136.025

Blackbushe: AFIS/A/G: 122.3

Blackpool: Tower: 118.4 Approach/Radar: 119.95 135.95 ATIS: 127.2

Bodmin: A/G: 122.7

Booker: See *Wycombe Air Park*

Boscombe Down: Tower: 130.75 Approach/ Radar: 130.0/126.7/130.0

Boulmer: A/G: 123.1

Bourn: A/G: 124.35

Bournemouth: Tower: 125.6 GMC: 121.7
  Approach/Radar: 119.475 118.65 ATIS:
  133.725
Breighton: A/G: 129.8
Brimpton/Walsing Lower Farm: A/G: 135.125
Bristol (Filton): Tower: 132.35 Approach/
  Radar: 122.725 127.975
Bristol (Lulsgate): Tower: 133.85 GMC:
  121.925 Approach/Radar: 125.65 136.075
  ATIS: 126.025
Brize Norton: Tower: 123.725   GMC: 121.725
  Approach/Radar: 124.275/127.25/119.0/13
  3.75/126.5 Ops: 130.075
Bruntingthorpe: A/G: 122.825
Caernarfon: A/G: 122.25
Cambridge: Tower: 122.2 Approach/Radar:
  123.6 124.975 ATIS: 134.6
Campbeltown: AFIS: 125.9
Cardiff: Tower: 125.0 Approach/Radar:
  126.625 125.85 ATIS: 132.475
Cark: A/G: 129.9
Carlisle: Tower/Approach: 123.6 ATIS:
  118.425
Chalgrove: A/G: 125.4
Chatteris: A/G: 129.9
Chetwynd: Tower/A/G: 121.1
Chichester (Goodwood): AFIS: 122.45
Chirk Microlights: 129.825
Chivenor: A/G: 130.2
Church Fenton: Tower: 122.1 GMC: 121.95
  Approach/Radar: 126.5/123.3
Clacton: A/G: 118.15
Clench Common Micolights (Devon): 129.825
Colerne: Approach: 120.075
Compton Abbas: A/G: 122.7
Coningsby: Tower: 124.675 GMC: 122.1
  Approach/Radar: 120.8/123.3
Cosford: Tower: 128.65 Approach: 135.875
Cottesmore: Tower: 122.1 130.2 Approach/
  Radar: 123.3
Coventry: Tower: 123.825 118.175 GMC:
  121.7 Approach/Radar: 123.825 136.15
  ATIS: 126.05
Cranfield: Tower: 134.925 Approach: 122.85
  ATIS: 121.875
Cranwell: Tower: 125.05 GMC: 121.775
  Approach/Radar: 119.375 123.3 ATIS:
  135.675
Cromer Microlight: 129.85
Crowfield: A/G: 122.775
Crowland/Spalding: A/G: 129.975

Culdrose: Tower: 122.1 Approach/Radar:
  134.05 123.3
Cumbernauld: A/G: 120.6
Damyns Hall (Hornchurch): A/G: 119.55
Deanland/Lewes: A/G: 129.725
Deenethorpe: 127.575
Defford (Croft Farm): A/G: 119.1
Denham: AFIS/A/G: 130.725
Derby: A/G: 118.35
Dishforth: Tower: 122.1
Doncaster Sheffield: Tower: 128.775
  Approach/Radar: 126.225 129.05 ATIS:
  134.95
Donna Nook Range: 122.75
Dublin: Tower 118.6 GMP: 121.875 GMC:
  121.8 Approach/Radar: 121.1 119.55 118.5
  119.925 126.25 119.55 ATIS: 124.525
Dublin Control: 124.65 129.129.175 136.05
  136.15
Dundee: Tower/Approach: 122.9
Dunkeswell: A/G: 123.475
Dunsfold: A/G: 119.1
Durham Tees Valley: Tower: 119.8 Approach/
  Radar: 118.85 128.85 ATIS: 132.375
Duxford: AFIS: 122.075
Eaglescott: A/G: 123.0
Earls Colne: A/G: 122.425
East Fortune Microlights: 118.775
East Midlands: Tower: 124.0 GMC: 121.9
  Approach/Radar: 134.175 120.125 ATIS:
  128.225
Edinburgh: Tower: 118.7 GMC: 121.75
  Approach/Radar: 121.2 128.975 ATIS:
  131.35
Eggesford: A/G: 123.5
Elmsett: A/G: 130.9
Elstree: AFIS/AG: 122.4
Elvington: A/G: 119.625
Enniskillen (St Angelo): A/G: 123.2
Enstone: A/G: 129.875
Eshott: A/G: 122.85
Eskmeals Range: 122.75
Essex Radar: See *London Stansted*
Exeter: Tower: 119.8 Approach/Radar:
  128.975 119.05 ATIS: 119.325
Fadmore: A/G: 123.3
Fairford: Tower: 119.15
Fair Isle: A/G: 118.025
Fairoaks: AFIS/AG: 123.425
Farnborough: Tower: 122.5 Approach/Radar:
  134.35 125.25 130.05 ATIS: 128.4

Felthorpe: A/G: 123.5

Fenland: AFIS/AG: 122.925

Fife/Glenrothes: A/G: 130.45

Fishburn Microlights (Co Durham): 118.275

Fowlmere: A/G: 135.7

Full Sutton: A/G: 132.325

Gamston: A/G: 130.475

Glasgow: Tower: 118.8 GMC: 121.7 Approach/Radar: 119.1 119.3 121.3 ATIS: 129.575

Gloucestershire: Tower: 122.9 Approach/ Radar: 128.55 120.975 ATIS: 127.475

Gormanston: Tower/Approach: 122.2

Great Yarmouth (North Denes): Approach/ Tower/A/G: 123.4

Guernsey: Tower: 119.95 GMC: 121.8 Approach/Radar: 128.65 118.9 124.5 ATIS: 109.4

Halfpenny Green: See *Wolverhampton-Halfpenny Green*

Halton: A/G: 130.425

Haverfordwest: A/G: 122.2

Hawarden: Tower: 124.95 Approach/Radar: 123.35 130.25

Henlow: A/G: 121.1

Henstridge: A/G: 130.25

Hibaldstow: A/G: 129.925

Highland Radar: 134.1 126.1

Hinton in the Hedges: A/G: 119.45

Hucknall: A/G: 130.8

Huddersfield (Crosland Moor): 128.375

Humberside: Tower: 124.9 Approach/Radar: 119.125 129.25 ATIS: 124.125

Husbands Bosworth: A/G: 127.575

Insch Microlights: 129.825

Inverness: Tower: 118.4 Approach/Radar: 122.6 ATIS: 109.2

Islay (Port Ellen): AFIS: 123.15

Isle of Man (Ronaldsway): Tower: 118.9 Approach/Radar: 120.85 118.2 125.3 ATIS: 123.875

Isle of Wight (Sandown): A/G: 119.275

Jersey: Tower: 119.45 GMC: 121.9 Approach/ Radar: 118.55 120.3 120.45 125.2 ATIS: 129.725 112.2

Kemble: AFIS: 118.9 Ops: 131.475

Kinloss: Tower: 122.1 Approach/Radar: 118.35/119.35

Kirkbride: A/G: 124.4

Kirkwall: Tower/Approach/AFIS: 118.3 ATIS: 108.6

Lakenheath: Tower: 122.1 Approach/Radar: 136.5 Ops (Civil transit): 128.9

Land's End (St Just): Tower/AG: 120.25

Langar: A/G: 129.9

Lasham: Base: 131.025 Approach (Farnborough): 125.25

Lashenden (Headcorn): A/G: 122.0

Leeds-Bradford: Tower: 120.3 Approach/ Radar: 123.75 121.05 ATIS: 118.025

Leeming: Tower: 120.5 Approach/Radar: 127.75/123.3

Lee-on-Solent: Tower: 120.225

Leicester: A/G: 122.125

Lerwick (Tingwall): AFIS: 125.3

Leuchars: Tower: 122.1 Approach/Radar: 126.5/123.3

Linton-on-Ouse: Tower: 122.1 Approach/ Radar: 118.55/123.3

Little Gransden: A/G: 130.85

Little Snoring: A/G: 118.125

Little Staughton: A/G: 123.925

Liverpool: Tower: 126.35 GMC: 121.95 Approach/Radar: 119.85 118.45 ATIS: 124.325

London (Battersea) Heliport: Tower: 122.9

London City: Tower: 118.075 118.4 GMC: 121.825 Approach/Radar: 132.7 128.025 ATIS: 136.35 Thames Radar: 132.7 Heathrow Director: 119.725

London Control: See Appendix 2

London/Gatwick: Tower: 124.225 134.225 GMP: 121.95 GMC: 121.8 Approach/Radar: 126.825 118.95 129.025 ATIS:136.525

London/Heathrow: Tower: 118.5 118.7 124.475 GMP: 121.975 GMC: 121.9 121.7 121.850 Radar: 119.725 120.4 127.525 134.975 125.625 Arr ATIS: 128.075 113.75 115.1 Dep ATIS: 121.935

London Mil: East: 135.275 Central: 128.7 Northwest: 127.45 West: 133.9 Southwest: 135.15

London Stansted: Tower: 123.8 125.55 GMP: 121.95 GMC: 121.725 Radar: 126.95 Essex Radar: 120.625 ATIS: 127.175 114.55

Londonderry (Eglinton): Tower: 134.15 Approach: 123.625

Long Marston: A/G: 129.825

Lossiemouth: Tower: 118.2 Approach/Radar: 123.3/119.35/118.9

Luton: Tower: 132.55 126.725 GMP: 121.675
GMC: 121.75 Approach/Radar: 129.55
128.75 Essex Radar: 129.55 ATIS: 120.575
Lydd: Tower: 128.525 Approach: 120.7 ATIS:
129.225
Lyneham: Tower: 119.225 GMC: 129.475
Approach/Radar: 118.425/123.4/123.3
Manchester: Tower: 118.625 119.4 GMP:
121.7 GMC: 121.85 Radar: 118.575 135.0
121.35 ATIS: 128.175 113.55
Manchester/Barton: AFIS: 120.25
Manchester Woodford: Tower: 120.7
Approach/Radar: 120.7 130.75 130.05
Manston: Tower: 119.925 Approach/Radar:
126.35 129.45 ATIS: 133.675
Marham: Tower: 122.1 Approach/Radar:
362.3/124.15/123.3
Merryfield: Tower: 122.1
Middle Wallop: Tower: 118.275 Approach/
Radar: 123.3
Mildenhall: Tower: 122.55 GMC: 121.8 Ops:
131.975
Mona: Tower: 119.175 AFIS: 118.95
Approach (Valley): 125.225
Netheravon: AFIS: 128.3 Salisbury Plain A/G:
122.75
Netherthorpe: A/G: 123.275
Newcastle: Tower: 119.7 GMC: 121.725
Approach/Radar: 124.375 125.825 ATIS:
118.375
Newquay: Tower: 134.375 GMC: 121.95
Approach/Radar: 133.4 128.725 ATIS: 127.4
Newtownards: A/G: 128.3
Northampton (Sywell): AFIS: 122.7
North Coates Microlights: 120.15
Northolt: Tower: 120.675 Approach/Radar:
126.45 130.35 125.875 129.125 ATIS:
125.125 Ops: 132.65
North Weald: A/G: 123.525 Glider Ops:
129.975
Norwich: Tower: 124.25 Approach/Radar:
119.35 128.325 ATIS: 128.625
Nottingham: A/G: 134.875
Oaksey Park: A/G: 132.225
Oban: AFIS: 118.05
Odiham: Tower: 122.1 Approach/Radar:
131.3/123.3
Old Buckenham: A/G: 124.4
Old Sarum: A/G: 123.2
Old Warden (display days only): A/G 130.7
Otherton Microlights (Staffs): 129.825

Oxford: Tower: 133.425 GMC: 121.95
Approach: 125.325 124.275 (Brize Radar)
ATIS: 136.225
Panshanger: A/G: 120.25
Pembrey: A/G: 124.4
Pembrey/Pendine Ranges: 122.75
Penzance Heliport: A/G: 118.1
Perranporth: A/G: 119.75
Perth: A/G: 119.8
Peterborough (Conington): A/G: 129.725
Peterborough (Sibson): A/G: 120.325
Plockton: A/G: 130.65
Plymouth: Tower: 118.15 Approach: 133.55
Plymouth Military Radar: 121.25/124.1
Pocklington: A/G: 129.9
Popham: A/G: 129.8
Predannack: Tower: 122.1 Approach
(*Culdrose*): 134.05
Prestwick: Tower: 118.15 121.8 Approach/
Radar: 120.55 119.45 ATIS: 121.125
Redhill: Tower: 119.6 ATIS: 136.125
Redlands Microlights (Wilts): 129.825
Rochester: AFIS: 122.25
Rufforth: A/G: 129.975
Rush Green/Hitchin: A/G: 122.35
St Athan: Tower: 118.125
Sandtoft: A/G: 130.425
Scatsta: Tower/Approach: 123.6 Radar: 122.4
Scilly Isles/St Mary's: Tower/Approach:
124.875
Scottish Control: See Appendix 2
Seething: A/G: 122.6
Shannon Control: 124.7 127.5 131.15 132.15
135.6 134.275 135.225 119.075
Shanwick Oceanic: 123.95 127.65 120.35
127.9
Shawbury: Tower: 122.1 Approach/Radar:
120.775/123.3
Sherburn-in-Elmet: A/G: 122.6
Shipdham: A/G: 132.25
Shobdon: AFIS/AG: 123.5
Shoreham: Tower/Approach: 123.15 125.4
ATIS: 125.3
Silverstone: A/G: 121.075
Sittles Farm (near Lichfield): 129.825
Skegness: A/G: 132.425
Sleap: A/G: 122.45
Southampton: Tower: 118.2 Approach/Radar:
128.85 ATIS: 113.35
Southend: Tower: 127.725 Approach/Radar:
130.775 128.95 ATIS: 136.05

Spadeadam Range: 128.725
Stapleford: A/G: 122.8
Stoke Microlights (near Southend): 129.825
Stornoway: Tower/Approach/AFIS: 123.5
  ATIS: 115.1
Strathallan: A/G: 129.9
Strubby Heliport: 118.75
Sturgate: A/G: 130.3
Sumburgh: Tower: 118.25 Approach/Radar:
  131.3 123.15 ATIS: 125.85
Sutton Microlights (near Ely): 129.825
Swansea: A/G: 119.7
Syerston: A/G: 125.425
Tain Range: 122.75
Tatenhill: A/G: 124.075
Teesside: See *Durham Tees Valley*
Tern Hill: Tower: 122.1
Thames Radar: 132.7
Thruxton: A/G: 130.45
Tibenham: A/G: 129.975
Tilstock: A/G: 118.1
Tiree: AFIS: 122.7
Topcliffe: Tower: 122.1 Approach/Radar:
  125.0 123.3
Tresco Heliport: A/G: 118.2
Truro: A/G: 129.8
Turweston: A/G: 122.175
Unst: AFIS/A/G: 130.35 Ops: 123.45
Valley: Tower: 122.1 Approach/Radar:
  125.225/123.3 ATIS: 120.725
Waddington: Tower: 122.1/121.3 Approach/
  Radar: 127.35/125.35/123.3

Wainfleet Range: 122.75
Walton Wood Heliport: A/G: 123.625
Warton: Tower: 130.8 Approach/Radar:
  129.525 129.725 ATIS: 121.725
Wattisham: Tower: 122.1 Approach/Radar:
  125.8/123.3
Wellesbourne Mountford: AFIS: 124.025
Welshpool: A/G: 128.0
West Freugh/Kirkcudbright Range:
  130.05/122.1
Weston on the Green: DZ: 133.65
West Wales (Aberporth): AFIS/AG:
  122.15
White Waltham: AFIS/AG: 122.6
Wick: Tower/Approach/AFIS: 119.7 ATIS:
  113.6
Wickenby: A/G: 122.45
Wittering: Tower: 125.525 Approach/Radar:
  130.2/123.3
Wolverhampton Halfpenny Green: AFIS:
  123.0
Woodford: See *Manchester Woodford*
Woodvale: Tower: 119.75 Approach:
  121.0
Wycombe Air Park: Tower: 126.55 GMC:
  121.775
Wyton: Tower: 119.975 GMC: 122.1
  Approach: 134.05
Yeovil (Westland): Tower/AG: 125.4
  Approach/Radar: 130.8
Yeovilton: Tower: 120.8 GMC: 122.1
  Approach/Radar: 127.35/123.3

Air band frequencies in numerical order

Note: Many of the offshore oil and gas field frequencies are shared between one or more installations; all current frequencies are listed below.

MHz

118.025	Leeds ATIS/Fair Isle A/G	118.25	Sumburgh Tower
118.05	Birmingham Radar/Oban AFIS	118.275	Wallop Tower/Fishburn
118.075	London City Tower/Barra AFIS		Microlights
118.10	Aberdeen Tower/Penzance	118.30	Birmingham Tower/Belfast
	Heliport A/G/Tilstock A/G		(Aldergrove) Tower/Kirkwall
118.125	St Athan Tower/Little Snoring A/G		Tower/Approach/AFIS
118.15	Plymouth Tower/Prestwick	118.35	Derby A/G/Kinloss Talkdown
	Tower/Clacton A/G	118.375	Newcastle ATIS
118.175	Coventry Tower	118.40	London City Tower/Blackpool
118.20	Southampton Tower/Ronaldsway		Tower/Inverness Tower
	Radar/Tresco Heliport A/G/Lossie	118.425	Carlisle ATIS/Lyneham Approach

118.45	Liverpool Radar	119.85	Liverpool Approach
118.48	London Control Clacton Sector	119.925	Manston Tower/Dublin Approach
118.50	Heathrow Tower/Dublin Approach	119.95	Blackpool Radar/Guernsey Tower
118.55	Jersey Radar/Linton Approach	119.975	Wyton Tower
118.575	Manchester Radar	120.075	Colerne Approach/Tyne Oil Platform
118.60	Dublin Tower		
118.625	Manchester Tower	120.125	East Midlands Radar
118.65	Bournemouth Radar	120.15	North Coates Microlights
118.70	Heathrow Tower/Edinburgh Tower	120.225	Solent Tower
		120.25	Barton AFIS/Panshanger A/G/
118.75	East Fortune Microlights/Strubby A/G		Lands End Tower/A/G
		120.30	Leeds Tower/Jersey Radar
118.775	Scottish Control	120.325	Sibson A/G
118.80	Glasgow Tower	120.35	Shanwick Oceanic
118.825	London Control (TC)	120.375	Beccles A/G
118.85	Durham Approach	120.40	Heathrow Radar
118.90	Ronaldsway Tower/Guernsey Radar/Kemble AFIS	120.425	Barkston Tower
		120.45	Jersey Radar
118.95	Gatwick Radar/Mona AFIS	120.475	London Control (TC)
119.00	Brize Zone	120.50	Leeming Tower
119.05	Aberdeen Approach/Exeter Radar	120.525	London Control (TC)
119.10	Glasgow Radar/Defford (Croft Farm) A/G/Dunsfold A/G	120.55	Prestwick Approach
		120.575	Luton ATIS
119.125	Humberside Approach	120.60	Cumbernauld A/G
119.15	Fairford Tower	120.625	Essex Radar
119.175	Mona Tower	120.675	Northolt Tower
119.20	Benbecula Tower/Approach/AFIS	120.70	Woodford Tower/Approach/Lydd Approach
119.225	Lyneham Tower		
119.275	Sandown A/G	120.725	Valley ATIS
119.30	Glasgow Radar	120.775	Shawbury Approach
119.325	Exeter ATIS	120.80	Coningsby Approach/Yeovilton Tower
119.35	Norwich Approach/Lossie Departures		
		120.85	Ronaldsway Radar
119.375	Barkston/Cranwell Departures	120.90	Belfast (Aldergrove) Radar/Benson Zone
119.40	Manchester Tower		
119.45	Jersey Tower/Prestwick Radar/ Hinton in the Hedges A/G	121.00	Woodvale Approach
		121.025	London Control (TC)
119.475	Bournemouth Radar	121.05	Leeds Radar
119.525	Scottish Control	121.075	Silverstone A/G
119.55	Damyns Hall (Hornchurch) A/G/ Dublin Approach	121.10	Chetwynd Tower/A/G/Dublin Approach/Henlow A/G
119.60	Redhill Tower	121.125	Prestwick ATIS
119.625	Elvington A/G	121.20	Edinburgh Radar
119.65	Aberporth Range	121.225	London Control
119.70	Newcastle Tower/Swansea A/G/ Wick Tower/Approach/AFIS	121.25	Plymouth Military Radar
		121.30	Glasgow Radar/Waddington Tower
119.725	Heathrow Radar		
119.75	Woodvale Tower/Perranporth A/G	121.325	Scottish Control
119.775	London Control (TC)	121.35	Manchester Radar
119.80	Durham Tower/Perth A/G	121.675	Luton GMP

121.70	Heathrow GMC/Manchester GMP/ Aberdeen GMC/Bournemouth GMC/Coventry GMC/Glasgow GMC
121.725	Stansted GMC/Newcastle GMC/ Brize GMC
121.75	Luton GMC/Belfast (Aldergrove) GMC
121.775	Wycombe ATIS/Cranwell GMC
121.80	Birmingham GMC/London City GMC/Guernsey GMC/Prestwick Tower/Benson GMC/Dublin GMC/ Mildenhall GMC
121.825	London City GMC
121.85	Heathrow GMC/Manchester GMC/ Aberdeen ATIS
121.875	Biggin Hill ATIS/Cranfield ATIS/ Dublin GMP
121.90	Heathrow GMC/East Midlands GMC/Edinburgh GMC/Jersey GMC
121.925	Birmingham GMP/Bristol (Lulsgate) GMC
121.935	Heathrow Dep ATIS
121.95	Oxford GMC/Newquay GMC/ Fenton GMC/Liverpool GMC/ Gatwick GMP/Stansted GMP
121.975	Heathrow GMP
122.00	Lashenden A/G/Baldonnel Approach/Offshore
122.05	Company Ops various
122.075	Duxford AFIS
122.10	Fenton Tower/Coningsby Approach/Cottesmore Tower/ Culdrose Tower/Dishforth Tower/ Kinloss Tower/Lakenheath Tower/ Leuchars Tower/Linton Tower/ Marham Tower/Merryfield Tower/ Odiham Tower/Predannack Tower/Shawbury Tower/Tern Hill Tower/Topcliffe Tower/Valley Tower/Waddington Tower/ Wattisham Tower/Wyton GMC/ Yeovilton GMC
122.125	Leicester A/G
122.15	West Wales AFIS/A/G
122.175	Turweston A/G/Offshore
122.20	Cambridge Tower/Haverfordwest A/G/Gormanston Tower/Approach
122.225	Offshore
122.25	Caernarfon A/G/Rochester AFIS/ Brent Radar

122.30	Blackbushe AFIS/A/G/Dublin Mil
122.325	Offshore
122.35	Flight Support Ops Ronaldsway etc/Execair Ops Glasgow/Audley End A/G/Rush Green A/G
122.375	Offshore
122.40	Scatsta Radar
122.45	Chichester (Goodwood) AFIS/ Sleap A/G/Wickenby A/G
122.50	Farnborough Tower/Mildenhall Tower
122.525	Ashcroft Farm A/G
122.60	Inverness Approach/White Waltham AFIS/A/G/Seething A/G/ Sherburn A/G
122.70	Sywell AFIS/Bodmin A/G/ Compton Abbas A/G/Tiree AFIS
122.725	Bristol (Filton) Radar
122.75	Donna Nook Range/Eskmeals Range/Tain Range/Pembrey Range/Salisbury Plain Range/ Wainfleet range
122.775	Crowfield A/G/Offshore
122.80	Stapleford A/G/Baldonnel Approach/Offshore
122.825	Belfast City Tower/Bruntingthorpe A/G
122.85	Cranfield Approach/Eshott A/G
122.90	Dundee Tower/Approach/London (Battersea) Heliport Tower
122.925	Fenland AFIS/A/G
123.00	Halfpenny Green AFIS/Eaglescott A/G/Offshore
123.05	Beverley/Linley Hill A/G
123.10	Baldonnel GMC/Boulmer A/G/ NATO/Intl Combined Scene of SAR
123.15	Islay AFIS/Shoreham Tower/ Approach/Sumburgh Radar
123.175	Badminton A/G
123.20	Barrow (Walney) AFIS/Old Sarum A/G
123.25	Bagby A/G/Bembridge A/G/ Offshore
123.275	Netherthorpe A/G
123.30	Barkston Talkdown/Fenton Talkdown/Coningsby Talkdown/ Cottesmore Director/Cranwell Radar/Culdrose Director/Kinloss Talkdown/Leeming Approach/ Leuchars Talkdown/Linton Talkdown/Lossie Approach/

	Lyneham Talkdown/Marham Talkdown/Wallop Radar/Odiham Talkdown/Shawbury Talkdown/ Topcliffe Talkdown/Valley Talkdown/Waddington Director/ Wattisham Director/Wittering Talkdown/Yeovilton Director
123.35	Hawarden Approach
123.40	Lyneham Zone
123.425	Fairoaks AFIS/A/G
123.45	Unst Ops
123.475	Dunkeswell A/G
123.50	Shobdon AFIS/A/G/Stornoway Tower/AFIS/A/G/Eggesford A/G/ Felthorpe A/G/Baldonnel Tower
123.525	North Weald A/G
123.55	Offshore
123.575	Belle Vue Microlights
123.60	Cambridge Approach/Carlisle Tower/Approach/Scatsta Tower/ Approach
123.625	Eglinton Approach/Walton Wood A/G
123.65	Offshore
123.725	Brize Tower
123.75	Leeds Approach/Salisbury Plain A/G
123.775	Scottish Control Antrim Sector
123.80	Stansted Tower
123.825	Coventry Tower/Approach
123.875	Ronaldsway ATIS
123.925	Little Staughton A/G
123.95	Shanwick Oceanic
124.00	East Midlands Tower
124.025	Wellesbourne AFIS
124.075	Tatenhill A/G
124.125	Humberside ATIS
124.15	Marham LARS/Plymouth Military Radar
124.225	Gatwick Tower
124.25	Norwich Tower
124.275	Brize Radar
124.325	Liverpool ATIS
124.35	Bourn A/G
124.375	Newcastle Approach
124.40	Old Buckenham A/G/Pembrey A/G/Kirkbride A/G
124.475	Heathrow Tower
124.50	Guernsey Radar/Scottish Control
124.525	Dublin ATIS
124.65	Dublin Control South

124.675	Coningsby Tower
124.825	Scotttish Control Dean Cross Sector
124.875	St Mary's Tower/Approach
124.90	Humberside Tower
124.925	London Control
124.95	Hawarden Tower/Manston Radar
124.975	Cambridge Radar
125.00	Cardiff Tower/Topcliffe Approach
125.125	Northolt ATIS
125.20	Jersey Radar
125.225	Valley Radar
125.25	Farnborough Radar
125.275	Anglia Radar
125.30	Ronaldsway Radar/Lerwick AFIS
125.325	Oxford Approach
125.35	Waddington Zone/Alderney Tower
125.40	Shoreham Tower/Approach/ Chalgrove A/G/Yeovil Tower/A/G
125.425	Syerston A/G
125.525	Wittering Tower
125.55	Stansted Tower
125.60	Bournemouth Tower
125.625	Heathrow Radar
125.65	Bristol (Lulsgate) Radar
125.675	Scottish Control Hebrides UCA
125.680	Scottish Control
125.725	Scottish Volmet
125.80	Wattisham Approach
125.825	Newcastle Radar
125.85	Cardiff Radar/Sumburgh ATIS
125.875	Northolt Talkdown
125.90	Campbeltown AFIS
126.025	Bristol (Lulsgate) ATIS
126.075	London Control Berry Head Sector
126.225	Doncaster Approach/Radar
126.25	Scottish Control/Dublin Radar
126.30	Scottish Control Dean Cross Sector
126.35	Liverpool Tower/London City ATIS/Manston Approach
126.45	Northolt Approach
126.50	Brize Talkdown/Fenton Approach/Leuchars Approach
126.55	Wycombe Tower
126.60	London Volmet North
126.625	Cardiff Radar
126.70	Boscombe Zone
126.725	Luton Tower
126.780	London Control North Sea Sector
126.825	Gatwick Radar
126.875	London Control

126.925	Scottish Control Montrose Sector	128.75	Luton Radar
126.95	Stansted Radar	128.775	Doncaster Tower
127.00	Dublin Volmet	128.85	Southampton Approach/Durham Radar
127.105	London Control Daventry Sector		
127.15	Benson Tower	128.90	Lakenheath Ops (Civil transit)
127.175	Stansted ATIS	128.925	Anglia Radar
127.20	Blackpool ATIS	128.95	Southend Radar
127.25	Brize Approach	128.975	Exeter Approach
127.275	Scottish Control West Coast Sector	129.025	Gatwick Radar
127.35	Waddington Zone/Yeovilton Radar	129.05	Doncaster Radar
127.40	Newquay ATIS	129.10	Scottish Control Rathlin Sector
127.425	London Control Worthing Sector	129.125	Northolt Departures
127.430	London Control Upper Sector	129.175	Dublin Control North
127.45	London Mil Northwest	129.205	London Control Daventry Sector
127.525	Heathrow Radar	129.225	Scottish Control Hebrides UCA/ Lydd ATIS
127.575	Deenethorpe A/G/Husbands Bosworth A/G		
		129.25	Humberside Radar
127.65	Shanwick Oceanic	129.375	London Control
127.70	London Control	129.40	Biggin Hill Approach/Offshore
127.725	Southend Tower	129.425	London Control
127.75	Leeming Approach	129.475	Lyneham Ground
127.825	London Control Worthing Sector	129.50	Brest Control
127.880	London Control Daventry Sector	129.55	Essex Radar
127.90	Shanwick Radio	129.575	Glasgow ATIS
127.975	Bristol (Filton) Radar	129.60	London Control
128.00	Welshpool A/G	129.70	Prestwick Handling
128.025	London City Radar	129.725	Jersey ATIS/Conington A/G/ Deanland A/G
128.05	Scottish Control		
128.075	Heathrow Arr ATIS	129.75	Manx Regional Ronaldsway/Jester Ops Gloucestershire
128.125	London Control North Sea Sector		
128.160	London Control Clacton Sector	129.80	Breighton A/G/Popham A/G/ Truro A/G
128.175	Manchester ATIS		
128.20	Belfast (Aldergrove) ATIS	129.825	Chirk Microlights/Clench Common Microlights/Insch Microlights/ Otherton Microlights/Redlands Microlights/Stoke Microlights/ Sutton Microlights/Long Marston A/G
128.225	East Midlands ATIS		
128.30	Aberdeen Radar/Newtownards A/G/Netheravon AFIS		
128.325	Norwich Radar		
128.375	Huddersfield Crosland Moor A/G		
		129.875	Enstone A/G
128.40	Farnborough ATIS	129.90	Chatteris A/G/Cark A/G/Langar A/G/Pocklington A/G/Strathallan A/G
128.425	London Control Dover Sector		
128.475	London Control		
128.50	Belfast (Aldergrove) Radar	129.925	Hibaldstow A/G
128.525	Lydd Tower	129.95	Brent Radar/Ballykelly DZ
128.625	Norwich ATIS	129.975	Crowland A/G/Bicester A/G/ Tibenham A/G/Glider Common Freq
128.60	London Volmet South		
128.65	Guernsey Radar/Cosford Tower		
128.675	Scottish Control	130.00	Boscombe Approach
128.70	London Mil Central	130.05	Farnborough Radar/Woodford Radar/West Freugh Range
128.725	Newquay Radar/Spadeadam Range		
		130.075	Brize Ops/FAL Ops Lydd

130.10	Ballarena Ops (Ballykelly)	132.25	Shipdham A/G
130.15	Offshore	132.30	London Control Worthing Sector
130.175	Company Ops various	132.325	Full Sutton A/G
130.20	Chivenor A/G/Cottesmore Radar/	132.35	Bristol (Filton) Tower
	Wittering Radar	132.375	Durham ATIS
130.25	Hawarden Radar/Henstridge A/G	132.425	Skegness A/G
130.275	Offshore	132.455	London Control
130.30	Sturgate A/G	132.475	Cardiff ATIS
130.35	Northolt Director/Unst AFIS/A/G	132.55	Luton Tower/Plymouth Approach
130.375	Far North Ops Wick	132.605	London Control Middle Sector
130.425	Sandtoft A/G/Halton A/G	132.65	Northolt Ops
130.45	Thruxton A/G/Fife A/G	132.840	London Control Upper Sector
130.475	Gamston A/G	133.175	London Control TC
130.50	Alderney GMC	133.675	Manston ATIS
130.55	Andrewsfield A/G	132.70	Thames Radar
130.575	Company Ops various	132.725	Scottish Control Central Sector
130.60	Servisair	132.840	London Control Lakes Sector
130.625	Isleavia Ops Ronaldsway/	132.860	London Control Lakes Sector
	Helicentre Ops	132.90	Temporary allocation for airshows,
130.65	Oceansky Manchester/Multiflight		etc
	Ops Leeds/Plockton A/G	132.95	London Control Berry Head Sector
130.725	Denham AFIS/A/G	133.005	Brest Control
130.75	Woodford Radar/Boscombe Tower	133.05	Scottish Control
130.775	Southend Approach	133.40	Newquay Approach
130.80	Yeovil Radar/Hucknall A/G/	133.425	Oxford Tower
	Heather Alpha	133.455	London Control Clacton Sector
130.85	Belfast City Approach/Little	133.480	Brest Control
	Gransden A/G	133.60	London Control Bristol Sector
130.90	Elmsett A/G	133.615	Brest Control
130.925	London Control TC	133.65	Weston DZ/Coast Guard
131.00	Birmingham Radar	133.675	Scottish Control Hebrides UCA
131.025	Lasham Base	133.705	London Control Lakes Sector
131.130	London Control Daventry Sector	133.725	Bournemouth ATIS
131.30	Odiham Approach/Sumburgh	133.75	Brize Director
	Approach	133.80	Scottish Control
131.325	Birmingham Radar	133.85	Bristol (Lulsgate) Tower
131.40	Southend Handling etc	133.90	London Mil West
131.425	Company Ops various	133.975	London Control TC
131.475	Kemble Ops/Gate Aviation Ops	134.05	Wyton Approach/Culdrose
131.50	Company Ops various		Approach
131.70	SAS Ground Services Manchester	134.10	Aberdeen Radar
131.725	ACARS/Datalink	134.125	London Control TC
131.75	LAS Liverpool etc	134.15	Eglinton Tower
131.80	Company Ops various	134.175	East Midlands Radar
131.825	ACARS Datalink	134.225	Gatwick Tower
131.875	Company Ops various	134.30	Scottish Mil
131.90	Company Ops various	134.35	Farnborough Radar
131.925	Company Ops Heathrow	134.375	Newquay Tower
131.975	Company Ops various	134.425	Scottish Control
132.15	Shannon Control	134.460	London Control Dover Sector
132.225	Oaksey Park	134.60	Cambridge ATIS

134.75	London Control Bristol Sector		135.70	Fowlmere A/G
134.775	Scottish Control Tyne Sector		135.85	London Control Lakes Sector
134.80	Biggin Hill Tower/Belfast City Radar		135.875	Cosford Approach
			135.925	Scottish Mil
134.875	Nottingham A/G		135.95	Blackpool Radar
134.90	London Control Dover Sector		136.00	Brest Control
134.925	Cranfield Tower		136.025	Birmingham ATIS
134.95	Doncaster ATIS		136.05	Southend ATIS/Dublin Control
134.975	Heathrow Radar		136.075	Bristol (Lulsgate) Radar
135.00	Manchester Radar		136.125	Redhill ATIS
135.05	London Control Worthing Sector		136.15	Coventry Radar/Dublin Control
135.125	Brimpton A/G		136.225	Oxford ATIS
135.15	London Mil Southwest		136.375	London Volmet Main
135.175	Aberdeen Radar		136.45	Benson Talkdown
135.255	London Control Bristol Sector		136.50	Lakenheath Approach
135.275	London Mil East		136.525	Gatwick ATIS
135.325	London Control Worthing Sector		136.575	Scottish Control
135.425	London Control Upper Sector		136.60	London Control
135.525	Scottish Control Dean Cross Sector		136.625	Belfast City ATIS
135.540	London Control Berry Head Sector		136.75	ACARS Datalink
			136.80	Company Ops various
135.580	London Control Lakes Sector		136.85	Company Ops various
135.60	Shannon Control		136.875	Company Ops various
135.675	Cranwell ATIS		136.90	ACARS Datalink

Appendix 4

UHF air band frequencies

THIS LISTING HAS been compiled from official sources available to the general public. There are of course many other allocations, including air-to-air, TADs, Ops and satellite communications. An anomaly is the use of parts of the sub-band 137.0–149.9MHz, officially allocated as 'Government mobile' for air band purposes. Note that some of the London Mil frequencies re-broadcast aircraft transmissions so that when a single controller is handling more than one channel, aircraft on one frequency are able to hear those on another and thus not inadvertently interrupt. An example is the Northwest ICF (Initial Contact Frequency) 277.625 on which civil aircraft transmitting on its sister VHF channel 127.45 can also be heard. London Mil has a number of unpublished UHF frequencies that are allocated by the ICF controller as required.

Frequencies of military airfields and radar units

Aberporth: Range: 338.925
ACMI Range North Sea: 252.1/340.55/290.95/359.4
Aldergrove: Tower/Approach: 278.35 Ops: 264.8
Barkston Heath: Tower: 281.225 GMC: 389.45 Approach (Cranwell): 280.775
PAR: 378.525 Radar: 355.95 282.6 ATIS: 293.45
Benson: Tower: 318.1 Approach/Radar: 376.65 356.125 PAR: 283.075 277.675
358.8 376.65
Boscombe Down: Tower: 338.475 GMC: 262.95 Approach/Radar: 233.85/371.825/282.675/256.5
  PAR: 369.25 ATIS: 275.725 Ops: 242.45
Boulmer: A/G: 249.625/282.8
Bristol Filton: Tower: 243.05 Approach/Radar: 341.325/336.475
Brize Norton: Tower: 379.75 GMC: 396.85 Approach/Radar: 389.575/297.8/264.775 PAR: 339.85
  Ops: 386.825 ATIS: 259.0
Cardiff: Approach/Radar: 251.375
Chetwynd: Tower/A/G: 356.25 Approach (Shawbury): 376.675
Chivenor: A/G: 252.8
Church Fenton: Tower: 234.1 GMC: 341.225 Approach/Radar: 233.45/338.7 PAR: 379.475
Colerne: Tower: 372.575 Approach: 374.825 ATIS: 277.85
Coningsby: Tower: 340.25 GMC: 279.075 Approach/Radar: 282.725/376.35/277.5
PAR: 281.125/341.2 ATIS: 280.3 Ops: 234.675/338.025
Cosford: Tower: 378.65 GMC: 241.4 Approach: 376.425
Cottesmore: Tower: 369.35 GMC: 308.825 Approach/Radar: 281.9/379.075/278.45/231.725 PAR:
  338.25/339.325 ATIS: 262.625
Cranwell: Tower: 268.625 GMC: 240.425 Approach/Radar: 280.775/275.675/284.325 PAR:
  338.275/378,.525 ATIS: 311.825
Culdrose: Tower: 297.775 GMC: 318.1 Approach/Radar: 378.55/241.4/369.225/313.6 PAR:
  293.825/296.675 ATIS: 231.85

Dishforth: Tower: 278.225 GMC: 371.975 Approach (Topcliffe): 293.775 Ops: 242.25
Donna Nook Range: 369.3 264.725
Eskmeals Range: 337.975
Fairford: Tower: 338.225 GMC: 234.25 Approach/Radar
(Brize): 297.8/264.775 Ops: 233.475/284.425 ATIS (Brize): 259.0
Holbeach Range: 231.375 375.225
Honington: Approach/Radar (Lakenheath): 337.6/264.675
Kinloss: Tower: 235.025 GMC:389.4 Approach/Radar (Lossie): 234.875/258.7/308.85 PAR: 279.15/240.475 Ops: 278.975 ATIS: 389.4
Lakenheath: Tower: 338.925 GMC: 375.45 Approach/Radar: 309.2/250.3/242.05 PAR: 256.425/3 60.075/269.675/315.7/386.75 Ops: 244.475/379.8/284.425 ATIS: 356.725
Leconfield: A/G: 369.175
Leeming: Tower: 368.925 GMC: 379.9 Approach/Radar: 386.575/262.95/231.45 PAR: 375.45/318.1 ATIS: 369.475 Ops: 259.025
Leuchars: Tower: 293.825 GMC: 275.375 Approach/Radar: 308.875/255.4/389.525/255.4 PAR: 379.475/298.2 Ops: 396.9 ATIS: 369.25
Linton-on-Ouse: Tower: 240.825 GMC: 278.325 Approach/Radar: 372.125/235.2/275.850/281.825 PAR: 369.025/375.575 ATIS: 283.725
London Mil: Initial Contact Frequency: East: 277.775 Central: 252.875 Northwest: 277.625 West: 280.350 Southwest: 278.6 Southeast: 275.625 Lichfield Corridor: 292.525
Lossiemouth: Tower: 279.05 GMC: 268.625 Approach/Radar: 234.875/277.875/258.7/308.85 PAR: 244.375/369.2 ATIS: 264.775 Ops: 369.3
Luce Bay Range: 368.975
Lyneham: Tower: 234.15 GMC: 369.2 Approach/Radar: 278.7/362.3/231.875/338.35 PAR: 240.825 Ops: 377.975 ATIS: 233.125
Manorbier Range: 279.125 369.3
Marham: Tower: 281.15 GMC: 336.35 Approach/Radar: 233.075/362.3/282.25/377.475 PAR: 298.825/234.325 Ops: 284.0 ATIS: 277.225
Merryfield: Tower: 378.525
Middle Wallop: Tower: 242.275 A/G: 357.025 Approach/Radar: 280.625/375.775 PAR: 369.025 ATIS: 240.975
Mildenhall: Tower: 370.25 GMC: 337.975 Approach (Lakenheath): 309.2/250.3 ATIS: 375.5 Ops: 308.85/313.55 Metro: 284.425 ATIS: 375.5
Mona: Tower: 234.325 Approach/Radar (Valley): 379.95/264.7
Moray Firth Range: 308.85
Netheravon: Tower: 313.475 A/G: 243.625 (Salisbury Plain)
Newcastle: Approach/Radar: 284.6
Northolt: Tower: 281.175 Approach/Radar: 371.6/369.675 PAR: 284.05 Ops: 311.575 ATIS: 300.35
Odiham: Tower: 258.725 GMC: 241.025 Approach/Radar: 234.35/339.225 PAR: 278.225 ATIS: 300.45 FIS: 372.375
Otterburn Range: 279.0
Pembrey Range: 264.725
Plymouth Military Radar: 281.475/370.85
Predannack: Tower: 278.675 Approach (Culdrose): 378.55
Prestwick: Ops: Navy Prestwick: 279.05
St Athan: Tower: 240.0 GMC: 241.125 Approach/Radar: 277.6/251.375 (Cardiff) PAR: 282.2 ATIS: 340.45
Salisbury Plain Ops: 243.625
Scampton: Tower: 281.325 GMC: 278.5 Approach (Waddington): 250.85 PAR: 377.075/241.825
Scottish Mil: 282.625 (ICF)
Shawbury: Tower: 378.45 GMC: 389.45 Approach/Radar: 282.0/231.7/376.675

PAR: 278.675 ATIS: 284.275
Spadeadam Range: 308.775 ATIS: 241.975
Stanford: A/G: 277.85
Tain Range: 339.8/279.125
Ternhill: Tower: 376.4 GMC: 279.025 Approach (Shawbury): 376.675
Topcliffe: Tower: 379.75 GMC: 241.875 Approach/Radar: 293.775/313.6 PAR: 278.05
Upavon: Tower: 242.025
Valley: Tower: 268.625 GMC: 266.8 Approach/Radar: 379.95/264.7/363.65 PAR: 313.55 SAR:
    252.8
Waddington: Tower: 256.675 GMC: 342.125 Approach/Radar: 250.85/259.525/378.5 PAR:
    308.625/231.8 ATIS: 291.675 Ops: 386.625
Wainfleet Range: 375.55 277.95
Warton: Tower: 264.75 Approach/Radar: 233.175/264.75/233.175/264.75/234.65
Wattisham: Tower: 378.575 Approach/Radar: 277.725/234.65 PAR: 368.925/314.425
West Freugh Range (Luce Bay): 368.975
Wittering: Tower: 372.225 GMC: 369.225 Approach/Radar: 234.075/278.45
PAR: 275.325/244.55
Woodford: Tower: 280.6/269.125 Approach/Radar: 369.075/358.575
Woodvale: Tower: 278.2 Approach: 282.575
Wyton: Tower: 372.2 GMC: 278.35 Approach: 369.525 ATIS: 279.15
Yeovil (Westland): Tower: 233.425 Approach/Radar: 372.325/300.675
Yeovilton: Tower: 375.575 GMC: 268.625 Approach/Radar: 234.3/259.075 PAR: 282.025/241.525
    ATIS: 283.925

Miscellaneous
NATO Common Frequencies: Tower: 257.8 Approach: 362.3 Radar: 344.0 PAR: 385.4 Fixer:
    317.5 Royal Navy Air/Ship: 278.3 Low Flying (NATO/RAF): 300.8
Army: 253.9 Distress: 243.0 Scene of Search: 282.8/156.0(FM)/156.8(FM)

UHF air band frequencies in numerical order

MHz

231.45	Leeming Director	234.325	Marham Talkdown/Mona Tower
231.70	Shawbury Director	234.35	Odiham Approach
231.725	Cottesmore Zone	234.65	Wattisham Director
231.80	Waddington Talkdown	234.675	Coningsby Ops
231.85	Culdrose ATIS	234.875	Lossie Approach
231.875	Lyneham Zone	235.20	Lossie Tower/Linton Zone
232.075	Marham Approach	240.00	St Athan Tower
233.125	Lyneham ATIS	240.425	Cranwell Ground
233.175	Warton Approach	240.475	Lossie Talkdown
233.425	Westland Tower (Yeovil)	240.825	Linton Tower/Lyneham Talkdown
233.45	Fenton Approach	240.975	Wallop ATIS
233.475	Fairford Ops	241.025	Odiham Ground/Shawbury
233.625	Cranwell ATIS		Talkdown
233.85	Boscombe Approach	241.125	St Athan Ground
234.075	Wittering Approach	241.40	Cosford Ground/Culdrose Radar
234.10	Fenton Tower	241.525	Yeovilton Talkdown
234.15	Lyneham Tower	241.825	Scampton Talkdown
234.25	Fairford Ground	241.875	Topcliffe Ground
234.30	Yeovilton Radar	241.975	Spadeadam ATIS

242.025	Upavon Tower	277.50	Coningsby Director
242.05	Lakenheath Radar	277.60	St Athan Approach
242.25	Dishforth Ops	277.625	London Mil (Northwest)
242.275	Wallop Tower	277.675	Benson Talkdown
242.45	Boscombe Ops	277.725	Wattisham Approach
242.475	Wittering ATIS	277.775	London Mil (East)
243.00	UHF Distress	277.85	Colerne ATIS
243.05	Filton Tower	277.875	Lossie Approach
243.625	Salisbury Plain A/G	277.95	Wainfleet Range
244.375	Lossie Talkdown	278.05	Topcliffe Talkdown
244.475	Lakenheath Ops	278.20	Woodvale Tower
244.55	Wittering Talkdown	278.225	Odiham Talkdown/Dishforth
244.60	Scene of SAR Control		Tower
249.625	Boulmer A/G	278.325	Linton Ground
250.30	Lakenheath Departure	278.35	Wyton Ground/Aldergrove Tower/
250.85	Waddington Approach		Approach
251.375	Cardiff Approach/Radar	278.45	Cottesmore/Wittering Departures
252.80	Chivenor A/G/Valley A/G/NATO	278.50	Scampton Ground
	Combined SAR Training	278.60	London Mil (Southwest)
252.875	London Mil (Central)	278.675	Shawbury Talkdown/Predannack
255.40	Leuchars Departures		Tower
256.425	Lakenheath Radar	278.70	Lyneham Approach
256.50	Boscombe Zone	279.00	Otterburn Range
256.675	Waddington Tower	279.025	Tern Hill Ground
257.80	Nato Common Tower	279.05	Lossie Tower/Prestwick Navy Ops
258.70	Lossie Director	279.075	Coningsby Ground
258.725	Odiham Tower	279.125	Tain Range/Manorbier Range
259.00	Brize ATIS	279.15	Lossie Talkdown/Wyton ATIS
259.025	Leeming Ops	280.30	Coningsby ATIS
259.075	Yeovilton Director	280.35	London Mil (West)
259.525	Waddington Zone	280.60	Woodford Tower
262.625	Cottesmore ATIS	280.625	Wallop Approach
262.95	Boscombe Ground/Leeming Zone	280.775	Cranwell Approach
264.70	Valley Radar	281.125	Coningsby Talkdown
264.725	Donna Nook Range/Pembrey	281.15	Marham Tower
	Range	281.175	Northolt Tower
264.75	Warton Tower/Approach	281.225	Barkston Heath Tower
264.775	Brize Director/Lossie ATIS	281.325	Scampton Tower
264.80	Aldergrove Ops	281.375	Holbeach Range
266.80	Valley Ground	281.475	Plymouth Radar
268.625	Valley Tower/Cranwell Tower/	281.825	Linton Departures
	Lossie Ground/Yeovilton Ground	281.90	Cottesmore Approach
269.125	Woodford Tower	282.00	St Athan Director/Shawbury
269.675	Lakenheath Radar		Approach
275.325	Wittering Talkdown	282.025	Yeovilton Talkdown
275.375	Leuchars Ground	282.25	Marham Zone
275.625	London Mil (Southeast)	282.525	Benson ATIS
275.675	Cranwell Radar	282.575	Woodvale Approach
275.725	Boscombe ATIS	282.60	Barkston Director
275.85	Linton Director	282.625	Scottish Mil
277.225	Marham ATIS	282.675	Boscombe Director

282.725	Coningsby Approach	338.275	Cranwell Talkdown
282.80	Boulmer A/G/Leconfield A/G/	338.35	Lyneham Director
	Valley SAR Ops/Scene of Search	338.475	Boscombe Tower
	freq	338.70	Fenton Director
283.075	Benson Talkdown	338.925	Lakenheath Tower/Aberporth
283.425	Doncaster Radar		Range
283.725	Linton ATIS	339.225	Odiham Director
283.925	Yeovilton ATIS	339.325	Cottesmore Talkdown
284.00	Marham Ops	339.80	Tain Range
284.05	Northolt Talkdown	339.85	Brize Talkdown
284.275	Shawbury ATIS	340.25	Coningsby Tower
284.325	Cranwell Director	340.45	St Athan ATIS
284.425	Fairford Metro/Lakenheath Metro/	341.225	Fenton Ground
	Mildenhall Metro	341.325	Filton Radar
284.60	Newcastle Radar	342.125	Waddington Ground
291.675	Waddington ATIS	344.00	Nato Common Radar
292.525	London Mil (Lichfield Corridor)	355.95	Barkston Heath Departures
293.45	Barkston Heath ATIS	356.125	Benson Director
293.775	Topcliffe Approach	356.25	Chetwynd A/G
293.825	Leuchars Tower/Culdrose	356.725	Lakenheath ATIS
	Talkdown	357.025	Wallop A/G
296.675	Culdrose Talkdown	358.575	Woodford Approach
297.775	Culdrose Tower	360.075	Lakenheath Radar
297.80	Brize Approach	362.30	Nato Common Approach
298.20	Leuchars Talkdown	363.65	Valley Director
298.825	Marham Talkdown	368.925	Leeming Tower/Wattisham
300.35	Northolt ATIS		Talkdown
300.45	Odiham ATIS	368.975	West Freugh Range (Luce Bay)
300.675	Westland Radar (Yeovil)	369.025	Wallop Talkdown/Linton
300.80	NATO Low-flying		Talkdown
308.625	Waddington Talkdown	369.075	Woodford Approach
308.775	Spadeadam Range	369.175	Leconfield A/G
308.825	Cottesmore Ground	369.20	Lyneham Ground/Lossie
308.85	Lossie Departures/Mildenhall Ops		Talkdown
308.875	Leuchars Approach	369.225	Wittering Ground
309.20	Lakenheath Approach	369.25	Boscombe Talkdown/Leuchars
311.575	Northolt Ops		ATIS
313.475	Netheravon AFIS	369.30	Lossie Ops/Donna Nook Range/
313.55	Valley Talkdown/Mildenhall Ops		Manorbier Range
313.60	Topcliffe Director/Culdrose	369.35	Cottesmore Tower
	Director	369.475	Leeming ATIS
315.70	Lakenheath Radar	369.525	Wyton Approach
318.10	Benson Tower/Leeming	369.675	Northolt Director
	Talkdown/Culdrose Ground	370.25	Mildenhall Tower
335.00	ILS Glidepath Transmitters	370.85	Plymouth Radar
336.475	Filton Director	371.60	Northolt Approach
337.975	Mildenhall Ground/Eskmeals	371.825	Boscombe Radar
	Range	371.975	Dishforth Ground
338.025	Coningsby Ops/Leuchars Ops	372.125	Linton Approach
338.225	Fairford Tower	372.20	Wyton Tower
338.25	Cottesmore Talkdown	372.225	Wittering Tower

372.325	Westland Approach (Yeovil)
372.375	Odiham ATIS
372.575	Colerne Tower
374.825	Colerne Approach
375.225	Holbeach Range
375.45	Lakenheath Ground/Leeming Talkdown
375.50	Mildenhall ATIS
375.55	Wainfleet Range
375.575	Linton Talkdown/Yeovilton Tower
375.775	Wallop Radar
376.35	Coningsby Approach
376.40	Tern Hill Tower
376.425	Cosford Approach
376.65	Benson Approach
376.675	Shawbury Low Level
377.075	Scampton Talkdown
377.475	Marham Radar
377.975	Lyneham Ops
378.45	Shawbury Tower
378.50	Waddington Director
378.525	Merryfield Tower/Barkston Heath Talkdown
378.55	Culdrose Approach
378.575	Wattisham Tower
378.65	Cosford Tower
379.075	Cottesmore Director
379.475	Leuchars Talkdown/Fenton Talkdown
379.75	Brize Tower/Topcliffe Tower
379.80	Lakenheath Ops
379.90	Leeming Ground
379.95	Valley Approach
385.40	Nato Common PAR
386.575	Leeming Approach
386.625	Waddington Ops
386.75	Lakenheath Radar
386.825	Brize Ops
389.40	Marham Ground/Lossie ATIS
389.45	Shawbury Ground/Barkston Heath Ground
389.525	Leuchars Director
389.575	Brize Radar
396.85	Brize Ground
396.90	Leuchars Ops

Appendix 5

ICAO aircraft type designators

THE DESIGNATORS BELOW are used for flight planning purposes and also by ATC on flight progress strips. The aircraft name or designation in full is normally used on R/T, but many of the abbreviated versions may also be heard. This list is a sample of a wide variety of types and gives an idea of how the system works.

A109	Agusta 109	BE76	Beech Duchess	GA7	Cougar
A310	Airbus A310	BH06	Bell Jet Ranger	GAZL	Gazelle
A318	Airbus A318	BN2P	Islander	H25B	HS125 800
A319	Airbus A319	BN2T	Turbine	HR20	Robin HR20
A320	Airbus A320		Islander	IL62	Ilyushin IL-62
A321	Airbus A321	C130	C-130 Hercules	IL76	Ilyushin IL-76
A333	Airbus A330-300	C152	Cessna 152	JS31	Jetstream 31
A345	Airbus A340-500	C172	Cessna 172	JS41	Jetstream 41
A3ST	Beluga	C208	Cessna	L188	Lockheed
AC12	Commander 112		Caravan		Electra
AC14	Commander 114	C310	Cessna 310	LJ24	LearJet 24
AN26	Antonov AN-26	C401	Cessna 401	LJ35	LearJet 35
AN72	Antonov AN-72	C421	Cessna 421	LJ60	LearJet 60
A124	Antonov AN-124	C500	Cessna	MD83	MD-83
AS65	Dauphin		Citation	P68	Partenavia P68
AJET	Alphajet	C550	Citation II	PA27	Piper Aztec
B733	Boeing 737-300	CL60	Challenger	PA28	Piper Cherokee
B734	Boeing 737-400	D228	Dornier 228	PA34	Piper Seneca
B738	Boeing 737-800	D328	Dornier 328	PA38	Piper Tomahawk
B74F	Boeing 747F	DH8D	Dash 8 400	PA30	Piper Twin
B74S	Boeing 747SP	E110	Bandeirante		Comanche
B753	Boeing 757-300	E121	Xingu	PA31	Piper Navajo
B762	Boeing 767-200	EC55	Eurocopter 155	PAYE	Piper Cheyenne
B773	Boeing 777-300	EUFI	Eurofighter		I/II
B462	BAe 146-200		Typhoon	PREM	Premier 1
BDOG	Bulldog	FA50	Falcon 50	S880	Rallye
BE9L	Beech King	F900	Falcon 900	SF34	Saab 340
	Air 90	FK10	Fokker 100	SW2	Merlin IIA
BE20	Super King	FK27	Friendship	SW4	Merlin IV/Metro
	Air 200	FK50	Fokker 50	TAMP	Tampico
BE40	Beechjet 400	FK70	Fokker 70	TOBA	Tobago
BE55	Beech Baron	GLF2	Gulfstream II	TOR	Tornado
BE60	Beech Duke	GLF4	Gulfstream IV	T154	Tupolev TU-154

Appendix 6

Aircraft radio call-signs

CALL-SIGN PREFIXES and three-letter codes are allocated by ICAO on a worldwide basis. The use of either is permitted but most operators tend to use the spoken prefix rather than the three-letter. Sometimes you will hear both in succession, especially when the controller is unable to understand an unfamiliar prefix in a foreign accent and uses the code on his flight progress strip instead! On HF frequencies, the three-letter code is often used in preference to the spoken prefix because it is easier to hear over the usual atmospherics and interference. As an example, I have heard a BA aircraft over Africa using BAW rather than the usual Speedbird.

The general advice from CAA to airline operators is: 'Many airlines continue to utilise their IATA commercial flight numbers as a call-sign suffix. However, because they tend to be allocated in batches of sequential and very similar numbers, call-sign confusion occurs. Several airlines have switched to alphanumeric systems with some success over recent years. However, if every operator adopts alphanumerics, the limited choices available within the maximum of four elements allowed in the call-sign suffix means that similar confusion to the numeric system is likely to result.

'Before changing to an effective numeric system, which involves a significant amount of work, especially for a large airline, it is recommended that operators review their existing numeric system to deconflict similar call-signs. Where there is no effective solution to those call-signs that have a potential for numeric confusion, alphanumerics can be adopted.'

The following is a summary of the guidelines for operators when allocating call-signs. Avoid use of similar flight numbers within the same company; co-ordinate advance planning, whenever possible, with other operators to avoid using similar numbers; after implementation, ensure that there is a tactical response to review and amend call-signs where necessary; consider starting flight number element sequences with a higher number, eg six and above; try to minimise use of call-signs involving four-digits and, whenever possible, use no more than three; try to avoid using alphanumeric call-signs which correspond to the last two letters of the destination's ICAO location indicator, eg ABC 96LL for a flight inbound to Heathrow where the location indicator is EGLL; if similar numbered call-signs are inevitable, allow a significant time and/or geographical split between aircraft using similar call-signs; when useful capacity in the allocation of flight numbers and alphanumerics has been reached, consider applying for and using a second company designator such as 'Shuttle'; avoid, whenever practicable, flight numbers ending in a zero or five, eg five may be confused visually with S, and zero when combined with two digits, ie 150, may be confused with a heading or level; avoid use of similar/reversed digits/letters in alphanumerics, eg ABC 87MB and ABC 78BM. Finally, avoid phonetic letters that can be confused with another airline designator prefix, eg D- (the airline) Delta.'

Requests for the registration of or change in a designator will only be recognised by ICAO when received from the state having jurisdiction over the aircraft operating agency. Conversely, when a designator is no longer required, ICAO should be informed immediately but undertake not to reassign it until a period of at least 60 days has elapsed. ICAO has just issued a safety bulletin highlighting the fact that the word 'Air' is used either as prefix or suffix in more than one in five radiotelephony designators in use worldwide. Furthermore, one of its derived translations, 'Aero' in the Spanish language, represents 270 cases worldwide. 'Avia' used by many Russian operators occurs 174 times, 'Jet' 155, 'Trans' 134, 'Express' and 'Cargo' 83 times each. Less numerous examples include 'Flight', 'Star', 'Service', 'Charter', and 'Wings'. The potential for call-sign confusion leading to dangerous situations is obvious. It will be interesting to see what ICAO does about this in the future.

In the case of individual flight numbers, a call-sign similarity group has been set up by Eurocontrol to tackle the ongoing problem of call-sign confusion which can lead to crews taking instructions meant for other aircraft, with obvious safety implications. Eurocontrol says that research has shown that over 80% of call-sign similarities could be resolved by a central management service. This would de-conflict call-sign similarities during the flight planning phases with the aid of a dedicated software application. The Central Flow Management Unit at Brussels is likely to be involved when this project is initiated. Currently, the airlines manage their own de-confliction programmes with varying amounts of success.

Military call-signs are further explained in Chapter 17, many being changed frequently for security reasons. This is not a problem for training aircraft, and many three-letter codes reflect their bases, examples being 'VYT' and 'WIT' for the Valley and Wittering Flying Training Units respectively. Many have been assimilated into the ICAO system. I have endeavoured to include as many as possible of the civil prefixes heard over Britain and further afield on HF, but the list is far from exhaustive.

R/T call-sign	Operator		
Abakan Avia	Abakan Avia (Russia)	Air Cadet	RAF Air Cadet Schools
Abex	Airborne Express (USA)	Air Canada	Air Canada
ABG	Abelag (Belgium)	Air China	Air China
Aceforce	Allied Command Europe	Airchina Freight	Air China Cargo
Actair	Air Charter & Travel	Air Discovery	Discovery Airways
Adria	Adria Airways	Airevac	USAF Ambulance
Adur	Premier School of Flying	Air Exports	EI Air Exports (Eire)
Aegean	Aegean Airlines	Air Force One	US President
Aer Arran	Aer Arran	Air Force Two	US Vice-President
Aerocaribbean	Aerocaribbean	Air France	Air France
Aerocharter	Aero Charter Midlands	Air Hong Kong	Air Hong Kong
Aeroflot	Aeroflot Russian Airlines	Air India	Air India
Aero Lloyd	Aero Lloyd	Air Kibris	Kibris Turkish (Cyprus)
Aeromexico	Aeromexico	Air Luxor	Air Luxor (Portugal)
Aeronaut	Cranfield University	Air Malta	Air Malta
Aeronord	Aeronord (Moldova)	Air Mauritius	Air Mauritius
Aer Turas	Aer Turas	Airmed	Air Medical Ltd
African Airlines	African Airlines (Kenya)	Air Mike	Continental Micronesia
African West	African West (Senegal)		(Guam)
Africa World	Africa One (Uganda)	Air Mil	Spanish Air Force
Aigle Azur	Aigle Azur	Air Nav	Air Navigation & Trading
Airafric	Air Afrique	Air Partner	Air Partner (UK)
Air Alpha	Air Alpha (Denmark)	Air Portugal	Air Portugal
Air Atlanta	Air Atlanta	Air Sweden	West Air Sweden
Air Baltic	Air Baltic	Air Tahiti	Air Tahiti
Air Berlin	Air Berlin	Airtax	Jet Options
Airbus Industrie	Airbus Industrie	Airtime	Airtime Charters

Air Tony	Spectrum Aviation	Bangladesh	Bangladesh Biman
Air Ukraine	Air Ukraine	Base	Budapest Air Service
Airventure	Airventure (Belgium)	Bavarian	ACM Air Charter
Air Zimbabwe	Air Zimbabwe		(Germany)
Albanian	Albanian Airlines	Beaupair	Aviation Beauport
Alitalia	Alitalia	Beauty	Jetairfly (Belgium)
All Charter	All Charter	Bee Med	British Mediterranean
All Nippon	All Nippon Airways		Airways
All Weather	CAA	Belarus Avia	Belavia
Ambasador	Caernarfon Airworld	Belvoir	British Parachute School
Amer Air	Amer Air (Austria)	Big A	Arrow Air (USA)
American	American Airlines	Binair	Binair (Germany)
Amex	Aero Market Express	Biscayne	Miami Air International
	(Spain)	Bizjet	Hamlin Jet
Amtran	American Trans Air	Bizz	Bizjet Ltd
Anglian	Anglian Flight Centres	Blackadder	Bournemouth Flight
Anglo	Anglo Cargo Ltd		Training
Applewood	Futura Gael (Ireland)	Blackbox	Boscombe Down DERA
Aravco	Aravco	Blue Berry	Blue Line (France)
Archer	Archer Aviation	Bluefin	Blue 1 Finland
Argentina	Aerolineas Argentinas	Blue Island	Blue Islands
Armyair	Army Air Corps	Blue Panorama	Blue Panorama (Italy)
Ascot	RAF Transport	Bluestrip	Farnair Hungary
Asiana	Asiana Airlines	Bluethunder	First Air
Aston	Chequair	Bond	Bond Helicopters
Atlanta	Air Atlanta Iceland	Bonus	Bonus Aviation
Atlantic	Air Atlantique	Braathens	Braathens (Norway)
Atlant-Soyuz	Atlant-Soyuz Air	Breeze	Breeze Aviation
Atlas Blue	Atlas Blue (Morocco)	Brintel	British Intl Helicopters
Audeli	Audeli Air Express (Spain)	Bristow	Bristow Helicopters
Augsburg Air	Augsburg Airways	British	BA Citiexpress
Augusta	Augusta Air (Germany)	British Global	British Global Airlines
Austrian	Austrian Airlines	British Medical	British Medical Charter
Austrian		Brittair	Brittair (France)
Ambulance	Austrian Air Ambulance	Broadway	Fleet Requirements Unit
Avcon	Execujet Charter (Switz)	Brunei	Royal Brunei Airlines
Aviaco	Aviaco (Spain)	Brymon	Brymon European
Avianca	Avianca (Columbia)	Buffalo Air	Buffalo Airways (USA)
Avon	Avon Flying School	Buzzard	Butane Buzzard Aviation
Avro	Woodford Flight Test	Cabair	Cabair Air Taxis
Axis	Axis Air (France)	Cactus	US Airways
Ayjay Services	AJ Services Ltd	Calibrator	Flight Precision Ltd
Ayline	Aurigny Air Services	Cam-Air	Cameroon Airlines
Baby	BMI Baby	Cameo	Cam Air Management
Backer	British Charter	Canforce	Canadian Armed Forces
Balado	Capital Aviation	Cargo	Safair Freighters (S Africa)
Balair	Balair (Switzerland)	Cargolux	Cargolux Airlines
Balkan	Balkan-Bulgarian	Carill	Carill Aviation Ltd
Balkan Holidays	Balkan Holidays	Carriers	Primavia Ltd
Balloon Virgin	Virgin Balloon Flight	Catcher	Rossair Europe (Holland)
Baltic	Baltic International (Latvia)	Catex	Catex (France)

Cathay	Cathay Pacific	Delta	Delta Airlines
Causeway	Woodgate Executive Air Charter	Denim	Denim Air (Netherlands)
		Diesel	Meridian Aviation
Cecil	Cecil Aviation	Dominicana	Dominicana
Cedarjet	Middle East Airlines	Donair	Donair Flying Club
Cega	Cega Aviation	Dragon	Dragonair (Hong Kong)
Celtic	Celtic West Air Charter	Dream Catcher	Dreamcatcher Airways
Challair	Challair (France)	Duke	Jubilee Airways
Channex	Jet2	Duo	Duo Airways
China Eastern	China Eastern Airlines	Dutchbird	Dutchbird
China Southern	China Southern Airlines	Early Bird	Charter Flug (Germany)
Chukka	Polo Aviation Ltd	Eastex	Eastern Air-Executive
Cimber	Cimber Air	Eastflite	Eastern Airways
Cirrus Air	Cirrus (Germany)	Easy	easyJet
City	KLM Cityhopper	Echelon	Euroceltic Airways
City-Jet	City-Jet Ireland	Ecuatoriana	Ecuatoriana (Ecuador)
Clickjet	Clickair (Spain)	Edelweiss	Edelweiss Air (Switz)
Clifton	Bristol Flying Centre	Egyptair	Egyptair
Cloud Runner	247 Jet Ltd	Ejay	Euro Executive Jet
Clue	HQ Euscom (USAF)	El Al	El Al
Coastguard	HM Coastguard	Electricity	SWEB Helicopter Unit
Coastrider	Base Regional (Netherlands)	Emerald	Westair Aviation (Ireland)
		Emery	Emery Worldwide (USA)
Comex	Comed Group	Emirates	Emirates
Compass	Compass International	Enimex	Enimex (Estonia)
Conair-Canada	Conair	Envoy	Flyjet (UK)
Condor	Condor Flugdienst	Eole	Airailes (France)
Connie	Kalitta Air (USA)	Estail	SN Brussels Airlines
Contactair	Contactair Flugdienst	Estonian	Estonian Air
Continental	Continental Airlines	Ethiopian	Ethiopian Airlines
Contract	Air Contractors Ireland	Etihad	Etihad Airways
Corsair	Corse Air (France)	Eurocat	Cat Aviation (Switz)
Corsica	Corse-Méditerranée	Eurocharter	European Aviation
Costock	East Midlands Helicopters	Eurocypria	Eurocypria Airlines
Cotam	French AF Transport	Eurofly	Eurofly (Italy)
Cott	Cottesmore FTU	Europa	Air Europa (Spain)
Coyne Air	Coyne Aviation	Eurotrans	European Air Transport
Cranwell	Cranwell FTU	Eurovan	Van Air Europe
Croatia	Croatia Airlines	Eurowings	Eurowings (Germany)
CSA Lines	Czech Airlines	Everflight	Eisele Flugdienst
Cubana	Cubana	Evergreen	Evergreen Intenational
Cugat	Corporatejets (Spain)	Exam	CAA Flight Examiner
Cyprus	Cyprus Airways	Executive	Night Express (Germany)
Dagobert	Quick Air Service (Germany)	Exel Commuter	Air Exel (Netherlands)
		Expert	Amira Air (Austria)
Dahl	Astair Air Cargo	Expo	Excel Airways
Danish	Danish Air Transport	Exxon	43rd Air Refuelling Wing
Danu	Danu (Lithuania)	Fairoaks	Fairoaks Flight Centre
Dark Star	Heliwhizz	Falcon	Falcon Air Cargo (Sweden)
Darta	Darta (France)	Falcon Jet	Falcon Jet Centre
Dartmoor	Airways Flight Training	Farnair Europe	Farnair Europe (Holland)

Farner	Farner Air Transport (Switz)	Gypo	Red Arrows Transit No 2 Section
Faroeline	Atlantic Airways	Gypsy	Eagle Aviation (UK) Ltd
Fedex	Federal Express	Hamburg Jet	Hamburg Airlines
Finedon	Fast Helicopters	Hamilton	Air Nova
Finesse	Finesse Executive	Hansaline	Lufthansa Cityline
Finnair	Finnair	Hapag Lloyd	Hapag-Lloyd
Firebird Team	Firebird Aerobatics	Harvard	Scientific Industries UK
First City	First City Air	Helimed	Helicopter Med
Flapjack	Heritage Aviation		Emergency
Flightline	Flightline	Helispeed	Biggin Hill Helicopters
Flightvue	AD Aviation	Hellas Jet	Hellas Jet (Greece)
Flo West	Florida West Airlines	Hemus	Hemus Air (Bulgaria)
Fly Cargo	African Intl (Swaziland)	Herky	37th Airlift Sqn
Fly Duo	Duo Airways	High Tide	Trans Euro Air
Flyhello	Hello AG (Switzerland)	Hiway	Highland Airways
Flying Group	Flying Service (Belgium)	Iberia	Iberia
Flying Olive	Aerodynamics Malaga	Iberworld	Iberworld Airlines
Flypast	Key Publishing	Icarfly	Icaro (Italy)
Flystar	Astraeus	Iceair	Icelandair
Formula	Formula One Management	Icebird	Icebird Airline (Iceland)
		Images	Air Images
Fraction	Netjets Europe	Indonesia	Garuda Indonesian
Franken Air	FAI Airservice (Germany)	Info	Independent Nuclear
Frans Air Force	French Air Force		Forces Observers
Freebird	Freebird Airlines (Turkey)	Interflight	Interflight
Funjet	LTE International (Spain)	Inver	Inversia Cargo (Latvia)
Gama	Gama Aviation	Iranair	Iran Air
Gauntlet	Boscombe Down Qinetic	Iraqi	Iraqi Airways
Gemini	Gemini Air Cargo (USA)	Irish	Irish Air Corps
Genex	Aviogenex	Isle Avia	Island Aviation
German Air Force	German Air Force	Jamaica	Air Jamaica
Germania	Germania	Janes	Janes Aviation
German Wings	German Wings	Japanair	Japan Airlines
Gestair	Gestair Executive Jet (Spain)	JAT	Jugoslovenski Aerotransport
Ghana	Ghana Airways	Javelin	Leeming FTU
Giant	Atlas Air (USA)	Jay-Dee	JD Aviation
Global Jet	Aero Business Charter (Germany)	Jaymax	J-Max Air Services
		Jayseebee	JC Bamford Excavators
Globespan	Flyglobespan	Jersey	Flybe
Gojet	Eurojet Aviation	Jester	Executive Aviation Services
Gold	28th Air Refuelling Sqn	Jetalliance	Jetalliance (Austria)
Goldcrest	Peach Air	Jet Connect	Jet Connection Frankfurt
Goosepool	Northern Aviation	Jet Executive	Jet Executive Dusseldorf
Goshawk	Markoss Aviation	Jetflite	Jetflite (Finland)
Gothic	Waltair (Sweden)	Jet Lift	Global Supply Systems
Grid	National Grid Co	Jet Management	Jet Management (Austria)
Griffon	The 955 Preservation Group	Jetnetherlands	Jetnetherlands
		Jet Nova	Jet Nova (Spain)
Gulf Air	Gulf Air	Jetplan	Jeppesen UK

Jetran Air	Jetran Air (Romania)	Lotus Flower	Lotus Air (Egypt)
Jetrider	Jetrider International (UK)	Loveair	London Flight Centre
Jet Set	First Choice Airlines	LTU	Lufttransport
Jets Personales	Jets Personales (Spain)	Lufthansa	Lufthansa
Jolly	USAF HH-53 Rescue	Luxair	Luxair
	Helicopters	Lyddair	Lyddair
J-Pat	Operational Support	Lynden	Lynden Air Cargo (USA)
	Airlift Command	Lynton	Lynton Aviation
Jordanian	Royal Jordanian	Lyon Helijet	Trans Helicopter Service
Jumprunner	Business Wings (Germany)	Macline	McAlpine Helicopters
Kabo	Kabo Air Travels (Nigeria)	Magna Air	Magna Airways (Austria)
Kalitta	Kalitta Flying Service	Mahan Air	Mahan Air (Iran)
	(USA)	Majan	Royal Omani Air Force
Karibu Air	Karibu Air (Denmark)	Malawi	Air Malawi
Kay-Jets	SmartJets (Greece)	Malaysian	Malaysian Airline System
Kenya	Kenya Airways	Malev	Malev (Hungary)
Kestrel	Mytravel Airways	Manhattan	Manhattan Air (UK)
Key Air	Key Airlines (USA)	Mann	Alan Mann Helicopters
King	King Aviation	Map Jet	Map-Management
Kingfisher	Kingfisher Airlines (India)		(Austria)
Kitty	Royal positioning flights	March	March Helicopters
Kittyhawk	32 (The Royal) Sqn (HM	Marshall	Marshall Aerospace
	the Queen on board or	Martin	Martin-Baker
	certain other members of	Mash	Foldpack Ltd
	the Royal Family)	Mavrick	Helicopter Training and
Kiwi	Royal New Zealand Air		Hire
	Force	Mayoral	Dominguez Toledo
KLM	KLM		(Spain)
Koreanair	Korean Airlines	Medic	Medical Air Services
Kuwaiti	Kuwait Airlines	Medivac	London Helicopter
Kyrgyz	Kyrgyzstan Airlines		Emergency Medical
LAN	LAN Chile		Service
Landmark	Grantex Aviation	Merair	Meridiana (Italy)
Latcharter	Latcharter (Latvia)	Meridian Cherry	Meridian (Ukraine)
Lauda	Lauda Air	Merlin	Rolls-Royce (Military)
LCN	Lineas Aereas Canarias	Mermaid	Air Alsie (Denmark)
Lead Air	Unijet (France)	Metman	Met Research Flight
Leopard	32 (The Royal) Sqn	Metropix	Metropix UK
	(Duke of York)	Midland	British Midland
Lester	Leicester Aero Club	Midnight	Sundt Air (Norway)
Libair	Libyan Arab	Mike Romeo	Air Mauritanie
Libyan Airways	Libyan Airways	Miniliner	Miniliner (Italy)
Lifeline	Aeromedicaire Ltd	Mitavia	RAF Avia (Latvia)
Lion King	Ducair (Luxembourg)	Monarch	Monarch Airlines
Lithuanian	Lithuanian Airlines	Montair	Montenegro Airlines
Livingston	Livingston (Italy)	Monty	Air Montgomery
Lizard	Plymouth School of	Moonflower	Neos (Italy)
	Flying	Moth	Tiger Fly
Logan	Loganair	Motion	Elbe Air Transport
Lomas	Lomas Helicopters		(Germany)
Lonex	London Executive Aviation	Mozambique	LAM-Mozambique

Mozart	Amadeus Air (Austria)	Palmer	Palmair
Mustang	London Heli Centres	Pander	National Luchtvaartschool
Myson	Myson Group		(Holland)
Namibia	Air Namibia	Para	Army Parachute Centre
NASA	National Aeronautics and	Pat	US Army Priority Air
	Space Administration		Transport
Nationwide	Nationwide Airlines	Philair	Philips Air Services
	(South Africa)	Philippine	Philippine Airlines
Navy	Royal or US Navy	Pipeline	Pipeline inspection flight
Neatax	Northern Executive	Planet	Planet Air
Neptune	Atlantic Airlines	Pleasure Flights	Manchester Helicopter
Netherlands			Centre
Air Force Royal	Netherlands AF	Podilia	Podilia-Avia (Ukraine)
Netherlands Navy	Netherlands Navy	Polar Tiger	Polar Air Cargo (USA)
Newpin	Raytheon Hawarden	Polestar	Polestar Aviation
Newsflight	Flying TV Ltd	Police	Police Aviation Services
New Zealand	Air New Zealand	Pollot	LOT (Poland)
Nimbus	Nimbus Aviation	Port	Skyworld Airlines (USA)
Nippon Cargo	Nippon Cargo Airlines	Portugalia	Portugalia
Nitro	TNT International	Powerline	Helicopter inspection
NOAA	National Oceanographic		flight
	and Atmospheric	Poyston	Haverfordwest Air Charter
	Administration	Prestige	Capital Aviation Trading
Norbrook	Haughey Air	Privatair	Privatair (Germany)
North Flying	North Flying (Denmark)	Proflight	Langtry Flying Group
Northolt	32 (TR) Squadron	Provost	Bearing Supplies Ltd
North Sea	North Sea Airways	Qantas	Qantas
	(Holland)	Qatari	Qatar Airlines
Northumbria	Northumbria	Quadriga	Windrose Air (Germany)
	Helicopters	Quick	Quick Airways (Holland)
Northwest	Northwest Orient	Quid	43rd Air Refuelling Sqn
Norton	Northants School of	Rabbit	Rabbit-Air Zurich
	Flying	Rafair	Royal Air Force
Norwegian	Royal Norwegian Air	Rainbow	32 (The Royal) Sqn (HRH
	Force		Prince Philip)
Nostru Air	Air Nostrum Symbol	Rangemile	Rangemile Ltd
	(Spain)	Ranger	Defence Products Ltd
Ocean Sky	Ocean Sky	Rapex	BAC Express
Olympic	Olympic Airways	Raven	Ravenair
Oman	Oman Royal Flight	Reach	USAF Air Mobility
Omega	Aeromega Ltd		Command
Omni	Omni Aviocau	Redair	Redhill Aviation
	(Portugal)	Red Devils	Red Devils Parachute
Onur Air	Onur Air (Turkey)		Team
Open Skies	Open Skies Commission	Red Dragon	Air Wales
	(UK)	Red Pelican	JDP France
Optic	Krystel Air Charter	Red Star	Goodridge UK
Osprey	PLM-Dollar Group	Relief	Relief Transport
Oxford	CSE Aviation		Services
Pacific	Air Pacific (Fiji)	Rescue	RAF Rescue
Pakistan	Pakistan International	Richair	Rich International

Rolls	Rolls-Royce (Bristol)
Romaf	Romanian Air Force
Royal Air Maroc	Royal Air Maroc
Royal Nepal	Royal Nepal Airlines
Roycar	Rolls-Royce Ltd
Rubens	VLM (Belgium)
Rushton	FR Aviation
Ryanair	Ryanair
Safiran	Safiran Airlines (Iran)
Saint Athan	St Athan MU
Saltire	Edinburgh Air Charter
Sam	Special Air Mission (USAF)
Samson	Samson Aviation
Santa	BA Santa Flights
Saudi	Saudi-Arabian Airlines
Saxonair	Saxonair (UK)
Scandinavian	Scandinavian Airlines System
Scanor	SAS Braathens
Scanvip	Air Express (Norway)
Scanwing	Malmo Aviation
Schreiner	Schreiner Airways
Scillonia	Isles of Scilly Sky Bus
Scout	N Ireland Air Support Unit
Selair	Sierra National Airlines (Sierra Leone)
Semitrans	Semitool Europe Ltd
Sentry	USAF AWACS
Seychelles	Air Seychelles
Shamrock	Aer Lingus
Shawbury	Shawbury FTU
Shell	Shell Aircraft
Shepherd One	Papal flight (Alitalia)
Shopair	Shoprite Group Ltd
Shuttle	British Airways Shuttle
Siberian	S7 Airlines
Silkair	Silkair (Singapore)
Silver	Sterling Helicopters
Silver Arrow	Silver Arrows (Luxembourg)
Silverline	Silver Air
Singapore	Singapore Airlines
Sirio	Sirio (Italy)
Sky Camel	KS Avia (Latvia)
Skydrift	Skydrift Aircharter
Sky Elite	European Business Jets
Skyjet	Panair Spain
Skyking	Skyking Ltd
Skyrunner	MSR Flugcharter

Sky Service	Sky Service (Belgium)
Skytravel	Travel Service Airlines (Czech Rep)
Skywork	Scottish Airways Flyers
Sloane	Sloane Aviation Ltd
Slovakia	Air Slovakia
Snoopy	Air Traffic Gmbh
Solidair	Solid Air (Holland)
Somalair	Somali Airlines
Southern Air	Southern Air Transport
Spacejet	Club 328
Spanair	Spanair
Spar	58th Airlift Sqn USAF
Special	Metropolitan Police Air Support Unit
Speedbird	British Airways
Speedway	Deutsche BA
Springbok	South African Airways
Standards	CAA Training Standards
Stapleford	Stapleford Flight Centre
Star	Star Aviation (UK)
Stardust	Northern Air Charter (Germany)
Starspeed	Starspeed (UK)
Star Wing	European Air Express (Germany)
Starway	XL Airways (France)
Sterling	Sterling European Airlines
Striker	Wittering FTU
Suckling	Scot Airways (Suckling)
Sudanair	Sudanair
Sunscan	Sun Air
Sunturk	Pegasus Airlines
Support	Prescott Support Co (USA)
Surinam	Surinam Airways
Surveyor	Cooper Aerial Surveys
Swallow	Air Southwest
Swedeforce	Swedish Armed Forces
Swedestar	City Airline
Swift	Swiftair (Spain)
Swiss	Swiss Airlines
Swiss Ambulance	Swiss Air Ambulance
Swissbird	Servair Private Charter
Synergy	Synergy Aviation
Syrianair	Syrian Arab Airlines
Tag Air	Tag Aviation (Switzerland)

Tajikair	Tajikair	Varig	Varig Brazil
TAM	TAM (Brazil)	Vectis	Pilatus Britten Norman
Tango Lima	Trans Mediterranean	Vega Airlines	Vega Airlines
Tarnish	BAe Warton		(Bulgaria)
Tarom	Tarom (Romania)	Vickers	Vickers Shipbuilding
Tayflite	Tayflite Ltd	Victor Victor	US Navy
Tayside	Tayside Aviation	Viking	Mytravel Airways
Tee Air	Tower Air		(Denmark)
Teessair	North British Airlines	Virgin	Virgin Atlantic
Tester	Empire Test Pilots School	Virgin Express	Virgin Express (Belgium)
Thai	Thai International	Virgin Nigeria	Virgin Nigeria
Thanet	TG Aviation Ltd	Visig	Visig (Spain)
Thomson	Thomsonfly.com	Vola	Volare (Italy)
Til	Tajikistan International	Volga-Dnepr	Volga-Dnepr Airlines
Tomcat	CCHT (Germany)	Vortex	Support Helicopter Force
Topcat	Helicopter Services	Vulcan	Waddington FTU
Topcliffe	Topcliffe FTU	Watchdog	Ministry of Fisheries
Top Jet	Thomas Cook Airlines	WDL	WDL Flugdienst
Topswiss	easyJet Switzerland	Welcomair	Welcome Air (Austria)
Trans Arabian	Trans Arabian (Sudan)	Westland	Westland Helicopters
Transat	Air Transat	Whitestar	Star Air (Denmark)
Transavia	Transavia (Holland)	Wildfox	Foxair (Italy)
Trans Europe	Air Transport	Wildgoose	Freshaer
	(Slovakia)	Wingwalker	Aerosuperbatics
Transoviet	Transaero Airlines	Witchcraft	Flugdienst Fehlhaber
Trident	Atlas Helicopters Ltd	Wizard	Micromatter
Triple A	Atlantique Air Assistance		Technology
Tropic	Tropair (UK)	Wizz Air	Wizz Air
Truman	Truman Air Charter	Wondair	Wondair on Demand
Tulip	Tuli Air (Netherlands)		(Spain)
Tunair	Tunisair	Woodstock	Oxford Air Services
Tune	435th Airlift Wing	World	World Airways
	(USAF)	World Express	DHL International
Turkair	Turkish Airlines	Worldgate	Lion Air Services
Twin Goose	Air Taxi Europe	Wycombe	Wycombe Air Centre
Twinjet	Twin Jet (France)	Xray	Xjet Ltd
Typhoon	Coningsby FTU	Yellow Cab	Hapag Lloyd Express
Tyrol Ambulance	Tyrol Air Ambulance	Yemeni	Yemen Airways
Tyrolean	Tyrolean Airways	Yeoman	Foster Yeoman
Tyroljet	Tyrolean Jet Service	Yorkair	Multiflight Ltd
Ukraine		Yugair	Air Yugoslavia
International	Air Ukraine International	Zambian	Zambia Airways
Uni Air	Uni Air (France)	Zap	Titan Airways
Union Jet	Eu Jet	Zebra	African Safari (Kenya)
Unique	Helicopter Management	Zigzag	Eagle Helicopters
	Ltd	Zimex	Zimex (Switzerland)
United	United Airlines	Zitotrans	Aviacon Zitotrans
UPS	United Parcel Service		(Russia)
	(USA)	Zoom	Zoom Airlines (Canada)
Uzbek	Uzbekistan Airways	Zorex	Zorex Air Transport
Vannin	Manx2		(Spain)

Suffixes to the flight number have various meanings:

A	Extra flight on the same route. If more than one, B, C etc., may be used
B	Freight
P	Positioning flight
T	Training flight
Heavy	Reminder to ATC that aircraft is wide-bodied with a strong vortex wake
Super Heavy	Airbus A380

Be aware that there are exceptions to these, such as British Airways' Shuttle call-signs, eg 'Shuttle 6M'. The letter suffixes change alphabetically for each service throughout the day.

ICAO Company Designators:
3-letter

code	Operator		
AAB	Abelag Aviation	ARD	ATA-Aerocondor (Portugal)
AAC	Army Air Corps	ARG	Aerolineas Argentinas
AAF	Aigle Azur	ATJ	Air Traffic Gmbh (Germany)
AAG	Atlantic Aviation	ATT	Aer Turas Teoranta
AAL	American Airlines	AUA	Austrian Airlines
AAR	Asiana Airlines	AUB	Augsburg Airways
ABG	Abakan Avia (Russia)	AUF	Augusta Air (Germany)
ABX	Airborne Express	AUI	Ukraine International
ACW	RAF Air Cadet Schools	AVA	Avianca
ADB	Antonov Airlines (Ukraine)	AVB	Aviation Beauport
ADI	Audeli Air (Spain)	AXY	Axis Air (France)
ADR	Adria Airways	AYZ	Atlant Soyuz
AEA	Air Europa	AZS	Aviacon Zitotrans (Russia)
AED	Air Experience Flight	AZW	Air Zimbabwe
AEE	Aegean Airlines	BAC	BAC Leasing
AEF	Aero Lloyd	BAF	Belgian Air Force
AFB	Belgian Air Force	BBB	Swedejet Airways
AFI	Africa One	BBC	Bangladesh Biman
AFP	Portuguese Air Force	BCR	British Charter
AGX	Aviogenex	BCS	European Air Transport
AHA	Air Alpha (Denmark)	BDN	Boscombe Down Qinetic
AHK	Air Hong Kong	BER	Air Berlin
AIK	African Airlines (Kenya)	BES	Aero Services Executive
ALK	Air Lanka	BGB	British Global Airlines
ALS	Air Alpe (France)	BGH	BH Air (Bulgaria)
AMC	Air Malta	BHL	Bristow Helicopters Group
AME	Spanish Air Force	BIH	British International Helicopters
AMK	Amerer Air	BLE	Blue Line (France)
AML	Air Malawi	BLF	Blue 1 Finland
AMR	Air America	BMA	British Midland
AMT	American Trans Air	BMM	Atlas Blue (Morocco)
AMX	Aeronaves de Mexico	BON	B & H Airways
ANA	All Nippon Airways	BPS	Budapest Air Service
ANE	Air Nostrum (Spain)	BRY	Brymon European
ANZ	Air New Zealand	BSK	Miami Air International
APW	Arrow Air	BVA	Buffalo Airways

BVR	ACM Air Charter (Germany)	EWG	Eurowings
BWA	Caribbean Airlines	EWW	Emery Worldwide
BWY	Fleet Requirements Air Direction	EXN	Exin (Poland)
	Unit	EXS	Jet2
BZN	Brize Norton FTU	EXT	Night Express (Germany)
CAO	Air China Cargo	EZS	easyJet Switzerland
CAZ	Cat Aviation (Switzerland)	FAF	French Air Force
CBY	Coningsby FTU	FAH	Farnair Hungary
CCA	Air China	FAT	Farner Air Transport
CEG	Cega Aviation	FBF	Fine Airlines (USA)
CFD	Cranfield University	FCN	Falcon Aviation (Sweden)
CFG	Condor Flugdienst	FDX	Federal Express
CFU	CAA Flying Unit	FFG	Flugdienst Fehlhaber
CIM	Cimber Air	FGN	Gendarmerie Nationale
CLG	Challair (France)	FHE	Hello AG (Switzerland)
CLI	Clickair (Spain)	FIN	Finnair
CLX	Cargolux Airlines	FJC	Falcon Jet Centre
CMI	Continental Micronesia	FJE	Flyjet (UK)
CNB	Cityline Hungary	FJI	Air Pacific (Fiji)
CNO	SAS Braathens	FLI	Atlantic Airways
COA	Continental Airlines	FNY	French Navy
CPA	Cathay Pacific	FPG	Tag Aviation (France)
CRL	Corse Air International	FRA	Flight Refuelling Aviation
CRN	Aero Caribbean	FSB	Flight Services International
CSA	Czech Airlines	FWC	Freeway Air (Netherlands)
CSN	China Southern Airlines	FXR	Foxair (Italy)
CTN	Croatia Airlines	FYG	Flying Service (Belgium)
CUB	Cubana	GAF	German Air Force
CWL	Cranwell FTU	GBJ	Aero Business Charter (Germany)
CYP	Cyprus Airways	GCO	Gemini Air Cargo
DAH	Air Algerie	GEC	Lufthansa Cargo
DAL	Delta Airlines	GES	Gestair (Spain)
DCN	German Federal Armed Forces	GFA	Gulf Air
DNC	Aerodynamics Malaga	GHA	Ghana Aiways
DRT	Darta (France)	GIA	Garuda Indonesian Airlines
DSR	DAS Air Cargo	GMI	Germania
DTA	TAAG Angola	GOT	Waltair (Sweden)
DUK	Ducair (Luxembourg)	GRL	Air Greenland
EAL	European Air Express (Germany)	HAF	Greek Air Force
EAX	Eastern-Air Executive	HLF	Hapag-Lloyd
EBF	MSR Flug-Charter	HLX	Hapag-Lloyd Express
EBJ	European Business Jets	HMS	Hemus Air
ECA	Eurocypria	HSK	Skyeurope
EFD	EFD Eisele Flugdienst	ICA	Icara (Italy)
EFF	Westair Aviation (Ireland)	ICE	Icelandair
EIA	Evergreen International	ICG	Icelandic Coastguard
EIN	Aer Lingus	ICL	CAL Cargo (Israel)
ENI	Enimex (Estonia)	IFA	FAI Airservice (Germany)
ESK	Skyeurope (Slovakia)	IFT	Interflight
ETH	Ethiopian Airline Corp	IMX	Zimex Aviation (Switzerland)
ETP	Empire Test Pilots School	INV	Inversia (Latvia)

IQQ	Caribbean Airways	MDJ	Jetran Air (Romania)
IRA	Iran Air	MDT	Sundt Air (Norway)
IRM	Mahan Air (Iran)	MEA	Middle East Airlines
IYE	Yemen Airways	MEM	Meridian (Ukraine)
JAF	Jetairfly (Belgium)	MET	Meteorological Research Flight
JAG	Jetalliance (Austria)	MGR	Magna Air (Austria)
JAL	Japan Airlines	MGX	Montenegro Airlines
JAT	Jugoslovenski Aerotransport	MMD	Air Alsie
JDP	JDP France	MND	Corporatejets (Spain)
JEF	Jetflite (Finland)	MNL	Miniliner (Italy)
JEI	Jet Executive Dusseldorf	MON	Monarch Airlines
JEP	Jets Personales (Spain)	MOZ	Amadeus Air (Austria)
JGX	Jet Management (Austria)	MPH	Martinair (Holland)
JKK	Spanair	MPJ	Map-Management (Austria)
JMP	Business Wings (Germany)	MRH	Marham FTU
JMS	Vista Jet (Austria)	MRT	Air Mauritanie
JNL	Jetnetherlands	MSR	Egyptair
JNV	Jetnova (Spain)	MTL	RAF Avia (Latvia)
KAC	Kuwait Airways	MYO	Dominguez Toledo
KAL	Korean Airlines	NAF	Royal Netherlands Air Force
KFR	Kingfisher Airlines (India)	NAN	National Airlines
KGA	Kyrgyzstan Airlines	NCA	Nippon Cargo
KHA	Kitty Hawk Air Cargo	NGA	Nigeria Airways
KIN	Kinloss FTU	NJE	Netjets Europe
KIS	Contactair Flugdienst	NMB	Air Namibia
KQA	Kenya Airways	NOW	Royal Norwegian Air Force
KSA	KS Avia (Latvia)	NPT	Atlantic Airlines
KSJ	SmartJets (Greece)	NRC	North Sea Airways (Holland)
LAA	Libyan Arab Airlines	NRN	Royal Netherlands Navy
LAM	Linhas Aereas Mocambique	NRP	Aeronord (Moldova)
LAN	LAN (Chile)	NTR	TNT Aviation
LAP	Lineas Aereas Paraguayas	NTW	Nationwide Airlines (South Africa)
LBC	Albanian Airlines	NVR	Novair (Sweden)
LBR	Elbe Air Transport	NVY	Royal Navy
LCN	Lineas Aereas Canarias	NWA	Nothwest Orient
LCS	RAF Leuchars	OAL	Olympic Airways
LDA	Lauda Air	OAV	Omni Aviocau (Portugal)
LEA	Unijet (France)	OCS	Ocean Sky
LGL	Luxair	ORF	Oman Royal Flight
LGO	Lego Company (Denmark)	OVA	Aero Nova (Spain)
LIL	Lithuanian Airlines	PAC	Polar Air Cargo
LKA	Alkair (Denmark)	PAL	Philippine Airlines
LOP	Linton-on-Ouse FTU	PAT	US Army Priority Air Transport
LOS	Lossiemouth FTU	PBU	Air Burundi
LOT	Lot Poland	PDA	Podilia-Avia (Ukraine)
LTC	Latcharter (Latvia)	PEA	Pan Europeenne (France)
LTU	Lufttransport	PGA	Portugalia
LYC	Lynden Air Cargo (USA)	PGT	Pegasus (Turkey)
MAH	Malev	PIA	Pakistan International
MAS	Malaysian Airline System	PJS	Jet Aviation (Switzerland)
MAU	Air Mauritius	PLC	Police Aviation Services

PNR	Panair (Spain)	SRG	SAR 22 Sqn
PSK	Prescott Support Co	SRR	Star Air (Denmark)
PSW	Pskovavia	SSV	Sky Service Airlines (Canada)
PTG	Privat Air Dusseldorf	STN	St Athan MU
QAH	Quick Airways (Holland)	SUD	Sudan Airways
QAJ	Quick Air Jet (Germany)	SUS	Sun Air of Scandinavia
QFA	Qantas	SVA	Saudi-Arabian Airlines
QNK	Kabo Air Travels (Nigeria)	SVF	Swedish Armed Forces
QSC	African Safari Airways	SWN	West Air Sweden
RAM	Royal Air Maroc	SWT	Swift Air (Spain)
RAX	Royal Air Freight (USA)	SWZ	Servair (Switzerland)
RAZ	Rijnmond (Holland)	SYR	Syrian Arab Airlines
RBA	Royal Brunei Airlines	SYS	Shawbury FTU
RBB	Rabbit Air (Switzerland)	TAM	TAM (Brazil)
RDK	Irish Air Transport	TAP	TAP (Portugal)
RFR	Royal Air Force	TAR	Tunis Air
RGL	Regional Airlines (France)	TAS	Lotus Airlines (Egypt)
RIA	Rich International	TAY	TNT
RJA	Royal Jordanian	TCN	Trans Continental (USA)
RJZ	Royal Jordanian Air Force	TCP	Transcorp Airways
RKA	Air Afrique	TCX	Thomas Cook Airlines
ROT	Tarom (Romania)	TEX	Catex (France)
RRL	Rolls-Royce (Military Aviation)	THA	Thai Airways
RRR	Royal Air Force (Air Transport)	THY	Turk Hava Yollari
RRS	Boscombe Down DERA	THZ	Trans Helicopter Service (France)
RTS	Relief Transport Services	TIL	Tajikistan International
RUA	Rwanda Airlines	TJS	Tyrolean Jet Service
RUS	Cirrus (Germany)	TJT	Twin Jet (France)
RVE	Air Venture (Belgium)	TLB	Atlantique Air Assistance
RYR	Ryanair	TLP	Tulip Air
RYT	Raya Jet (Jordan)	TMA	Trans Mediterranean Airlines
SAY	Scot Airways (Suckling)	TOF	Topcliffe FTU
SAZ	Swiss Air Ambulance	TOW	Tower Air
SBI	S7 Airlines (Russia)	TRA	Transavia (Holland)
SCH	Schreiner Airways	TRT	Trans Arabian Air Transport
SCW	Malmo Aviation (Sweden)	TSC	Air Transat (Canada)
SDJ	Club 328	TSO	Transaero Airlines
SDR	City Airline (Sweden)	TSV	Tropair Air Services
SEY	Air Seychelles	TVS	Travel Service (Czech Republic)
SFR	Safair Freighters	TWE	Transwede
SGF	Swiss Government Flights	TWG	Air Taxi Europe
SHF	Support Helicopter Flight NI	TYR	Tyrolean Airways
SIA	Singapore Airlines	TYW	Tyrol Air Ambulance
SIO	Sirio (Italy)	UAA	Leuchars UAS/AEF
SKS	Sky Service (Belgium)	UAD	Colerne UAS/AEF
SLD	Silver Air (Czech Republic)	UAE	Emirates
SLK	Silkair (Singapore)	UAG	Cambridge UAS/AEF
SLM	Surinam Airways	UAH	Newton UAS/AEF
SOX	Solid Air (Holland)	UAJ	Glasgow UAS/AEF
SPC	Skyworld Airlines (USA)	UAM	Woodvale UAS/AEF
SRD	SAR 22 Sqn	UAO	Benson UAS/AEF

UAQ	Leeming UAS/AEF	VLL	Valley SAR Training
UAU	Boscombe Down UAS/AEF	VLM	VLM
UAV	Wyton UAS/AEF	VRE	Volare Aircompany (Ukraine)
UAW	St Athan UAS/AEF	VSG	Visig (Spain)
UAX	Church Fenton UAS/AEF	VTA	Air Tahiti
UAY	Cosford UAS/AEF	VYT	Valley FTU
UGA	Uganda Airlines	WAD	Waddington FTU
UPA	Air Foyle	WDG	Min of Ag & Fish
UYC	Cameroon Airlines	WDL	WDL Aviation
UZB	Uzbekistan Airways	WFD	Woodford Flight Test
VAS	Aviatrans (Russian Fed)	WHE	Westland Helicopters
VCN	Execujet Charter (Switzerland)	WIT	Wittering FTU
VDA	Volga-Dnepr Airline	WLC	Welcome Air (Austria)
VEA	Vega Airlines (Bulgaria)	WNR	Wondair (Spain)
VEX	Virgin Express (Belgium)	WOA	World Airways
VGN	Virgin Nigeria	WTN	Warton Flight Ops
VHM	Charter Flug (Germany)	XLF	XL Airways (France)
VIR	Virgin Atlantic	XPE	Amira Air (Austria)
VKG	Mytravel Airways (Denmark)	YRG	Air Yugoslavia

Appendix 7

UK SSR Code Assignment Plan

MOST CODES ARE assigned by ATC units but some can be selected by the pilot where the situation requires or allows it. An example is 7000, the Conspicuity Code which, as the name implies, makes an aircraft not in receipt of an ATC service more conspicuous. This can be very useful to a controller providing radar service outside controlled airspace. For IFR flights the squawk code is assigned as part of the airways clearance and remains the same throughout the flight. Airfield radar units are allocated a block of codes to assign at their discretion for local traffic. Some non-radar-equipped ATC units will allocate squawk codes, notably towers who assign 7010 to circuit training traffic. The main reason is that the aircraft will show up on flight deck TCAS displays. This will provide an alert in the event of an inexperienced pilot wandering too close to the final approach, despite being instructed to hold well clear. Another example is London Information which does not have access to radar but does assign 0027 to all aircraft that receive a service from them. This tells other radar-equipped ATC units that a specific aircraft is listening on the London Information frequency in case they need to contact that aircraft. SSR codes can provide many clues to aircraft operation and are thus very useful to virtual radar box enthusiasts.

UK SSR Code Assignment Plan

Codes/ Series	Controlling Authority/Function
0000	SSR data unreliable
0001	Height Monitoring Unit
0002	Ground Transponder Testing
0003-0005	Not allocated
0006	British Transport Police ASU
0007	Off-shore Safety Area (OSA) Conspicuity
0010	Aircraft operating outside of Birmingham Controlled Airspace Zone and monitoring Birmingham Radar frequency
0011	Surrey/Sussex Air Ambulance (HMD60)
0012	Aircraft operating outside of Heathrow/ London City/Gatwick CAS and monitoring Thames/Gatwick Radar frequency
0013	Aircraft operating outside of Luton/Stansted CAS and monitoring Luton/Essex Radar frequency
0014	Kent Air Ambulance (HMD21)
0015	Essex Air Ambulance (HMD07)
0016	Thames Valley Air Ambulance (HMD24)
0017	Virgin HEMS (HMD27)
0019	Air Ambulance Helicopter Emergency Medivac
0021	Fixed-wing aircraft (Receiving service from a ship)
0022	Helicopter(s) (Receiving service from a ship)
0023	Aircraft engaged in actual SAR Operations
0024	Radar Flight Evaluation/Calibration
0025	Not allocated

0026	Special Tasks (Mil) - activated under Special Flight Notification (SFN)
0027	London AC (Swanwick) Ops Crossing/Joining CAS
0030	FIR Lost
	An aircraft receiving a radar service from D & D centre
0032	Aircraft engaged in police air support operations
0033	Aircraft Paradropping
0034	Antenna trailing/target towing
0035	Selected Flights - Helicopters
0036	Helicopter Pipeline/Powerline Inspection Flights
0037	Royal Flights - Helicopters
0040	Civil Helicopters North Sea
0041-0042	Greater Manchester Police ASU
0043-0044	Metropolitan Police ASU
0045	Sussex Police ASU
0046	Essex Police ASU
0047	Surrey Police ASU
0050	Chiltern Police ASU (Western Base)
0051	Chiltern Police ASU (Eastern Base)
0052	Norfolk Police ASU
	West Yorkshire Police ASU
0053	Suffolk Police ASU
	South Yorkshire Police ASU
0054	Cambridgeshire Police ASU
	Merseyside Police ASU
	South and East Wales Police ASU
0055	Northumbria Police ASU
	Cheshire Police ASU
0056	Northumbria Police ASU
	North Midlands Police ASU
0057	Strathclyde Police ASU
	Humberside Police ASU
	East Midlands Police ASU
0060	West Midlands Police ASU
0061	Lancashire Police ASU
	Western Counties Police ASU
0062-0077	No 1 Air Control Centre
0100	NATO Exercises
0101-0117	Transit (ORCAM) Brussels
0120-0137	Transit (ORCAM) Germany
0140-0177	Transit (ORCAM) Amsterdam
0200	NATO Exercises
0201-0213	TC Stansted/TC Luton
0201-0217	RAF Leuchars
0201-0257	Ireland Domestic
	RNAS Yeovilton
0220	RAF Leuchars Conspicuity
0220-0237	RAF Shawbury
0221-0247	RAF Leuchars
0224-0243	Anglia Radar
0240	RAF Shawbury Conspicuity
0241-0246	RAF Shawbury
0244	North Denes Conspicuity
0245-0267	Anglia Radar
0247	Cranfield Airport - IFR Conspicuity Purposes
0260	Liverpool Airport Conspicuity
0260-0261	Coventry Airport Conspicuity
0260-0261	Oil Survey Helicopters - Faeroes/Iceland Gap
0260-0267	Westland Helicopters Yeovil
0260-0267	RAF Northolt
0261-0267	Liverpool Airport
0262-0267	Coventry Approach
0270-0277	Superdomestic - Ireland to UK, Germany and Benelux
0300	NATO Exercises
0301-0377	Transit (ORCAM) UK
0400	NATO Exercises
0401	RAF Leeming Conspicuity
0401	Shoreham Approach Procedural
0401-0420	Birmingham Approach
0401-0430	Exeter Approach
0401-0437	Ireland Domestic
0401-0467	RAF Lakenheath
0402-0426	RAF Leeming
0421-0446	Farnborough Radar/LARS
0427	RAF Leeming (Topcliffe) Conspicuity
0430-0443	Edinburgh Approach
0447	Farnborough LARS - Blackbushe Departures
0450-0456	Blackpool Approach
	Farnborough Radar/LARS
0457	Blackpool Approach (Liverpool Bay and Morecambe Bay Helicopters)
0460-0466	Blackpool Approach
	Farnborough LARS - Fairoaks Departures
0460-0467	Farnborough Radar/LARS
0467	Blackpool Approach (Liverpool Bay and Morecambe Bay Helicopters)
0470-0477	Not allocated
0500	NATO Exercises
0501-0577	Transit (ORCAM) UK
0600	NATO Exercises

0601-0637	Transit (ORCAM) Germany	2601-2637	RAF Cranwell
0640-0677	Transit (ORCAM) Paris	2601-2645	MoD Boscombe Down
0700	NATO Exercises	2601-2657	Irish Domestic Westbound
0701-0777	Transit (ORCAM) Maastricht		departures and Eastbound arrivals
1000	IFR GAT flights operating in	2621-2630	Aberdeen (Sumburgh Approach)
	designated Mode S Airspace	2631-2637	Aberdeen (Northern North Sea
1001-1077	Transit (ORCAM) Spain		Off-shore)
1100	NATO Exercises	2640-2657	Aberdeen (Northern North Sea
1101-1137	Transit (ORCAM) Rhein		Off-shore - Sumburgh Sector)
1140-1176	Transit (ORCAM) UK	2641-2642	RAF Cranwell - Lincolnshire
1177	London AC (Swanwick) FIS		AIAA
1200	NATO Exercises	2646-2647	MoD Boscombe Down - High
1201-1277	Channel Islands Domestic		Risks Trial
1300	NATO Exercises	2650	MoD Boscombe Down
1301-1327	NATO - Air Policing (Air Defence		Conspicuity
	Priority Flights)	2650-2653	Leeds Bradford Approach
1330-1357	Transit (ORCAM) Bremen	2651-2657	MoD Boscombe Down
1360-1377	Transit (ORCAM) Munich	2654	Leeds Bradford Conspicuity
1400	NATO Exercises	2655-2677	Leeds Bradford Approach
1401-1407	UK Domestic	2660-2675	Middle Wallop
1410-1437	Superdomestic - Shannon to UK	2660-2677	Aberdeen (Northern North Sea
1440-1477	Superdomestic - Dublin to UK		Off-shore)
1500-1577	NATO Exercises	2676-2677	Middle Wallop Conspicuity
1600-1677	NATO Exercises	2700	NATO Exercises
1700-1727	NATO Exercises	2701-2737	Transit (ORCAM) Shannon
1730-1746	Newquay Approach	2740-2777	Transit (ORCAM) Zurich
1730-1756	RAF Coningsby	3000	NATO Aircraft receiving a service
1730-1767	RAF Spadeadam		from AEW aircraft
1747	Newquay Conspicuity	3001-3077	Transit (ORCAM) Zurich
1757	RAF Coningsby Conspicuity	3100	NATO Aircraft receiving a service
1760-1777	RAF Coningsby		from AEW aircraft
1760-1777	RNAS Yeovilton Fighter Control	3101-3127	Transit (ORCAM) Germany
2000	Aircraft from a non-SSR	3130-3177	Transit (ORCAM) Amsterdam
	environment, or on the	3200	NATO Aircraft receiving a service
	aerodrome surface in accordance		from AEW aircraft
	with certain conditions	3201-3216	UK Domestic (London AC
2001-2077	Transit (ORCAM) Shannon		(Swanwick) Special Sector Codes)
2100	NATO Exercises	3217-3220	UK Domestic
2101-2177	Transit (ORCAM) Amsterdam	3221-3257	Superdomestic - UK to Oceanic
2200	NATO Exercises		via Shannon/Dublin
2201-2277	Superdomestic UK to France,	3260-3277	UK Domestic
	Spain, Portugal, Canaries and S	3300	NATO Aircraft receiving a service
	Africa		from AEW aircraft
2300	NATO Exercises	3301-3304	Swanwick (Military) Special Tasks
2301-2337	Transit (ORCAM) Bordeaux	3305-3307	London D&D Cell
2340-2377	Transit (ORCAM) Brest	3310-3367	Swanwick (Military)
2400-2477	NATO Exercises	3370-3377	UK Domestic
2500	NATO Exercises	3400	NATO Aircraft receiving a service
2501-2577	Transit (ORCAM) Karlsruhe		from AEW aircraft
2600	NATO Exercises	3401-3457	Superdomestic – UK to Germany,
2601-2620	Glasgow Approach		Netherlands and Benelux

3460-3477	Transit (ORCAM) Germany to UK	3740-3745	RAF Brize Norton
3500	NATO Aircraft receiving a service from AEW aircraft	3740-3747	RAF Valley
		3750	RAF Valley - VFR VATA East
3501-3507	Transit (ORCAM) Luxembourg	3750-3763	TC Gatwick
3510-3537	Transit (ORCAM) Maastricht	3751	RAF Valley - VFR VATA West
3540-3577	Transit (ORCAM) Berlin	3752	RAF Valley - RIFA
3600	NATO Aircraft receiving a service from AEW aircraft	3753	RAF Valley - Low-level helicopters
3601-3623	RAF Benson	3754	RAF Valley - Special tasks
3601-3632	Scottish ATSOCA Purposes	3755	RAF Valley
3601-3634	RAF Waddington	3755-3762	RAF Wittering Approach
3601-3643	Cardiff Approach	3756-3765	RAF Valley - VATA IFR Traffic
3601-3647	Jersey Approach	3764-3767	Gatwick Tower
3624	RAF Benson Conspicuity	3767	Newcastle Approach Conspicuity
3640-3653	RAF Odiham	3770-3777	Not allocated
3640-3665	RAF Marham	4000	NATO Aircraft receiving a service from AEW aircraft
3640-3677	Aberdeen (Northern North Sea Off-shore)	4001-4077	Transit (ORCAM) Aix-en-Provence
3641-3677	BAe Warton	4100	NATO Aircraft receiving a service from AEW aircraft
3645	Cardiff Approach - St Athan Conspicuity	4101-4127	Transit (ORCAM) Frankfurt
		4130-4177	Transit (ORCAM) Dusseldorf
3646-3657	Cardiff Approach	4200	NATO Aircraft receiving a service from AEW aircraft
3660-3665	Solent Approach (Southampton)		
3666	Solent Radar Conspicuity	4201-4214	Heathrow Domestic
	RAF Marham - Visual Recovery	4215-4247	Superdomestic - Shannon inbound UK
3667	RAF Marham - FIS Conspicuity		
3667-3677	Solent Approach (Southampton)	4250	Manston Conspicuity
3700	NATO Aircraft receiving a service from AEW aircraft	4250-4257	Belfast City Approach
		4250-4267	Aberdeen Approach
3701-3710	BAe Woodford	4250-4277	BAe Bristol Filton
3701-3710	Norwich Approach		Humberside Approach
3701-3717	Military aircraft under service from RN AEW aircraft in South West Approaches	4251-4267	Manston Approach
		4300	NATO Aircraft receiving a service from AEW aircraft
3701-3736	RAF Brize Norton	4301-4307	UK Domestic
3701-3747	Guernsey Approach	4310-4323	UK Domestic (Gatwick Special Sector Codes)
	RAF Lossiemouth		
3711	Woodford Entry/Exit Lane (Woodford Inbounds and Outbounds)	4324-4337	UK Domestic (Manchester Special Sector Codes)
		4340-4353	UK Domestic (SCoACC Special Sector Codes)
3712	Woodford Entry/Exit Lane (Manchester Inbounds)	4354-4377	UK Domestic
3713	Manchester VFR/SVFR (Outbounds)	4400	NATO Aircraft receiving a service from AEW aircraft
3720	RAF Cottesmore Conspicuity		
3720-3727	RAF Valley	4401-4427	Superdomestic - Brussels FIR to UK FIR
3720-3766	Newcastle Approach		
3721-3754	RAF Cottesmore	4430-4477	Superdomestic - UK to Eire and Oceanic
3730-3736	RAF Valley		
3737	RAF Valley - Visual Recovery	4500	NATO Aircraft receiving a service from AEW aircraft
	RAF Brize Norton Approach Conspicuity		

4501	Wattisham Conspicuity	5271-5277	Transit (ORCAM) Channel Islands
4501-4515	RAF Lyneham	5300	NATO Aircraft receiving a service from AEW aircraft
4501-4520	Prestwick Approach		
4501-4547	RAF Linton-on-Ouse	5301-5377	Transit (ORCAM) Barcelona
4502-4547	Wattisham Approach	5400	NATO Aircraft receiving a service from AEW aircraft
4510	Prestwick Approach Conspicuity		
4516-4517	RAF Lyneham Conspicuity	5401-5477	UK Domestic
4520-4524	RAF Lyneham	5500	NATO Aircraft receiving a service from AEW aircraft
4530-4542	MoD Aberporth		
4530-4567	Plymouth (Military) Radar	5501-5577	Transit (ORCAM) Barcelona
4550-4567	Isle of Man	5600	NATO Aircraft receiving a service from AEW aircraft
4550-4572	East Midlands Approach		
4573	East Midlands Approach Conspicuity	5601-5647	Transit (ORCAM) Paris
		5650-5657	Transit (ORCAM) Luxembourg
4574	Not allocated	5660-5677	Transit (ORCAM) Reims
4575	RAF Leeming/RAF Linton-on-Ouse	5700	NATO Aircraft receiving a service from AEW aircraft
	Southend Airport Conspicuity	5701-5777	Transit (ORCAM) Geneva
4576-4577	RAF Colerne Conspicuity	6000	NATO Exercises
4576-4577	Vale of York AIAA Conspicuity	6001-6006	Not allocated
4600	NATO Aircraft receiving a service from AEW aircraft	6007	London (Military) Radar
		6010-6037	UK Domestic
4601	Hawarden Conspicuity	6040-6077	London (Military) Radar
4601	RAF Wyton QGH Approach	6100	NATO Exercises
4602-4607	Hawarden Approach	6101-6157	London (Military) Radar
4610-4617	Bristol Approach	6160	Doncaster Sheffield Conspicuity
4610-4667	Scottish (Military) Radar	6160-6175	Inverness Approach
4620	Bristol VFR Conspicuity	6160-6176	Cambridge Approach
4621-4637	Bristol Approach	6160-6177	Plymouth (Military) Radar
4640-4666	Farnborough LLARS	6161-6177	Doncaster Sheffield Approach
4667	Farnborough LLARS Conspicuity	6176	Inverness IFR Conspicuity
4670-4676	TC Stansted/TC Luton	6177	Cambridge Conspicuity
4670-4677	RAF Coningsby RWS	6177	Inverness VFR Conspicuity
4677	Carlisle Airport Conspicuity Luton Airport Conspicuity	6200	NATO Exercises
		6201-6227	Superdomestic - Dublin inbound UK
4700	NATO Aircraft receiving a service from AEW aircraft	6230-6247	Superdomestic - UK to Scandinavia and Russia
4701- 4777	Special Events (activated by NOTAM)	6250-6257	Superdomestic - UK to Amsterdam and Iceland
5000	NATO Aircraft receiving a service from AEW aircraft	6260-6277	Superdomestic - Amsterdam to UK, Eire and Iceland
5001-5012	TC Non-Standard Flights	6300	NATO Exercises
5013-5077	UK Domestic	6301-6377	Superdomestic - UK to France
5100	NATO Aircraft receiving a service from AEW aircraft	6400	NATO Exercises
		6401-6457	Swanwick (Military) Radar
5101-5177	CRC Boulmer	6460-6477	UK Domestic
5200	NATO Aircraft receiving a service from AEW aircraft	6500	NATO Exercises
		6501-6577	CRC Scampton
5201-5260	Transit (ORCAM) UK	6600	NATO Exercises
5261-5270	Transit (ORCAM) Dublin to Europe	6601-6677	Transit (ORCAM) Germany

6700	NATO Exercises
6701-6747	Transit (ORCAM) Reims
6750-6777	Transit (ORCAM) Aix-en-Provence
7000	Conspicuity code
7001	Military Fixed-wing Low Level Conspicuity/Climbout
7002	Danger Areas General
7003	Red Arrows Transit/Display
7004	Conspicuity Aerobatics and Display
7005	Not allocated
7006	Autonomous Operations within TRA
7007	Open Skies Observation Aircraft
7010	Operating in Aerodrome Traffic Pattern
7011-7013	Not allocated
7014-7027	UK Domestic
7030-7045	RNAS Culdrose
7030-7046	TC Thames/TC Heathrow
7030-7047	Aldergrove Approach
7030-7066	Durham Tees Valley Airport
7030-7077	Aberdeen (Northern North Sea Off-shore)
7046-7047	RNAS Culdrose Conspicuity
7047	TC Thames (Biggin Hill Airport Conspicuity)
7050-7057	TC Thames/TC Heathrow
7050-7077	RNAS Culdrose
7067	Durham Tees Valley Airport Conspicuity
7070-7076	TC Thames/TC Heathrow
7100	London Control (Swanwick) Saturation Code
7101-7177	Transit (ORCAM) Brussels
7200	RN Ships
7201-7247	Transit (ORCAM) Vienna
7250-7257	UK Superdomestic for destinations in France and Barcelona FIR
7260-7267	Superdomestic - Shannon/Dublin to France and Spain
7270-7277	Plymouth Radar Superdomestic for destinations in UK and France
7300	Not allocated
7301-7307	Superdomestic - Shannon Eastbound landing UK
7310-7327	Superdomestic - UK to Netherlands
7330-7347	Superdomestic - Netherlands to UK
7350	Norwich Approach Conspicuity
7350-7361	MoD Ops in EG D701 (Hebrides)
7350-7365	Manchester Approach
7350-7367	RNAS Culdrose
7350-7376	Bournemouth Approach/LARS
7351-7377	Norwich Approach
7362	MoD Ops in EG D702 (Fort George)
7363	MoD Ops in EG D703 (Tain)
7366	Aircraft operating within 5nm of Manchester CTR and maintaining a listening watch only on the Manchester Approach frequency
7367-7373	Manchester Approach
7374	Dundee Airport Conspicuity
7375	Manchester TMA and Woodvale Local Area (Woodvale UAS Conspicuity)
7377	Bournemouth Radar Conspicuity
7400	MPA/DEFRA/Fishery Protection/METMAN (Civil Contingency) Conspicuity
7401	Scottish FIS
7402-7437	UK Domestic
7440-7477	Superdomestic Spain and France to UK, Ireland, Iceland and North America
7500	Special Purpose Code - Hijacking
7501-7537	Transit (ORCAM) Geneva
7540-7547	Transit (ORCAM) Bremen
7550-7577	Transit (ORCAM) Paris
7600	Special Purpose Code - Radio Failure
7601-7607	Superdomestic - Shannon/Dublin to Nordic States
7610-7617	Superdomestic - Ireland to UK
7620-7657	Superdomestic - UK to USA, Canada and Caribbean
7660-7677	Superdomestic - UK to USA, Canada, Canaries and Caribbean.
7700	Special Purpose Code - Emergency
7701-7717	Superdomestic - UK to France and Spain
7720-7727	Transit (ORCAM) Munich
7730-7757	Superdomestic - Shannon Eastbound landing UK
7760-7775	Superdomestic - UK to Channel Islands
7776-7777	SSR Monitors

Appendix 8

Magazines for the enthusiast and air band listener

ALMOST EVERY PART of the British Isles has an active aviation society, many of which produce a magazine or newsletter detailing local aircraft movements and overflights. Most now have websites but unfortunately the addresses sometimes change or the site becomes defunct. A web search should soon come up with the new address. I have included several web addresses where no other contact exists.

Addresses for enthusiasts' magazines

Air-Britain News and Air-Britain Digest, David Crook (Membership Secretary), 36 Nursery Road, Taplow, Maidenhead, Berkshire SL6 0JZ

Air Link, Lincolnshire Aviation Society, wwwlincsavsoc.co.uk

Air North, Northeast Branch of *Air-Britain*, Andrew Murray (Membership Secretary), 12 Burnside Road, Cullercoats, North Shields NE30 3LE

Avgas, Wirral Aviation Society, www.geocities. com/wirralaviation

Aviation Ireland, Aviation Society of Ireland, aviationsociety@ireland.com

Aviation Letter, John R. Roach, 8 Stowe Crescent, Ruislip,Middlesex HA4 7SS

Aviation News & Review, LAAS International, www.laasdata.com

Channel Islands Aviation News, Can Pastilla, 5 Rue du Douit, Guernsey, CI GY6 8AY

Hawkeye, Gatwick Aviation Society Membership Secretary, 144 The Crescent, Horley, Surrey RH6 7PA

Humberside Air Review, Humberside Aviation Society, PG Wild (Secretary), 37 Church Drive, Leven, East Yorkshire HU17 5LH

Irish Air Letter, 20 Kempton Way, Dublin 7, Ireland

Leuchars Aviation Group, www. leucharsaviationgroup.co.uk

Osprey, Solent Aviation Society, webmaster@ solent-aviation-society.co.uk

SCAN, Scottish Air News Central Scotland Aviation Group, join@scottishairnews.co.uk

Scramble, Dutch Aviation Society, www.scramble.nl

SWAG MAG, South West Aviation Group, Michael Screech (Editor), 4 West Meadow Road, Saunton Park, Braunton, Devon EX33 1EB

Ulster Air Mail, Ulster Aviation Society, Keith Lloyd (Membership Secretary), 14D Coolmoyne House, Dunmurry, Belfast BT17 9EW

Valley Aviation Society, www. valleyaviationsociety.net

Winged Words, The Aviation Society, Alan Birtles, TAS Registrar, The Aviation Society, PO Box 36, Manchester M46 9YW

Wolverhampton Aviation Group, www. wolverhamptonaviationgroup.co.uk

X-Air Society, Exeter Airport, www.btinternet. com/n.C.C.Evans/xair.htm

There are two commercial magazines that publish air band information in a regular column. One is *Aviation News* wherein appears my ATC News column. The other is *RadioUser Magazine* whose content includes my Airband News column, Godfrey Manning's Sky High, along with Kevin Paterson's Military Matters and SBS Files.

Index